BECOMING
ABRAHAM LINCOLN

BECOMING ABRAHAM LINCOLN

The Coming of Age of Our Greatest
President

RICHARD KIGEL

Skyhorse Publishing

Skyhorse Publishing books may be purchased in bulk at special discounts for sales promotion, corporate gifts, fund-raising, or educational purposes. Special editions can also be created to specifications. For details, contact the Special Sales Department, Skyhorse Publishing, 307 West 36th Street, 11th Floor, New York, NY 10018 or info@skyhorsepublishing.com.

Skyhorse® and Skyhorse Publishing® are registered trademarks of Skyhorse Publishing, Inc.®, a Delaware corporation.

Visit our website at www.skyhorsepublishing.com.
10 9 8 7 6 5 4 3 2 1

Library of Congress Cataloging-in-Publication Data is available on file.

Jacket design by Rain Saukas
Jacket illustration: *Lincoln the Rail Splitter*, J. L. G. Ferris

Print ISBN: 978-1-5107-1730-5
Ebook ISBN: 978-1-5107-1731-2

Printed in the United States of America

Dedication

While I was teaching in Brooklyn, I went hunting for books about famous people who came from dire poverty but, through their passion for reading and learning, educated themselves and made their mark in the world. The first person I thought of was Lincoln. I looked but found no books on Lincoln's young manhood in backwoods America that described in detail how he picked up his extraordinary reading and writing skills.

As C. S. Lewis once said to J. R. R. Tolkien, "If they won't write the kind of books we want to read, we shall have to write them ourselves."

This book is dedicated to students everywhere who, like Lincoln, find themselves stuck in an atmosphere with "absolutely nothing to excite ambition for education," and still they come to school, eager to learn, determined to excel, and willing to work.

Lincoln himself knew the power of words and saw a kind of magic in their vast reach. Words transcend barriers, enabling us to "exchange thoughts with one another" and "converse with the dead, the absent and the unborn, at all distances of time and space."

If we can isolate the one quality that made Lincoln great, it would be his hunger for reading. "The things I want to know are in books," he said. "My best friend is the man who will get me a book I ain't read."

—Richard Kigel

Table of Contents

———∽∽∽———

My childhood's home I see again,
And sadden with the view;
And still, as memory crowds my brain,
There's pleasure in it too.
O Memory! Thou midway world
'Twixt earth and paradise,
Where things decayed and loved ones lost
In dreamy shadows rise.

—*Abraham Lincoln, 1844*

Preface

———⊶⊷———

Becoming *Abraham Lincoln* is biography at its purest. The story of Abraham Lincoln is told by those most qualified to tell it: the men and women who knew Lincoln in Kentucky, Indiana, and Illinois from the day he was born until he turned twenty-five.

This biography uses only primary source material that historians regard as authentic, observations and statements by individuals who were in a position to tell us what they saw and heard. Here are the actual words of those who grew up with Lincoln—his friends and family. They are the real eyewitnesses to history.

A note about the quotations and sources: most of the statements were collected by William Herndon, Lincoln's law partner and friend, in the years following Lincoln's death. The responses came in original handwritten letters and transcribed interviews. Because of the low literacy levels of many of his subjects, sometimes these statements are difficult to understand. Often they used no punctuation and wrote in fragments of thoughts. Misspellings were common and names and places were often confused. "Lincoln" was sometimes spelled "Linkhorn" or "Linkern." Lincoln's grandmother "Lucy" was sometimes "Lucey." Some respondents referred to themselves in the third person. Lincoln himself did in his biographical writings.

In the nineteenth century there were no standards in journalism. It was up to each writer to determine how to present the material. The result can be jarring and inconsistent. Sometimes, Lincoln's cousin Dennis Hanks sounds like an uneducated country bumpkin and other times like an eloquent diplomat. This is entirely due to differences in literary technique of the writer. Some interviewers who reported on his words prioritized clarity, so they sanitized his language. Other interviewers sought to convey his habitual language patterns and dialect. All of it was perfectly acceptable to nineteenth-century readers.

In spite of all these difficulties, we are able to obtain a vivid, authentic account of Lincoln's childhood and adolescence in the actual words of those who knew him best. We see Lincoln as he was, according to law partner Billy Herndon, "just as he lived, breathed, ate and laughed in this world."

Suppose we could gather all those who knew Lincoln as a child and young man together in one room. We would certainly question them: What was Abraham Lincoln like? What did he say? What did he do? Their observations and statements quoted here would most likely be the words they use when they tell us what they know about Abraham Lincoln.

INTRODUCTION

"I saw him this morning about 8:30."

———⊷⊶———

When Walt Whitman went to Washington, DC, in 1862 to find his brother, a Union soldier wounded at the Battle of Fredericksburg, he ended up staying for two years. Visiting battlefield camps and field hospitals, he served as a compassionate nurse, tending to the sick, wounded, and dying, handing out fruit, sweets, and plugs of tobacco to Union and Rebel soldiers and civilians black and white. He talked to them, read to them, and helped them write letters to their loved ones. He stayed with them at night so they would not be alone in their agony.

"From the first I kept little notebooks for impromptu jottings in pencil," Whitman wrote.[1] "I took notes as I went along, often as I sat talking . . . writing while the other fellow told his story."[2]

Whitman wanted America to know the devastating price paid by the American soldier. "Future years will never know the seething hell," he wrote.[3] "I am more than ever convinced that it is important for those of us who were on the scene to put our experiences on record."[4]

Whitman was a newspaperman, editor of the *Brooklyn Daily Eagle* and the *Brooklyn Times*. "My idea," he said, "is a book of the time, worthy of the time."[5] So he "wrote, wrote, wrote,"[6] scribbling in his notebooks, describing sights, sounds, scenes, events, recording his impressions of the moment. "You want to catch the first spirit, to tally its birth," he said. "By writing at the instant, the very heartbeat of life is caught."[7]

Often while walking near the White House, Whitman would see President Lincoln passing by. "A hoosier Michel Angelo," he wrote, "so awful ugly it becomes beautiful, with its strange mouth, its deep-cut criss-cross lines and its doughnut complexion."[8]

Whitman described one of these momentary encounters in his notebook. On August 12, 1863, he wrote:

> *I see the President almost every day as I happen to live where he passes to and from his lodgings out of town. . . . I saw him this morning about 8:30 coming in to business, riding on Vermont Avenue near L Street. He always has a company of twenty-five or thirty cavalry with sabers drawn and held upright over their shoulders. . . . Mr. Lincoln on the saddle generally rides a good sized, easy going gray horse; is dressed in plain black, somewhat rusty and dusty; wears a stiff black hat and looks about as ordinary in attire, etc. as the commonest man.*[9]

Once, the president noticed the stranger standing alone by the side of the road. For a fleeting moment, their eyes met. The poet's pen flashed.

> *They passed me once very close and I saw the President in the face fully as they were moving slowly; and his look, though abstracted, happened to be directed steadily in my eye. He bowed and smiled . . . We have got so that we exchange bows and very cordial ones.*[10]

A poet's eye runs deep. His vision penetrates the surface of things, touching the essence. Whitman looked upon one of the most familiar faces of all time—it was well known even then—and saw into his soul.

I see very plainly Abraham Lincoln's dark brown face, with the deep cut lines, the eyes always to me, with a deep latent sadness in the expression. . . . None of the artists or pictures have caught the deep though subtle and indirect expression of this man's face. There is something else there.[11]

Poets see what others miss. In what seems plain and ordinary, they find something exceptional. With their probing scrutiny and mystical insight, they glimpse the future. Whitman knew that one day Americans would celebrate the greatness of this president.

I have fancied, I say, some such venerable relic of this time of ours, preserved to the next or still the next generation of America. I have fancied, on such occasion, the young men gathering around; the awe, the eager questions: "What! Have you seen Abraham Lincoln—and heard him speak—and touched his hand?"[12]

Any historical account of Lincoln's life faces problems with his formative years. Reliable primary source evidence is largely absent. We have few documents that were written at the time. While Lincoln was growing up, nobody around him was scribbling notes and observations as Whitman did. The story of young Lincoln can only be told in anecdotes and reminiscences by those who knew him, collected some forty years later.

Old memories make historians cringe. "The very materials we use to forge biography—letters, journals, diaries, interviews, recollections and the like—were all recorded by people who filtered things through their own perceptions and sensibilities," cautions Lincoln biographer Stephen B. Oates.[13]

Building a biography from remembrance has pitfalls. "Not only is it often vague and ambiguous, it is notoriously subject to the aberrations of memory, the prejudices of the informant, the selective character of the reporting and the subtle transformations that occur when a story is either resurrected from the depths of the past or recalled repeatedly over time," wrote contemporary historian Douglas L. Wilson.[14]

In the field of Lincoln biography, when it comes to his early life, the long memories of old men and women are all we have. "The historian must use reminiscence," wrote Lincoln scholar James G. Randall, "but he must do so critically."[15]

In his own book on young Lincoln, *Honor's Voice* (Random House, 1998), historian Wilson lists the criteria for judging whether an informant's testimony has value:

- Is it likely that a reported event actually occurred?
- Is it supported by the weight of the evidence?
- Does it offer specific details?
- Does the informant have a reputation for reliability?
- Does the informant have any prejudices?
- Was the informant in a position to know what happened?[16]

By these standards, Whitman's scribbled, poetic eyewitness accounts are indeed authentic. But it doesn't take a poet to give a vivid description that re-creates the life of the moment. Simple unsophisticated men and women can affect us deeply by their richly textured, highly detailed accounts of an event. When they are honest and real, we feel the power in their words.

Words. Lincoln has inspired oceans of them. "More words have been written about him, it's been estimated, than about any other figure in the history of the world with the exception of Jesus," Michiko Kakutani reported in the *New York Times*.[17]

Historians agree that Lincoln himself produced more words than Shakespeare and the Bible combined. Yet he left precious little writing on his childhood and growing up.

"I have no confidence in biographies," Lincoln told law partner Billy Herndon in their Springfield office one day. "You don't get a true understanding of the man."[18]

"I know he thought poorly of the idea of attempting a biographical sketch," said journalist John Scripps, who wrote the candidate's life story for the 1860 presidential campaign. "The chief difficulty I had to encounter," recalled Scripps, "was to induce him to communicate the homely facts and incidents of his early life."[19]

"Why Scripps," Lincoln said, "It is a great piece of folly to attempt to make anything out of my early life. It can all be condensed into a single sentence and that sentence you will find in Gray's Elegy: 'The short and simple annals of the poor.' That's my life and that's all you or anyone else can make of it."[20]

Because he was a candidate for president, Lincoln dashed off some background notes for Scripps.

"Herewith is a little sketch, as you requested," wrote Lincoln. "There is not much of it, for the reason I suppose, that there is not much of me."[21]

Lincoln wrote two autobiographical accounts totaling less than a dozen pages. It was the only autobiography he left the world.

Since Lincoln never really told his story, his law partner Herndon would. "If Mr. Lincoln could speak to me this day," Herndon wrote, "he would say 'Tell the truth. Don't varnish me.'"[22]

It became Herndon's mission.

"I think I knew Lincoln well," he said. "Thousands of stories about the man I rejected because they were inconsistent with the nature of the man."[23]

Wilson reminds us that Herndon "has long been in the doghouse of Lincoln scholarship." Among other faults he can be cited for: "claiming credit for influencing Lincoln on important issues" and "for intuitive psychologizing." [24]

"It was in this process of guessing, of analyzing and inferring from known facts that Herndon went astray," wrote Lincoln scholar Paul Angle.[25]

Herndon was guilty of myth making. He believed he understood Lincoln and claimed to know the inner workings of his mind. He thought he could fathom the mysteries of the man.

"I know Lincoln better than I know myself," he declared.[26] "My opinions are formed from the evidence before you and in a thousand other things, some of which I heard from Lincoln, others are inferences springing from his acts, from what he said and from what he didn't say."[27]

Unfortunately, "opinions" and "inferences" based on what someone "said" and "didn't say" are not history. This is speculation and supposition, more fantasy than fact. The great value of Herndon's portrait of Lincoln becomes clear when he avoids musing and hypothesizing and instead offers what he actually saw and heard for himself. It is then that William Herndon becomes a true biographer.

"When Herndon relates a fact as of his own observation, it may generally be accepted without question," Angle wrote.[28]

In telling the real story of Lincoln, no man gave us a more authentic portrait than Billy Herndon. His extensive collection of letters and interviews provided a live chorus of real voices. These were the people who knew Lincoln. They could tell the Lincoln story as they saw it, heard it, and lived it.

It was Billy Herndon who searched them out, visited their homes, prodded their memories, asked them questions, and preserved their words. It was Herndon and his informants who "wrote, wrote, wrote." They may not have caught "the first spirit" as Whitman did, but their vivid recording of recollected sights, scenes, sounds, events, and impressions of a moment in time sometimes, magically, catches "the very heartbeat of life."

In a sense, they are the real Lincoln biographers. It is their history, word for word, as it flowed from their lips and spilled from their pens. If they could come back today, and somehow sit among us and tell us what Lincoln was really like, this may be what they have to say.

Herndon left an extraordinary record of raw, unedited, eyewitness testimony on young Lincoln.

"I do not recall another case in history where, immediately after the death of a great personage, the facts of his personal life were collected so carefully, thoroughly and impartially by a lifelong friend and intimate professional associate as the facts about Lincoln were gathered by William H. Herndon," wrote Lincoln biographer Albert Beveridge.[29]

While Herndon was all too willing to offer opinions, theories, and beliefs about Lincoln, all the evidence shows him to be an honest man. "Nowhere in his intimate letters . . . did Herndon ever suggest the inclusion of a saying or anecdote which he knew to be false," wrote Donald, biographer of both Lincoln and Herndon.[30]

"Herndon was certainly not a liar," said Angle. "Surpassing even his devotion to Lincoln was his passion for truth. Never, knowingly, would he distort a fact."[31]

"I have gone into his credibility as if I were trying a murder case," said Beveridge.[32] "In all my investigation, his character shines out clear and stainless. He was almost a fanatic in his devotion to truth. Wherever he states a fact as such, I accept it—unless other indisputable and documentary proof shows that his memory was a little bit defective."[33]

Today, Lincoln lives in the words of those who knew him. One thing about the man during his time on earth—he loved to talk. He enjoyed the company of many friends. He loved shooting the breeze. While he was spinning his yarns, joking, discussing, debating, or sharing secrets, someone was listening. Often, that person was Billy Herndon.

"Herndon saw more of Lincoln and heard more from Lincoln's lips than any other human being, excepting Lincoln's wife," said Beveridge.[34]

His biography, *Herndon's Lincoln: The True Story of a Great Life*, finally appeared in 1889. Weeks before he died, Billy Herndon left his final statement on the extraordinary historical record he gave the world.

"I felt it my religious duty to tell all that I knew about Lincoln . . . I did this to benefit my fellow man . . . I drew the picture of Mr. Lincoln as I saw him and knew him. I told the naked God's truth and I'll stand by it. . . . Pay or no pay, as to my book, I shall give to the world the facts of Lincoln's life, truly, faithfully and honestly. The great future can then write its own book."[35]

Perhaps even Abraham Lincoln would be interested in a biography like this. Like Whitman, he knew the power of words and marveled at their reach, seeing a kind of magic that enables us to "exchange thoughts with one another . . . to converse with the dead, the absent and the unborn, at all distances of time and space."[36]

"History is not history unless it is the truth," said Lincoln.[37] "For people who like that sort of book, this is the sort of book they would like."[38]

CHAPTER 1

"My good friend is gone."

———⊗⊗⊗———

Good news. It was the message he was waiting for, the report he longed so desperately to hear. After five brutal years of war, unspeakable devastation, and catastrophic numbers of dead, the nation was exhausted and demoralized. At long last, the suffering would soon be over.

President Lincoln received word from his generals that the Union army had marched unopposed into Richmond, Virginia, taking control of the capital of the rebel Confederacy. It was Monday, April 3, 1865.

The next day the president with his young son Tad steamed downriver to Richmond on a US Navy gunship. They passed silent scars of war floating in the water, shattered wagons, smoking hulks of boats, parts of rifles and cannons, and dead horses. When they landed in Richmond, the dockhands immediately recognized the tall gaunt man in the stovepipe hat. The newly freed slaves there knew who he was. One old man threw down his shovel, fell on his knees, and cried, "Bless the Lord! There is the great Messiah! Glory Hallelujah!"

A jubilant crowd of black men and women surrounded him, calling his name and shouting, "Bless the Lord! Father Abraham's come!"

Intoxicated by their first sweet taste of freedom, some tried to kiss the president's feet.

"Don't kneel to me," Lincoln told them. "That is not right. You must kneel to God only and thank him for the liberty you will hereafter enjoy."[1]

A dozen armed sailors walked with the president as the procession made its way through the center of a ravaged, battle-worn city. His bodyguard, William Crook, recalled the scene.

"Every window was crowded with heads," he remembered. "But it was a silent crowd. There was something oppressive in those thousands of watchers without a sound, either of welcome or hatred."

Crook remembered the president's appearance at his moment of triumph. "I stole a look sideways at Mr. Lincoln. His face . . . had the calm . . . of a brave man . . . ready for whatever may come."[2]

The president's party entered a two-story Colonial building with stately pillars in front. It was the Confederate White House.

Lincoln sank wearily into the chair Jefferson Davis used as president of the Confederate States of America. Captain Barnes remembered that the president looked "pale and haggard, utterly worn out."

"I wonder if I could get a glass of water," Lincoln said.[3]

Twelve days later, early in the morning of April 15, 1865, as a cold gloomy rain fell in the nation's capital, Lincoln died after he was shot in the back of his head while at the theater.

"My good friend is gone . . .," Billy Herndon wrote. "The news of his going struck me dumb, the deed being so infernally wicked—so monstrous—so huge in consequences that it was too large to enter my brain. . . . It is . . . grievously sad to think of one so good, so kind, so loving, so honest, so manly and so great, taken off by the bloody murderous hand of an assassin."[4]

The nation mourned their departed president. Americans from all walks of life came to see the funeral train. The demand for Lincoln stories grew. People needed to hear his reassuring words again, to recall his stories and jokes, to find comfort in his wisdom. Lincoln was gone and America missed him. People were hungry for more Lincoln.

It was Billy Herndon they called on to talk about Lincoln: "You knew him," people would say. "What was he like? What did he tell you? What was he thinking?"

Billy Herndon was the junior partner in the law firm of Lincoln & Herndon from 1844 until the day in 1861 when Lincoln left Springfield, Illinois, for Washington as president-elect. They shared work on court cases and ran political campaigns. Together they managed the birth of the modern Republican Party. They spent long days and evenings debating and analyzing fine points of law, literature, science, philosophy, or any topic that struck their nimble minds.

Herndon, a reader like Lincoln, was always bringing books to the office so they could discuss new ideas. "I brought with me additional sermons and lectures by Theodore Parker," he said. "One of these was a lecture on 'The Effect of Slavery on the American People' delivered in the Music Hall in Boston and which I gave to Lincoln who read and returned it. He liked especially the following expression, which he marked with a pencil . . . 'Democracy is direct self-government, over all the people, for all the people, by all the people.'"[5]

Herndon admired Lincoln as a man and loved him as a friend. "He was so good and so odd a man, how in the hell could I help study him!" he wrote.[6] "Sometimes it appeared to me that Lincoln's soul was just fresh from the presence of its creator."[7]

Who could possibly know more about Lincoln than Billy Herndon? Who else was with him almost every day? Who could describe him with more authority than Billy Herndon?

When Mr. Lincoln walked he moved cautiously but firmly, his long arms, his hands on them hanging like giant's hands, swung down by his side. He walked with even tread; his toes, the inner sides of his feet, were parallel if not a little pigeon-toed . . . In walking, Mr. Lincoln put the whole foot flat down on the ground at once, no landing on the heel. He lifted his foot all at once, not lifting himself from the toes and hence had no spring or snap or get up to his walk.[8]

Was there anyone who looked more studiously at Lincoln's face? Who else could leave for posterity a detailed portrait of his living features, an accurate description of his color, his expressions, his every wrinkle and furrow?

His forehead was narrow but high. His hair was dark, almost black and lay floating where his fingers put it or the winds left it, piled up and tossed about at random. His cheek bones were high, sharp and prominent. His jaws were long, upcurved and massive, looked solid, heavy and strong. His nose was large, long and blunt, a little awry toward the right eye. . . . His eyebrows cropped out like a huge jutting rock out of the brow of a hill. His face was long, narrow, sallow and cadaverous, flesh shrunk, shriveled, wrinkled and dry, having on his face a few hairs here and there. . . . His ears were large and ran out nearly at right angles from the sides of his head, caused by heavy hats. . . . There was the lone mole on his right cheek just a little above the right corner of his mouth.[9]

Herndon knew that providence blessed him with a unique vantage point on Lincoln's life. If the nation needed the Lincoln story, he was the man to tell it. "Would to God the world knew what I do," he wrote.[10]

Seeing Lincoln as I see him, he is a grand character. I see him in my mind from his cradle to his grave and I say Lincoln's life seems a grand march over the forces and resistances of nature and man. . . .[11]

Many of our great men and our statesmen, it is true, have been self-made, rising gradually through struggles to the topmost round of the ladder. But Lincoln rose from a lower depth than any of them."[12]

Billy Herndon vowed to keep the soul of his friend alive for future generations. "Soon after Mr. Lincoln's assassination I determined to gather up all the facts of his life—truly, honestly and impartially, whatever it might cost in money or infamy—and to give the facts to the world as I understood them," he wrote.[13]

"I am writing Mr. L's life," he decided, "a short little thing giving him in his passions, appetites and affections, perceptions, memories, judgments, understanding, will, acting under and by emotions, just as he lived, breathed, ate and laughed in this world."[14]

Herndon wrote dozens of letters to people in Kentucky and Indiana who may have known young Abe and his family, asking for information they may have had about the president.

Herndon said he was interested in hunting down the "facts and truth of Lincoln's life—not fictions—not fables—not floating rumors—but facts—solid facts and well attested truths."[15]

A month after Lincoln was shot, Herndon was out in the country-side, seeking old-timers who knew Lincoln when he lived in New Salem thirty years before.

"When I met a man or woman who knew anything good or bad and was willing to tell it, I generally took notes then and there of what was said about Lincoln. . . .[16] I have been with the people, ate with them, slept with them and thought with them—cried with them too."[17]

Today, the basic source for what we know about the early life of Abraham Lincoln comes from the determined effort by William Herndon to gather all the statements he could about Lincoln from people who were there with him.

CHAPTER 2

"I have heard much of this blessed good woman."

⸺◦◦◦⸺

Billy Herndon met Dennis Hanks on June 13, 1865, at a Chicago fair featuring the original Lincoln log cabin. While Herndon witnessed much of Lincoln's early career as a lawyer and helped him rise to national prominence, no one knew more about the boy Lincoln than Dennis Hanks.

Dennis was a likeable old codger who loved to ramble on about the days of his youth in the backwoods of Kentucky and later Indiana with his cousin Abe. He knew the Lincoln family well, lived with them, worked with them, joked with them, and buried them. Amid the confusion of names and relations—at least eight women were named Nancy Hanks including Dennis's mother and Abe's mother—Dennis tried his best in his homespun way to set the record straight about who was who.

"My mother and Abe's mother's mother was sisters," he told Herndon. "My mother's name was Nancy Hanks. (This was Abe's aunt.) Abe's grandmother was Lucy Hanks which was my mother's sister. The woman that raised me was Elizabeth Sparrow, the sister of Lucy and Nancy. The other sister, her name was Polly Friend, so you see that there was four sisters that was Hankses."[1] The four Hanks sisters were Lucy (Abe's grandmother), Nancy (Dennis's mother), Elizabeth (who raised Dennis), and Polly.

He never tired of digging up old memories and homespun yarns in that simple countrified backwoods twang, reminding people that he, Dennis, grew up in a wild country with the president. Hanks told his story to Herndon at the fair that day, and Billy copied every word. His handwritten statement ran nineteen pages.

"Want to know what kind o' boy Abe Lincoln was?" Dennis drawled years later. "Well, I reckon old Dennis Hanks is the only one livin' that knowed him that arly. Knowed him the day he was born an' lived with him most of the time till he was twenty-one an' left home fur good."[2]

Herndon knew Dennis Hanks was sitting on a treasure, a rare kind of eyewitness testimony that makes history real. Yet he was wary. "You must watch Dennis," he warned. "Criticize what he says and how he says it. . . .[3] What he says about anything must be taken with much allowance. . . .[4] Dennis loves to blow."[5]

Lawyer Herndon knew the common legal standard that juries can disregard the entire testimony of a witness who makes even one false statement. He was skeptical because he caught Dennis in a bit of deception.

"Dennis has got things mixed up," Herndon complained. "He purposely conceals all things that degrade the Hankses."[6]

Loyal Dennis tried to hide a family embarrassment from posterity, the scandalous beginnings of Nancy Hanks, Abe's mother. Dennis loved Nancy like a sister, even though she was sixteen years older. They grew up together as close cousins, both removed from their mothers, the Hanks sisters, Lucy and Nancy, at an early age.

Nancy (Abe's mother) and Dennis came to live with Aunt Betsy (Elizabeth Hanks) and Uncle Tom Sparrow. Dennis, mindful of the Lincoln family reputation, claimed the Sparrows were Nancy's rightful parents to spare her the embarrassment of being born out of wedlock. "Those things about Abe's being a bastard is false. . . . If you call hir Hanks you make hir a base born child which is not true,"[7] Dennis wrote to Herndon when his facts were challenged. "Her madin name—Nancy Sparrow."[8]

Dennis made a valiant effort to conceal the truth. When the Sparrows married in 1791, Nancy Hanks, Lincoln's mother, was already seven years old. Yet Dennis stuck to his story, offering his own fanciful explanations.

"Calling her Hanks probily is my fault," Dennis claimed. "I always told hir she looked more like the Hankses than Sparrows. . . . You know about families. They will always have Nick Names for one or another."[9]

Dennis Hanks knew his place in history. He had a starring role in the life of a national hero, a man whose story would be told and retold for generations. Eager for his contributions to be noticed, he may have been guilty of stretching his case. "I taught Abe his first lesson in spelling, reading and writing," he bragged.[10] "I no this," he continued. "I am the man that can tell all about it."[11]

"Now William," he prodded Herndon just in case he missed the point, "Be shore and have my name very conspikus . . ."[12] I will say this much to you. If you don't have my name very frecantly in your book, it won't gaw of [go off] at all."[13]

Dennis was right. No man, not Billy Herndon, not anyone, could talk about the raw details of Lincoln's boyhood with more authority. Dennis Hanks was there with them. He knew the Lincolns intimately. But even Dennis wasn't sure the whole story should be told. "I don't want to tell all the things that I know," he said. "It would not look well in history."[14]Despite major flaws, historians accept the testimony of Dennis Hanks as reliable and authentic. Said Pulitzer-Prize–winning Lincoln biographer Albert Beveridge, "Dennis Hanks is watchful in the extreme in exalting the Hanks and Lincoln families. But aside from his boastfulness and championship of his clan, his statements are accurate. Luckily, it is easy to distinguish between fact and imagination in his letters and interviews."[15]

When Herndon met Lincoln's stepmother Sarah Bush Lincoln on September 8, 1865, he could talk to the one person who had the greatest impact on young Abe as he grew up.

"When I first reached the home of Mrs. Lincoln and was introduced to her by Colonel A. H. Chapman, her grandson by marriage, I did not expect to get much out of her," said Herndon. "She seemed so old and feeble. She asked me my name two or three times and where I lived as often. . . . She breathed badly at first but she seemed to be struggling at last to arouse herself or to fix her mind on the subject.

"Gradually, by introducing simple questions to her about her age, marriage, Kentucky, Thomas Lincoln, her former husband (Daniel Johnston), her children, grandchildren . . . she awoke, as it were, a new being. Her eyes were clear and calm.[16]

"She told me then that Mr. Lincoln, when a boy, used to keep an arithmetical copybook in which he put down his worked out sums. She likewise then told me that the boy Abraham was in the like habit of putting down in another copybook—his literary one—all things that struck him, such as fine oratory, rhetoric, science, art, etc. . . . Read them, looked at them over and over, analyzed, thoroughly understanding them. He would translate them into his boyish language and would tell his schoolmates, friends and mother what they meant . . . and his schoolmates, friends and mother must hear or he would 'bust wide open.'

"The information thus given me by the good old lady, the kind and loving step-mother—God bless her—put me on nettles. . . . We commenced the search and found this, the arithmetical copybook. . . . We could not find the other book. It is lost and lost forever as our search was thorough. Mrs. Lincoln gave me the book with her own hands or by the hand of her grandson. . . .[17]

"Ate dinner with her," continued Herndon. "Ate a good hearty dinner, she did. When I was about to leave, she arose, took me by the hand, wept and bade me goodbye, saying: 'I shall never see you again and if you see Mrs. Abraham Lincoln and family, tell them I send them my best and tenderest love. Good-bye my good son's friend. Farewell."[18]

A few days later, Herndon found Nat Grigsby in Gentryville, Indiana. Herdon listened and took notes as Abe's boyhood friend spoke of their days together when they were young. On September 14, 1865, Nat Grigsby went with Herndon to visit the grave of Nancy Hanks Lincoln, Abraham Lincoln's mother.

"I started from Nat Grigsby's house with him as my guide and friend throughout the trip," related Herndon. "Started to find Mrs. Lincoln's grave. It is on a knob, hill or knoll about a half-mile south-east of the Lincoln house. . . . Landed at the grave. Tied my horse. The grave was—is—on the very top or crown of the hill. . . . The grave is almost indistinguishable. It has sunk down, leaving a kind of hollow. There is no fence around the graveyard and no tomb, no headboard to mark where she lies.

"Mrs. Lincoln's body—her ashes—lie just 15 feet west of a hollow hickory stump and just 18 feet . . . from a large white oak tree. . . . Mrs. Lincoln is buried between two or more persons, said to be Hall and his wife on the one hand and some children on her left hand. . . .[19]

"At her head, close to it, I pulled a dogwood bush and cut or marked my name on it. . . . After looking at the grave and contemplating in silence the mutations of things—death—immortality—God—I left, I hope . . . a better man—at least if but for one moment. . . .

"God Bless her! If I could breathe life into her again, I would do it. Could I only whisper in her ear: 'Your son was President of the United States from 1861 to 1865' I would be satisfied.

"I have heard much of this blessed good woman. I stood bareheaded in reverence at her grave. I can't say why, yet I felt in the presence of the living woman . . . 'God bless her,' said her son to me once, and I repeat that which echoes audibly in my soul: 'God bless her.'"[20]

CHAPTER 3

"Injuns!"

⸺⧳⧳⧳⸺

By the end of 1781, the War for Independence was over. British troops under General Cornwallis surrendered to General George Washington, and a new nation was born.

These new United States, joined by the Articles of Confederation, held the promise of greatness. Beyond the settlements on the eastern shore, a vast continent was yet to be explored. It seemed endless, a glorious wonderland of natural beauty. Raw and untouched, the land was as fresh as the day it was made. Men heard this new country calling in the song of the prophet Isaiah: *For ye shall go out with joy and be led forth with peace: the mountains and the hills shall break forth before you into singing and all the trees of the field shall clap their hands.*

Adventuresome Americans dared to carve through walls of timber to reach into the heart of a virgin land. Daniel Boone left civilization behind, moving out from the towns of Virginia, heading west into the unknown forest. Colonel Boone and his men hacked a path through the trees and mountains and called it "Wilderness Road." They chiseled a settlement out of the woods. Men and women came and brought their families, and they all watched it grow.

It was called "Kaintuckee," the native's term for "dark and bloody ground." Peaceful Cherokee Indians lived there, roaming the woods for centuries, rightful heirs to the land, until they grew alarmed at the destruction of the forest stillness and their Mother Earth. They rose in anger to drive the white men out.

Still, the Americans came. They pushed to the rough borders of their world to face new lives of danger and daily toil. They found the outer edge of man's rule of law and government and there set out to build a nation.

When Daniel Boone returned home, he was a genuine American hero, a valiant soldier in the battle to tame a wild country. He had been to another world and back, preparing the way for others to follow. He called it "a second paradise,"[1] blue grass shimmering over moist black earth, clear winding streams jumping with fish, herds of wild game running everywhere. He moved his family to Kentucky and urged his friend Abraham Lincoln to sell his Virginia farm and come along.

This Abraham Lincoln never knew that his name would go down in history as a beacon for the nation, that the name Abraham Lincoln would inspire generations to come, that his grandson would become an American icon standing for freedom, honesty, and decency. This Abraham Lincoln was a captain in the Virginia Militia during the Revolution. His brother, Jacob Lincoln, fought with Washington at Yorktown and saw the British surrender. Captain Abraham fought no battles with the British. Instead, he led patrols into the Virginia countryside to defend the community from the terror attacks of angry Cherokee warriors.

Grandfather Abraham Lincoln put stock in the words of Daniel Boone. Lincolns and Boones had been friends for generations. When the Boone family came to America from England and settled in Pennsylvania, their neighbors were Lincolns. Some Boones and Lincolns married. When Abraham Lincoln spoke to Daniel Boone, it was like talking to a kinsman.

Seventeen eighty-one was the first year of a growing young nation. Restless families looked west for new beginnings. Abraham Lincoln sold his Virginia farm, packed up his belongings, and with his wife, Bathsheba, and their five children—Mordecai, Josiah, Mary, Nancy, and baby

Thomas—followed the moving stream of American pioneers along the Wilderness Road to a "second paradise" in Kentucky.

"The first inhabitants of Kentucky, on account of the hostility of the Indians, lived in what were called forts," wrote an early Kentucky settler.[2] Abraham Lincoln moved his family to a settlement known as Hughes Station on Floyd's Creek. Cabins were set together, side by side, forming a large closed-in courtyard. Here children could romp with the chickens, goats, and pigs while the men practiced their military drills.

Abraham Lincoln filed a claim for nearly two thousand acres of open Kentucky land.

> *"Surveyed for Abraham Linkhorn, 400 acres of land in Jefferson County, by virtue of a Treasury Warrant No. 3334 on the fork of Floyd's Fork, now called the Long Run, beginning about two miles up the said fork . . . at a sugar tree standing on the side of the same marked DS-B and extending there East 300 poles to a Poplar and Sugar Tree, North 213 and a third poles to a Beech and Dogwood, West 300 poles to a white Oak and Hickory, South 213 and a third poles to the beginning. May 7th, 1785."*[3]

Daniel Boone surveyed another five hundred acres for his friend. The name "Abraham Linkhorn" or "Abraham Linkern" appeared often on official documents of the day. "They were called Linkhorn," an old friend said. "That proves nothing as the old settlers had a way of pronouncing names as they pleased."[4]

Frontier life was hard. Food and clothing came from the creatures of the forest. Chores were never-ending. Great forests had to be cleared, the soil plowed and prepared for bearing fruits and vegetables. Dark surprises lurked in every new morning. Would rainstorms wash their crops away? Would drought wither them? Would fever strike and weaken the men and take one of the women or children? Would the livestock survive ravaging bears and mountain lions? Would they hear savage war whoops of rampaging Indians?

One day in May 1786, a bloody surprise arrived at the door of the Lincoln family. The pioneer father and his three boys were just outside the fort working to clear a plot of land. A rifle shot rang out and Abraham Lincoln fell dead.

"Injuns!" the boys screamed in terror and lit out in different directions.[5]

The killing of Grandfather Abraham became legend in the Lincoln family for generations. They told the story over and over again whenever the men swapped Indian tales. Years later Dennis told his daughter Harriet and her husband, Colonel A. H. Chapman, about the death scene.

"Grandfather was working in the field laying up the last rails when an Indian shot him," Chapman recalled. "Josiah ran to a stockade some four miles. Mordecai ran to the house, got a rifle, ran upstairs or aloft, put his gun through the port hole. Saw the Indian with Thomas."[6]

"The Indian ran out from his hiding place and caught Thomas, the father of Abraham," Dennis went on. "Mordecai, the oldest brother of Thomas . . . shot the Indian through the holes in the fort. The Indian dropped Thomas, ran and was followed by the blood the next day and found dead. Mordecai said the Indian had a silver half-moon trinket on his breast at the time he drew his 'bead' on the Indian, that silver being the mark he shot at. He said it was the prettiest mark he held a rifle on."[7]

Tom Lincoln, father of the sixteenth president of the United States, was fatherless at age eight. He received no inheritance. By law, all the Lincoln property went to the eldest son, Mordecai. Uncle Mord became a well-to-do Kentucky farmer, but he never lost his hatred for Indians. He was known as one of the most ruthless Indian fighters of his day.

"Young Mord Lincoln swore eternal vengeance on all Indians, an oath which he faithfully kept," said Colonel Chapman. "Afterwards during times of profound peace with the Indians, killed several of them. In fact, he invariably done so when he could—without it being known that he was the person that done the deed."[8]

Of his father, Abraham Lincoln wrote: "Thomas, the youngest son . . . by the early death of his father, and very narrow circumstances of his mother, even in childhood, was a wandering labor boy and grew up literally without education. He never did more in the way of writing than to bunglingly write his own name."[9]

Tom grew into a strong, sturdy man, taking odd jobs wherever he could. "Thomas Lincoln was not a lazy man," said Abe's friend Nat Grigsby, "but . . . a piddler, always doing but doing nothing great. Was happy, lived easy and contented."[10]

"I have known him near fifty years," said Dennis Hanks. "No better man than old Tom Lincoln. . . ."[11] He was a man who took the world easy, did not possess much envy. He never thought that gold was God and the same idea runs through the family."[12]

"Was strictly a moral man, never used profane or vulgar language," said Colonel Chapman.[13]

"Always asked grace at the table. Read the Bible," said Harriet. She knew the Lincolns. The family resemblance was easy to spot. "Abraham L. inherited his father's features rather than his mother's," she said.[14]

Dennis agreed. "Very much like Abe, his son. He had a broader face than Abe.[15] He was a large man of great muscular power. His usual weight 196 pounds. I have weighed him many a time. He was five feet ten and a half inches high and well proportioned. . . . He was built so compact that it was difficult to find or feel a rib in his body."[16]

Tom made a name for himself in the neighborhood when the men gathered at the general store to share news, spin yarns, and gossip. "He didn't drink or swear or play cards or fight," said Dennis. "An' them was drinkin' and cussin' quarrelsome days. Tom was popylar an' he could lick a bully if he had to,"[17] adding that "He was a man of great strength and courage—not one bit of cowardice about him."[18]

Dennis told the story of how Tom earned his reputation. "One time while on a visit to some friends at Hardinburgh, he had a desperate fight with a man named Hardin, a noted bully and desperado. Thomas Lincoln whipped Hardin easily without receiving a scratch or bruise. This is the only fight he ever had. After his encounter with Hardin, no one else ever tried his manhood in a personal combat."[19]

Tom made friends in Elizabethtown and found steady work. His brother Mordecai gave Tom some of his inheritance so he could buy a little farm, settle down, and gain some respectability. In 1805, the County Court appointed Tom as a Patroller, whose job was to capture slaves traveling without a permit. Patrollers could administer ten lashes on the bare back of any slave. At that time there were few slaves in the county, so the Patrollers protected the settlers from hostile Indians and strangers who happened to ride through those parts of Kentucky.

The captain of the Patrollers was Christopher Bush, head of one of the leading families of Elizabethtown. He had six sons and three daughters, all built from sturdy stock. "There was no backout in them," neighbors said.[20] Tom became friendly with one of the Bush sons, Isaac Bush, and his young sister Sarah, whom everyone called Sally. Though he was ten years older, Tom was sweet on Sally Bush. He thought she was the marrying kind.

"Lincoln had been acquainted with her and proposed marriage to her before either of them had ever married but had been rejected by her," Colonel Chapman said.[21]

In March 1806, Tom and Isaac Bush were hired to build a flatboat and make the dangerous journey down the Mississippi to New Orleans to sell a load of goods. Said Chapman, "They walked the entire distance across the country from New Orleans back to their homes in Kentucky."[22]

While the boys were away, Sally Bush married Daniel Johnston. When they returned, Tom and Isaac brought special wedding gifts for the bride.

Elizabethtown was swelling with new settlers. Homes, stores, and churches had to be put up from hewn logs. Joseph Hanks was the only carpenter in town, and he had all the construction work he could handle. When he went looking for a reliable assistant, he found a good man in Tom Lincoln. Learning the trade under Joseph Hanks, Tom became a craftsman in wood.

"Thomas Lincoln—then called 'Linkhorn' but it was always spelled 'Lincoln'—was a house carpenter by trade," said Samuel Haycraft, son of the founder of Elizabethtown. "Done the joiners work on my father's house and the entire joiners work on the house of Hardin Thomas. The work still exists to show for itself (nearly sixty years later)."[23]

"Thomas Lincoln often and at various times worked for me," recalled William Wood. "Made cupboards and other household furniture for me. He built my house, made floors, run up the stairs, did all the inside work for my house."[24]

Now with steady, respectable work and a small place of his own, Tom was looking for a good wife, a wily Kentucky woman who could "toss a pancake off a skillet up through the top of a chimney and run outdoors and catch it coming down."[25] He found his woman the day he met Joseph Hanks's young niece, Nancy Hanks.

CHAPTER 4

"Purty as a pitcher."

———❦———

Two years after Grandfather Abraham Lincoln staked his claim to the black Kentucky earth, another caravan of pioneer Americans left Virginia for Kentucky. Among them was a teenage mother and her suckling babe. The baby's father, a well-bred Virginia gentleman, wanted no part of them. So mother and daughter joined the sweeping tide heading west, seeking to make a new life in the second paradise.

Baby Nancy Hanks was only a few months old, a bundle in her mother's arms, when she was carried through the Indian country along the Wilderness Road. Her mother, Lucy Hanks, a high-spirited nineteen-year-old, was coming to stay with her older sister, Rachel, who had the good sense to marry a wealthy farmer named Richard Berry. The Berry plantation was a mile and a half from the home of Bathsheba Lincoln, Grandfather Abraham's widow.

Young Lucy Hanks was "not very much of a talker, very religious and her disposition was very quiet."[1] Yet soon after she arrived at her new Kentucky home, the young mother found herself at the center of a storm of gossip. Folks accused her of being a loose woman, shameless with men and wild in her ways, and filed a suit in court charging Lucy Hanks with the crime of displaying immoral tendencies.

Now that she was starting a new life in Kentucky, Lucy fell in love with a kind and gentle man, a Revolutionary War veteran named Henry Sparrow. When they decided to get married, she stated her intentions in a note presented to the court.

I do sertify and I am of age and give my approbation freely for Henry Sparrow to git out Lisons this or enny other day. Given under my hand this day. April 26, 1790.Lucey Hanks [2]

The suit against her was dropped, and on April 3, 1791, they married. Together, Lucy and Henry Sparrow brought eight children into the world. Lucy was one of the few women of the time who could read and write, and she took care to see that this skill was passed to her children. Her deep religious worship was passed on to three of her sons, who later became traveling Ministers of God.

Family played an important role when it came to raising children on the frontier. When the everyday struggles of backwoods living became too much to bear—too many hungry bellies, too many small bodies to clothe, clean, and care for—there were always aunts and uncles ready to open their hearts and homes for their own blood. Family was family—your brother's son was your son, your aunt was like a mother, your cousins became your brothers and sisters.

So it was that Lucy's first child, Nancy Hanks, born in 1784, passed her childhood years with the Berry family. It was a pleasant and comfortable home for a young pioneer girl. Richard Berry was well respected in the community and owned a large plantation with a stock of cattle, horses, and a few slaves. He even owned some feather beds.

While Nancy was growing up with the Berrys, a cousin of hers joined them. Sarah Mitchell was the daughter of another of Lucy's sisters. She was twelve years old when Indians ambushed her family on their way to Kentucky. They tomahawked her mother to death and carried Sarah along with them to Canada. Sarah's father led a search party but drowned in the Ohio River. After five years, the Indians finally released the girl under the terms of a peace treaty. Orphaned and homeless, she came to live with her aunt.

"Sarah Mitchell and Nancy Hanks were first cousins . . . reared and educated by Uncle Richard Berry. These two girls grew up together, went to school together and became known as sister cousins,"[3] Sarah's granddaughter later wrote. Nancy tried to help Sarah make up for her lost years. Nancy was particularly talented at spinning flax, and Sarah was her pupil.

When Nancy was a teenager, Tom and Betsy Sparrow took her under their wing. Tom was Henry Sparrow's brother, Betsy was Lucy's sister—another Sparrow-Hanks love match. They loved Nancy as their own daughter, and she became known in the neighborhood as Nancy Sparrow.

Young Dennis Hanks, born out of wedlock in 1799 to another of Lucy's sisters, came to live with them. "The woman that raised me was Elizabeth Sparrow, the sister of Luccy and Nancy," said Dennis.[4] "I am a base born child. My mother was Nancy Hanks, the aunt of A. Lincoln's mother."[5]

Cousins Nancy and Dennis Hanks grew up with the Sparrows as brother and sister. They rose in the morning together and did their chores side by side. Dennis Hanks could tell the world about the mother of Abraham Lincoln.

"She was purty as a pitcher an' smart as you'd find 'em anywhar. . . ."[6] Mrs. Lincoln, Abraham's mother, was . . . affectionate—the most affectionate I ever saw—never knew her to be out of temper. . . . She seemed to be immovably calm."[7]

"I knew Mrs. Nancy Lincoln—or Nancy Sparrow—before marriage," John Hanks remembered. "Abraham's mother and I were cousins. Abraham and I are second cousins. . . . She was a tall slender woman, dark skinned, black hair and eyes. Her face was sharp and angular, forehead high. She was beyond all doubt an intellectual woman. . . . Her nature was kindness, mildness, tenderness . . . Abraham was like his mother very much. . . ."[8] He was tall like his mother. Abraham was six feet four inches in height. His mother was five feet ten inches in height."[9]

Lincoln rarely spoke of his mother. In his campaign biography, Herndon was "struck with Lincoln's meager reference to his mother. He even fails to give her maiden or Christian name."[10]

Whatever secret feelings her memory stirred remained locked in his heart. Even in private conversation no one could recall Lincoln talking about his mother. "I only remember one time when Mr. Lincoln ever referred to it," recalled Herndon. "It was about 1850 when he and I were driving in his one-horse buggy to the court in Menard County, Illinois. . . . During the ride he spoke, for the first time in my hearing, of his mother. . . ."[11]

"Lincoln all at once said: 'Billy, I'll tell you something. But keep it a secret while I live. My mother was a bastard, was the daughter of a nobleman, so called, of Virginia. My mother's mother was poor . . . and she was shamefully taken advantage of by the man.'[12] He said, among other things, that she was the illegitimate daughter of Lucey Hanks and a well-bred Virginia farmer. . . . He argued that from this last source came his power of analysis, his logic, his mental activity, his ambition. . . . He believed that his better nature and finer qualities came from this broad-minded, unknown Virginian. The revelation, painful as it was, called up the recollection of his mother, and as the buggy jolted over the road, he added ruefully—'God bless my mother. All that I am or ever hope to be I owe to her'—and immediately lapsed into silence."[13]

In the early part of the nineteenth century, America was a wild country. Decent, God-loving folks struggled to carve a community out of the woods. It was in this harsh, primitive world that Tom Lincoln and Nancy Hanks found each other. The glue that brought them together was their faith in God. Like their neighbors, they were drawn to backwoods revival meetings. People came to sit in candlelit huts, listening to the traveling preacher wail, quiver, cry, jump, and sing, all in praise of the Lord.

Religious revival meetings were a big event on the frontier. When a preacher came to town, folks flocked to hear him. Bible readings brought comfort and helped the people hold their faith against the terrors of a dark unknown. They were reminded that trials as well as blessings come from the Lord and that the supreme satisfaction to be found on this earth was to do God's will. The preachers excited them and opened their hearts. They supplied all the entertainment there was. Preaching was their theater, their drama, their show.

Like his neighbors, Abe loved the spectacle of the revival meetings. "When I hear a man preach," he said, "I like to see him act as if he were fighting bees." [14]

Tom Lincoln's favorite preacher was the Reverend Jesse Head, a fiery disciple of decency and justice, well known for his bold and passionate sermons on the evils of slavery. He was a carpenter, like Tom, and he would not stand for any guff. Drunken or disorderly worshipers who were moved to disrupt the word of God soon found themselves face to face with the good reverend, who would not hesitate to grab a ruffian by his coat and toss him out.

Reverend Jesse Head joined Tom Lincoln and Nancy Hanks in holy matrimony on June 12, 1806. They were married in the Berry home. Sarah Mitchell was Nancy's guardian and gave her away. A wild Kentucky-style celebration lasted all day and into the night. A wedding guest remembered the party.

"We had bear meat, venison, wild turkey and ducks, eggs wild and tame, maple sugar lumps tied on a string to bite off for coffee or whiskey, syrup in big gourds, peach and honey, a sheep that the two families barbecued while over coals of wood burned in a pit and covered with green boughs to keep the juices in and a race for the whiskey bottle."[15]

The newlyweds made their home in Elizabethtown, living in a log cabin near the courthouse. Tom worked diligently at his trade, building cabinets, door and window frames, and coffins. He had a hand in putting up many of the cabins, stores, and churches in the area. His reputation as an honest, reliable craftsman grew. A friend said that "Tom had the best set of tools" in the county.[16]

One of Tom's jobs was to build a new sawmill for the town. When the job was nearly finished, the owner of the sawmill refused to pay Tom for his services. He brought Tom to court, claiming that he didn't have to pay because the timbers Tom put up were not cut square and true. The judge threw out the suit. Tom won his pay and the respect of the community, who began to look to him as a man whose word was his bond.

The Lincoln family was growing. On February 10, 1807, Nancy gave birth to a baby girl. They named her Sarah in honor of Nancy's "sister-cousin." Tom bought a piece of land from his friend Isaac Bush about fourteen miles outside of Elizabethtown on the Big South Fork of Nolin's Creek. They moved to their new home in the fall of 1808. By then, Nancy was growing bigger again, and before the winter was out, the Lincolns had their second child.

CHAPTER 5

"Nancy's got a boy baby."

———— ∞ ————

February 12, 1809. A cold Sabbath Sunday in the dead of winter. A fine day for great souls to appear in the world. On this day, across a great ocean, a baby boy came into the home of a physician. He became a giant among men, his name celebrated into the next century, most remembered for looking backward into the wheels of time to advance our understanding of how humans evolved on this planet. The baby, born to Dr. and Mrs. Darwin, was named Charles.

That same morning in the backwoods of Kentucky, Tom Lincoln was poking logs in the fireplace to keep the flames crackling. He made sure Nancy was tucked tightly in bed under some warm bear-skins. Then he headed to the Sparrow place to tell Nancy's sister Betsy the news. For nine-year-old Dennis Hanks, it was a day to remember.

"I ricollect Tom comin' over to our house one cold mornin' in February an' sayin' kind o' slow an' sheepish: 'Nancy's got a boy baby,'" Dennis said. "Mother got flustered an' hurried up her work to go over to look after the little feller, but I didn't have nothin' to wait fur, so I jist tuk an' run the hill two miles to see my new cousin. . . .[1]

"You bet I was tickled to death. Babies wasn't as plenty as blackber-ries in the woods o' Kaintucky. Mother came over an' washed him an' put a yaller flannen petticoat an' linsey shirt on him, an' cooked some

27

dried berries with wild honey fur Nancy, an' slicked things up an' went home. An' that's all the nuss'n either of em' got. . . .[2]

"'What you goin' to name him, Nancy?'" I asked her.

"'Abraham,' she says, 'after his gran'father that come out to Kaintucky with Dan'l Boone.'"[3]

The Lincoln baby was born "in a hunter's hut not fit to be called a home,"[4] a neighbor wrote. Tom cut the timber for the house from the woods around it. There was one small window and a chimney made of packed-down clay. The earth was their floor.

On Abraham's first night, Dennis Hanks stayed with him, huddling under a bearskin by the fireplace. That night he could hear baby Abraham crying in the dark and the quick footsteps of a new mother hurrying to comfort him.

Dennis asked if he could hold the baby. "I was the second man who touched Lincoln after his birth," he said.[5] "Well, now, he looked jist like any other baby at fust, like a red cherry-pulp squeezed dry in wrinkles. An' he didn't improve none as he growed older. Abe was never much for looks."[6]

Nancy eased the baby into Dennis's arms. "Be keerful, Dennis," she said, "fur you air the fust boy he's ever seen."

"I sort o' swung him back and forth. . . . With the talkin' and the shakin' he soon begun to cry and then I handed him over to my Aunt Polly who wuz standin' close by."

Dennis had a feeling about his new cousin. "He'll never come to much," he declared solemnly. "I'll tell you he wuz the puniest, cryin'est little youngster I ever saw."[7]

The cabin on Nolin's Creek was home for the Lincoln family for three years. Nearby was the Rock Spring, a moss-covered ledge high above the cool flowing water. Nancy often climbed the ledge with baby Abraham and his sister Sarah. They listened to the bubbling stream as Nancy sweetly chanted her favorite hymns and lullabies.

> *"Come thou fount of every blessing.*
> *Tune my ear to sing Thy praise."* [8]

"Praise the mount, O, fix me on it!
Mount of God's unchanging love."[9]

The land at Nolin's Creek was hard and stubborn, mostly clay and stones beneath the thick underbrush. Every season Tom's crops were poor and withered. Folks said the land had "the barrens."

Dennis remembered those difficult times: "Pore? We was all pore, them days. But the Lincolns was poorer than anybody. Choppin' trees, an' grubbin' roots, an' splittin' rails, an' huntin' an' trappin' didn't leave Tom no time to put a . . . floor in his cabin. It was all he could do to git his family enough to eat and kiver 'em." [10]

In the spring of 1811, the Lincolns moved ten miles northeast to Knob Creek, "one of the prettiest streams I ever saw," remarked one longtime resident. "You can see a pebble in ten foot of water."[11]

Little Abraham was just beginning to talk. The sound of words rang all around him. Rough Kentucky voices, his father's and the neighbors', filled the air in homespun conversation, and his mother patiently showed him things and gave everything a name.

Abe heard their jabbering, listened to the way they formed their words. A family without much was "pore." You went to school to "larn" and get an "eddication." When you ran errands you "brung" things back. In summertime you "swum" in the "crick." Sometimes a stray dog "follered" you home. If you acted against your better judgment, you were "hornswoggled." When you met your friend you said, "howdy." If he came from over "yonder," you might ask him "whar" he'd been.

Abe grew up hearing the voices of old Kentucky sages, the backwoods wisdom of everyday folks telling tales of gypsy magic to help them through unknown dangers and uncertain days. If you kill the first snake you see in the spring, you will defeat all your enemies that year. If your right foot itches, you will certainly go on a journey. A dog crossing your path is bad luck unless you hook your two little fingers together and pull till the dog is out of sight. If you feel your ears burning, someone is surely spreading gossip about you. If you can make your first finger and your pinkie meet over the back of your hand, you will get married.

Life in the woods was a drama of bitter surprises. Nature's round of birth and death followed its own secret rhythm. Nancy became pregnant again not long after the Lincolns arrived at Knob Creek. A baby boy was born, and she named him Thomas for his father. The baby lived for three days. Tom whipsawed some logs into a little coffin and laid the doll-like body to rest on a grassy hilltop near the cabin. A flat stone marked the grave, chiseled with the letters *TL*.

Abe learned to be at home in the woods. It was his playground. The little creatures darting along the tangled forest floor were his playmates. Dennis remembered: "Abe was right out in the woods, about as soon's he was weaned, fishin' in the crick, settin' traps fur rabbits an' muskrats, goin' on coon-hunts with Tom an' me an' the dogs, follerin' up bees to find bee-trees an drappin' corn fur his pappy."[12]

He was a shirt-tail boy. During the warm months, his only covering was the long prickly woolen shirt he wore as he dutifully did his chores. He filled the woodbox, cleaned the fireplace, carried water buckets, and gathered nuts and berries. He hoed the ground with his father and helped him plant seeds. He learned the feel of cool earth between his toes and blisters burning on his hands.

One of Abe's first memories was working out in the field. One Saturday he was helping his father with spring planting. "I dropped two seeds every other hill and every other row," Abe recalled. "The next Sunday morning there came a big rain in the hills. It did not rain a drop in the valley, but the water coming down through the gorges washed ground, corn, pumpkin seeds and all clear off the field."[13]

The main road from Louisville to Nashville ran by the Lincoln cabin. It was a well-traveled road. Abe and his sister Sarah could watch a daily procession of pioneer caravans of covered wagons, peddlers pushing their wares, traveling preachers, circuit judges and soldiers, scores of black men and women shuffling in their chains, prodded by rifle-waving "slave-ketchers" on high horses. It seemed the whole world was passing

by. Abe could watch backwoods America parading before him and dis-
appear into the far-off dust of the road.

Abe never forgot a small incident that happened on that road. "I had
been fishing one day and caught a little fish which I was taking home. I
met a soldier in the road and having been always told at home that we
must be good to soldiers, I gave him my fish."[14]

Even before young Abe could read, Nancy interested him in Bible
stories. The upright, magical men and women of the Old and New
Testament stirred his boyish imagination. "Lincoln's mother learned him
to read the Bible, study it and the stories in it . . . repeating it to Abe and
his sister when very young," said Dennis. "Lincoln was often and much
moved by the stories."[15]

"It was her custom on the Sabbath when there was no religious worship in the neighborhood—a thing of frequent occurrence—to employ
a portion of the day in reading the Scriptures aloud to her family," his
campaign biographer wrote during the presidential election. "After
Abraham and his sister had learned to read, they shared by turns in this
Sunday reading. This practice, continued faithfully through a series of
years, could not fail to produce certain effects. . . . There are few men in
public life so familiar with the Scriptures as Mr. Lincoln."[16]

Said Abe: "The Fundamental truths reported in the four gospels as
from the lips of Jesus Christ that I first heard from the lips of my mother
are settled and fixed moral precepts with me."[17]

There was plenty of Indian talk to fire his dreams. They heard endless
stories of Daniel Boone—how he was chased by Indians and swung forty
feet on a grapevine so they would lose his trail; how he ran backward in
the woods so the Indians following his tracks would think he was going
where he'd already been. Nancy spoke of her cousin Sarah, how her family was massacred, how she lived with the Indians for five years before
coming home.

One story that cut deeply into the boy's heart was told time and time
again by Tom Lincoln—the story of the ambush and murder of
Grandfather Abraham. Lincoln later confided, "The story of his death by

the Indians and of Uncle Mordecai, then fourteen years old, killing one of the Indians, is the legend more strongly than all others imprinted upon my mind and memory."[18]

When Abe lived on the Knob Creek farm, his best friend was Austin Gollaher. They made a rowdy bunch—Austin, Sarah, Dennis, and Abe. Dennis was the chief rascal and mischief-maker, but Abe and Austin and their friends were always happy to follow along. "It was their custom to climb up the high knobs and trees," said one of the gang.[19]

Once, their antics nearly proved tragic. Austin recalled: "One Sunday my mother visited the Lincolns, and I was taken along. Abe and I played around all day. Finally, we concluded to cross the creek to hunt for some partridges young Lincoln had seen the day before. The creek was swollen by a recent rain and in crossing on the narrow foot-log, Abe fell in.

"Neither of us could swim. I got a long pole and held it out to Abe, who grabbed it. Then I pulled him ashore. He was almost dead and I was badly scared. I rolled and pounded him in good earnest. Then I got him by the arms and shook him, the water meanwhile pouring out of his mouth. By this means, I succeeded in bringing him to and he was soon all right.

"Then a new difficulty confronted us. If our mothers discovered our wet clothes, they would whip us. This we dreaded from experience and determined to avoid. It was June, the sun was very warm, and we soon dried our clothing by spreading it on the rocks about us. We promised never to tell the story. . . ."[20]

Austin had a crush on Abe's sister, Sarah. "She was a very pretty girl," he remembered. "Sallie [Sarah] Lincoln was about my age. She was my sweetheart. I loved her and claimed her, as boys do. I suppose that was one reason for my warm regard for Abe. When the Lincoln family moved to Indiana, I was prevented by circumstances from bidding goodbye to either of the children, and I never saw them again." [21]

Nearly fifty years later, in the midst of his fiery trial as leader of a bleeding nation at war, President Lincoln found a moment's comfort reliving childhood memories of growing up in the backwoods of Kentucky. When Dr. Jesse Rodman, an old Kentucky neighbor, came to

Washington, the President took time out to meet him. Lincoln asked about the folks he knew and especially one in particular. "Where is my old friend and playmate Austin Gollaher?"

The president explained why he was so eager to find his friend. "He played a dirty trick on me once and I want to pay him up."

Lincoln told the whole story. "One Sunday, Gollaher and another boy and myself were out in the woods on Knob Creek playing and hunting around for young squirrels. I climbed up a tree and left Austin and the other boy. Gollaher shut his eyes like he was asleep and I noticed his hat sat straight with the reverse side up. I thought I would shit in his hat. Gollaher was watching and when I let the load drop he swapped hats and my hat caught the whole charge."

When Lincoln finished, Dr. Rodman recalled how "The President laughed heartily," clearly enjoying the memory of his old friend.

Said Lincoln, "I would rather see Gollaher than any man living."[22]

CHAPTER 6

"It was a wild region."

———◈———

Pioneer Americans were roving vagabonds. Their roots were never deep. The dark uncertainties of life on the edge of civilization drove them from one safe haven to the next. Tom and Nancy Lincoln, married ten years, had already packed their worldly belongings four times to move to more fertile soil. A neighbor once asked Tom why he worked so hard to fix up his place when he would soon be leaving it. He answered, "I ain't going to let my farm find it out."[1]

The Knob Creek farm proved to be as disappointing as the others. "The thirty acre farm in Kentucky was knotty, knobby as a piece of land could be, with deep hollows, ravines . . . knobs as thick as trees," said Dennis.[2]

"From this place," wrote Abe, referring to himself in the third person, "he removed to what is now Spencer County, Indiana, in the autumn of 1816, Abraham then being in his eighth [actually seventh] year. This removal was partly on account of slavery, but chiefly on account of the difficulty in land titles in Kentucky."[3]

In the early days, when Daniel Boone and his band of adventurers began taming the Kentucky wilderness, they needed a way to set apart each man's claim. The settlers made boundaries to separate one man's land from his neighbor's, carving letters in trees, marking large stones, and noting meandering creeks as borders. Those markers didn't last. Trees grew bark to cover the letters, rainstorms moved the stones, and

35

creeks dried up. Boundaries changed. Land ownership became vague and confusing. "In the unskillful hands of the hunters and pioneers of Kentucky," one observer wrote, "surveys . . . were piled upon each other, overlapping and crossing in endless perplexity."[4]

Tom Lincoln had seen dozens of acres taken away from his farms due to faulty surveying. Now a wealthy Philadelphia family was bringing Tom and nine of his neighbors to court claiming rightful ownership of the entire Knob Creek valley.

The early years of the nineteenth century saw the new United States embroiled in raging debates over the institution of slavery. Congress passed the Act Prohibiting Importation of Slaves in 1807. No new slaves could enter the country, although an illegal slave trade continued to flourish. The law did nothing to stop the sale of millions of Africans already enslaved in the United States, who would remain in bondage for the next six decades.

Kentucky was a state where it was legal for one man to keep another as personal property. Some defended this as a natural right. Others were deeply offended by its inhuman brutality. It was a hot issue.

Passionate arguments set neighbor against neighbor. The South Fork Baptist Church, where the God-fearing folks of Knob Creek went to worship, was forced to close its doors because the congregation could not meet in peace. Church records said fifteen members "went off from the church on account of slavery."[5]

The Reverend William Downs, who gave Tom his Christian baptism in Knob Creek, was prohibited from preaching his antislavery sermons at any church meeting or at the home of any of its members. Reverend Downs led several families, including the Lincolns, in establishing the Little Mount Church, where they could damn the evils of slavery in a nation that would later sacrifice the blood of her children to destroy it.

Many Kentucky families, whose consciences could not bear the sight of men and women in chains, crossed the Ohio River to settle in Indiana, a heavily wooded territory then applying to the United States Congress for statehood. The citizens of Indiana drew up a constitution firmly declaring that "no alteration of this constitution shall ever take place so as to introduce slavery or involuntary servitude in the state." [6]

Tom's brother Josiah Lincoln brought his family across the river into Indiana and sent back glowing reports of his prosperity. "Thomas Lincoln, the father of Abraham, had a notion in his head, formed a determination to sell out his place and move to Indiana," said Dennis.[7]

According to Colonel Chapman, "During the summer of 1816 he traded his little place for 400 gallons of whiskey."[8] "Mr. Lincoln got $300 and took it, the $300, in whiskey," added Dennis.[9]

Tom was not a drinking man. He acquired the liquor as a wise investment. Whiskey was a valuable commodity, used as an alternate for money on the frontier.

"He cut down trees—made a kind of flatboat out of yellow poplar," said Dennis. "He made the boat on the Rolling Fork at the mouth of Knob Creek. Loaded his household furniture, his tools, whiskey and other effects, including pots, vessels, rifles on the boat."[10]

He set his "crazy craft" in the water, and young Abe and Sarah waved good-bye to their father as he poled his way down Knob Creek to the Salt River, heading toward the great waters of the Ohio.[11] Tom's crude boat could not handle the river's rough currents. "His boat was capsized and all he had in it was thrown into the river," said Chapman. "He succeeded in saving most of his whiskey, a few tools and a few other goods. He then got his boat righted and loading what he had saved from the wreck, he again started on his journey in quest of a new home. He finally landed at Thompson Ferry on the Indiana side of the Ohio River."[12]

He left his belongings with a man named Posey and sold him the boat. Then, carrying only an ax and a hunting knife, he headed into the woods on foot.

"Indiana is a vast forest,"[13] an early explorer wrote in his diary. Giant trees—oak, elm, sycamore, willow, poplar, maple, ash, hickory, beech, and walnut—all grew together, tightly packed, some twenty feet around and a hundred feet high. A thick layer of brush wove the trees together in an impenetrable net along the forest floor. Tom followed a narrow trail as far as he could until the way became impassable.

"Thomas Lincoln, when he landed in Indiana, cut his way to his farm with an ax, felling the forest as he went," wrote Abe's childhood friend Nat Grigsby.[14] He hacked and sliced and cleared a new trail, covering sixteen miles through dense underbrush, until he came upon a promising patch of land near Little Pigeon Creek. This would be his home.

Tom Lincoln notched the trees, piled up brush, and lit a fire to mark the location so he could purchase the land on credit for two dollars an acre according to the US Government Land Law of 1800. He set up a small temporary shelter, a hunter's "half-faced camp." It was a small shed, about fourteen feet square, made of log poles. Dry brush and packed leaves covered the roof and three sides. The front was wide open.

Then he "Started back to Kentucky for his family, walking the entire distance—eighty miles," Chapman said.[15]

After Tom had returned home, he loaded up a borrowed wagon with pots, pans, kettles, blankets, a spinning wheel, farm tools, the family Bible, and their good feather bed. They could leave behind their cupboards, bureaus, tables, and chairs, since Tom would easily fashion new ones from the forest wood.

On December 11, 1816, Indiana became the nineteenth state of the United States. About this time the Lincoln family paid a solemn visit to the grave of their departed son, baby Thomas, and said good-bye to their Kentucky friends and neighbors. Dennis Hanks traveled with the Lincolns and later wrote about the journey. "I went myself with them. Backwards and forwards to Indiana and back to Kentucky and back to Indiana and know the story of all the facts well," he said.[16]

In four days, the travelers reached the ferry that carried them across the Ohio River. It was an awesome sight, nothing like Knob Creek, a stream so small even young Abe could cross it on a log while reaching in to pull out a fish or a bullfrog. The great Ohio was like a vast ocean, busy with the smoking newfangled steamboats, whose distant shores seemed to stretch into blue eternity.

On the Indiana side, Tom retrieved their belongings, and the rugged pioneer family pressed on through some of the roughest terrain any traveler could face. "This country at that time was a perfect wilderness without roads or bridges," said Nat Grigsby. "Thomas Lincoln and his little family had to cut a road through the heavy forests of timber which was unbroken by the hand of man."[17]

"I will jest say to you that it was the brushest country that I have ever seen," Dennis said later, ". . . all kinds of undergrowth . . . matted together so that as the old saying goes you could drive a butcher knife up to the handle in it."[18]

They followed the narrow trail Tom blazed through the woods, but it was not nearly wide enough for their wagon. The menfolk ripped through tangles of vines to make an opening large enough for a wagon to squeeze through. The rickety wooden wagons carried the family through mounds of mud and flowing streams, across gullies, and over rocks and stumps, until they reached the little parcel of land in the woods that would be home to the Lincolns for the next fourteen years.

"We reached our new home about the time the state came into the Union," Abe wrote. "It was a wild region, with many bears and other wild animals still in the woods. There I grew up."[19]

Frigid winter winds stung their faces as they came upon Tom's pole shed. The men piled logs and brush in front of the open side of the shed and kept a big bonfire alive day and night to keep the family warm and frighten away bears and panthers they found hovering around the edge of the camp.

Here they passed an Indiana winter, rough even for a pioneer family. Soaking rains and driving blizzards blasted their shelter. Nasty winds whipped choking smoke from the bonfire, burning their eyes.

The pole shed was "not much better'n a tree," said Dennis. "I've seen Injun lodges that'd beat pole-sheds all holler fur keepin' out the weather. I don't see how the women folks lived through it. Boys are half wild anyhow, an' me 'n Abe had a bully good time. . . ."[20]

CHAPTER 7

"Constantly handling that most useful instrument."

———— ✇ ————

"We, Lincoln's family, including Sally and Abe and myself, slept and lodged in this cabin [the pole-shed] all winter and till next spring," Dennis recalled. "We, in the winter and spring, cut down brush, underwood trees, cleared ground, made a field of about six acres on which we raised our crops. We all hunted pretty much all the time, especially when we got tired of work, which was very often, I will assure you. We did not have to go more than four or five hundred yards to kill deer, turkeys and other wild game."[1]

The woods around the Lincoln homestead were teeming with creatures of the forest. Raccoons, squirrels, opossum, skunks, deer, bears, wolves, wildcats, and panthers—all came to the salt-lick near their cabin to rub their tongues against the wet rocks. Honking ducks and geese flew over their heads. Wild Carolina parakeets lined the treetops, brightening the forest with their yellow and green feathers and shrill cries. Millions of passenger pigeons darkened the sky. Flocks of wild turkeys often came right upon them, almost into their cabin.

That winter young Abe killed his first creature. "He done it with his father's rifle," more by accident than skill, since turkeys were "too numerous to mention," according to Dennis.[2] The shooting incident left a lasting impression on the boy, and he included it in his notes for his campaign biography.

"At this place Abraham took an early start as a hunter, which was never much improved afterward," Dennis wrote. "A few days before the completion of his eighth year . . . a flock of wild turkeys approached the new log cabin, and Abraham with a rifle-gun, standing inside, shot through a crack and killed one of them. He has never since pulled a trigger on any larger game."[3]

Hunting was part of everyday life. The pioneers needed wild game for food and clothing. Some beasts were a menace to livestock and dangerous to human life. In Indiana, the men of the community often banded together to hunt down herds of animals. It was necessary for their safety and they enjoyed the sport of it.

"There was a great many deer licks," said Abe's friend David Turnham, "and Abe and myself would go to these licks sometimes and watch . . . to kill deer, though Abe was not so fond of a gun as I was."[4]

Abe had no enthusiasm for taking the lives of animals, even for food. But the sporting hunts fascinated him. Thirty years after the Lincolns first set foot in Indiana, his memory stirred up an incident he had witnessed, and he was moved to write about it.

THE BEAR HUNT

A wild-bear chase, didst never see?
Then hast thou lived in vain.
Thy riches bump of glorious glee,
Lies desert in thy brain.
When first my father settled here,
'Twas then the frontier line;
The panther's scream filled night with fear
And bears preyed on the swine.
But woe for Bruin's short lived fun,
When rose the squealing cry;

Now man and horse, with dog and gun,
For vengeance, at him fly.
A sound of danger strikes his ear;
He gives the breeze a snuff.
Away he bounds with little fear,
And seeks the tangled rough.
On press his foes, and reach the ground,
Where's left his half munched meal;
The dogs, in circles, scent around,
And find his fresh made trail . . .
Now to elude the eager pack,
Bear shuns the open ground;
Though matted vines, he shapes his track
And runs it, rough and round . . .
And fresh recruits are dropping in
To join the merry corps;
With yelp and yell—a mingled din—
The woods are in a roar.
And round and round the chase now goes,
The world's alive with fun;
Nick Carter's horse, his rider throws,
And more, Hill drops his gun.
Now sorely pressed, bear glances back,
And lolls his tired tongue;
When as, to force him from his track,
An ambush on him sprung.
Across the glade he sweeps for flight,
And fully is in view.
The dogs, new-fired, by the sight,
Their cry and speed renew.
The foremost ones, now reach his rear.
He turns, they dash away;
And circling now, the wrathful bear,
They have him full at bay.

At top of speed, the horse-men come,
All screaming in row
"Whoop! Take him, Tiger. Seize him Drum."
Bang—bang—the rifles go.
And furious now, the dogs he tears,
And crushes in his ire.
Wheels right and left, and upward rears,
With eyes of burning fire.
But leaden death is at his heart,
Vain all the strength he plies.
And, spouting blood from every part,
He reels and sinks, and dies.[5]

There was plenty of work to be done in order to make their little homestead livable. "The country was very rough," David said, "so thick with brush that a man could scarcely git through on foot."[6] It was, according to Abe, an "unbroken forest, and the clearing away of surplus wood was the great task ahead. Abraham, though very young, was large for his age, and had an ax put into his hands at once, and from that till within his twenty-third year he was almost constantly handling that most useful instrument."[7]

He helped Tom and Dennis chop logs for their new cabin forty yards from the pole shed. He trimmed the branches off logs, hacked away brush from the ground, and dug up the soil for planting. It was up to Abe and Sarah to fetch water from the spring a mile away.

Their days were long and filled with endless chores. They lived simply. "We wasn't much better off'n Injuns," said Dennis, "except we tuk an interest in religion and polytics. We et game an' fish an' wild berries an' lye hominy an' kep' a cow. Sometimes we had corn enough to pay fur grindin' meal an' sometimes we didn't. . . .When it got so we could keep chickens an' have salt pork an' corn dodgers . . . an' molasses an' have jeans pants an' cowhide boots to wear we felt as if we was gettin' along in the world. . . .

"Abe was runnin' 'round in buckskin moccasins an' breeches, a tow-linen shirt an' coonskin cap. Yes, that's the way we all dressed them days. . . . Most of the time we went b'arfoot. . . . Them moccasins wasn't no putection against the wet. Birch bark with hickory bark soles stropped on over yarn socks beat buckskin all holler fur snow. Me 'n Abe got purty handy contrivin' things thataway."[8]

When the family gathered at the dinner table "dog-tired and hog-hungry," Tom would lead the family in a simple prayer: "Fit and prepare us for humble service, we beg for Christ's sake. Amen."[9]

"One day they had nothing for dinner but roasted potatoes," recalled Harriet Hanks Chapman, Abe's niece. "After Grandpa L got through returning thanks, which duty he never neglected—if he only had dry bread or potatoes he would ask the same blessing when he sat down to eat—so this time Uncle Abraham put on a long face and looked up at his father."

"Papa," complained Abe, "I call these [potatoes] very poor blessings."[10]

"Sometimes potatoes was used as a treat," recalled their neighbor Elizabeth Crawford. "I must tell you that the first treat that I ever received in old Mr. Lincoln's house, that was our President's father's house, was a plate of potatoes washed and pared very nicely and handed round. It was something new to me for I never had seen a raw potato ate before. I looked to see how they made use of them. They took a potato and ate them like apples."[11]

The land was not always so miserly toward them, and soon they had a healthy crop of corn and other vegetables. The corn had to be ground into flour for use in baking bread. One of Abe's greatest pleasures was the daylong visit to the mill, some sixteen miles away. It was a chance to get away from the farm, a welcome break in the day-to-day routine. The mill was a place to see new faces, hear fantastic tales, and learn the latest news.

"When we got there, the mill was a poor concern," recalled Dennis.[12] It was "pulled by a bag-o'-bones hoss. Abe used to say his hound could eat meal faster'n that mill could grind it an' then go hungry for supper. But it was a good place fur visitin' an' swappin' yarns. Other men'd be comin' in an' have to wait all day, mebbe, an' they'd set on a rail fence . . . crackin' jokes or argyin' polytics. Abe'd come home with enough news an' yarns to last a week."[13]

It was at the mill, Abe recalled, that he was "kicked by a horse and apparently killed for a time."[14] On that day, he rode to the mill with a bag of corn atop an old flea-bitten gray mare. He arrived late in the day and had to wait till it was nearly dark for his turn.

Customers had to provide their own horsepower, so Abe hitched up his tired old beast to the mill machinery. The gears cranked up and started spinning. The old mare was in no hurry. Abe grew impatient and used his whip, barking at the old horse, "Get up, you old hussy!"[15] In the midst of his exclamation, the ornery beast let an angry hoof fly, striking the boy's forehead. He went sprawling to the ground, bleeding, senseless. The miller thought he was dead and sent for his father. Tom Lincoln came and they carried the boy's lifeless body to a wagon for the trip home.

Morning came. Abe began to stir. His tongue began to roll. His body twitched, and suddenly he was wide awake and blurting out the words "you old hussy." It was the unfinished part of the sentence interrupted by the old horse's heel.

"Just before I struck the old mare," Abe explained, "my will through the mind had set the muscles of my tongue to utter the expression 'Get up, you old hussy' and when her heels came in contact with my head the whole thing stopped half-cocked, as it were, and was only fired off when mental energy or force returned."[16]

Years later, Billy Herndon recounted how deeply the mishap impressed Abe: "He often referred to it and we had many discussions in our law office over the psychological phenomenon involved in the operation." Herndon concluded that "Mr. Lincoln considered this one of the remarkable incidents of his life."[17]

CHAPTER 8

"I am going away from you, Abraham."

———— ✕✕✕ ————

In the fall of 1817, the Lincolns took up residence in their new cabin. Nancy was overjoyed when her Uncle Tom and Aunt Betsy Sparrow moved from Kentucky to Indiana to join them along with their adopted son, Dennis Hanks.

"Lived on Thomas Lincoln's place," said Dennis, "in that darn little half-face camp."[1]

The summer of 1818 was hot and dry. Much of the grass in the cow pastures was parched and brittle, scorched by a searing sun. Cattle, finding the grass inedible and hungry for fresh greens, discovered a tall white-flowered weed called snakeroot flourishing in the shadows of the trees. The cows flocked to the shade and grazed on the moist plant in cool comfort. Soon these cows would be stricken with severe trembling, and within three days they would be dead.

Anyone who drank the milk of a cow that ate the snakeroot weed would soon come down with the same symptoms. They would experience dizziness, nausea, vomiting, stomach pains, cold hands, cold feet, and a ghoulish white coating to the tongue and mouth. The patient would slip into a coma. After about a week the siege would be over. Most victims did not survive.

The discovery of milk sickness among them was enough to fill a pioneer community with dread. The toll on human life and livestock was staggering. When a family was relocating, as the Lincolns did, the first question they asked was if milk sickness was around.

In the fall of 1818, one of Tom Lincoln's cows began trembling. Within days, Tom Sparrow came down with the disease. On September 21, he wrote his last will and testament, giving all his worldly belongings to his wife "Elizabeth Sparrow so she can do as she pleases with it until her death." Then the "whole property is to fall to Dennis Hanks when he comes of age."[2] A healthy Nancy Lincoln signed the document as a witness by making an X.

"The Milk Sick was very prevalent among the settlers this year. Nearly all that were attacked with it died," said Colonel Chapman. "There was no physician in the county at that time. The nearest one was at Yellow Banks, Kentucky, thirty miles distant."[3]

In a week, both Tom and Betsy Sparrow were dead from milk sickness. Nancy Lincoln nursed them in their final days. When a neighbor, Mrs. Brooner, came down with a white mouth, Nancy was at her bedside, easing her misery until the end.

"Thomas Lincoln made all the coffins for those that died in that neighborhood about that time," Chapman recalled. "The lumber was green and cut with a whipsaw. There was scarcely enough will in the neighborhood that fall to bury those that died."[4]

"'Pears to me," said Dennis, "like Tom was always makin' a coffin fur someone."[5]

Then the dreaded milk sick came to Nancy Lincoln. She grew weak and took to her bed. The gentle soul who nursed the others now needed care herself. "I sat up with her all one night," recalled a neighbor, William Wood.[6]

Nancy sank rapidly. "She struggled on day by day," remembered Dennis, "a good Christian woman . . . She knew she was going to die and called the children to her dying side. . . ."[7]

"I am going away from you, Abraham," she whispered to her son, "and I shall not return."[8]

"[She] told them to be good and kind to their father, to one another and to the world, expressing a hope that they might live as they had been taught by her—to love men . . . and worship God," remembered Dennis.[9]

On October 5, 1818, just two weeks after the dread disease infected her stepfather and mother, Nancy Lincoln died. "O Lord, O Lord," wailed Dennis. "I'll never furgit the mizry in that little green log cabin in the woods when Nancy died."[10]

Nancy's body lay in the cabin until it was ready for burial while the family tried to get on with life. Tom Lincoln, who had made so many coffins for his neighbors that season, now had to make one for his beloved wife.

"Me 'n Abe helped Tom make the coffin" Dennis remembered. "He tuk a log left over from buildin' the cabin, an' I helped him whipsaw it into planks an' plane 'em together with pegs Abe'd whittled. . . . We laid Nancy close to the deer-run in the woods. Deer was the only wild critters the women wasn't afeerd of."[11]

The coffin traveled by sled up the side of a little hill near the Lincoln cabin and was lowered into the ground beside the new graves of Tom and Betsy Sparrow and Mrs. Brooner. Just days after he watched his mother laid to rest on that very spot, Mrs. Brooner's son returned for Nancy's burial. "I remember very distinctly that when Mrs. Lincoln's grave was filled, my father, Peter Brooner, extended his hand to Tom Lincoln and said, 'We are brothers now.'"[12]

An elder of the Little Pigeon Baptist Church recited a simple Christian prayer, and Tom followed the custom of the day by laying stones at the head and the foot of the grave. On the headstone he carved the initials *N. L.*

Young Abe was not satisfied with the meager ceremony his mother received on the day of her burial. The boy scrawled a letter to an old family friend, the pastor at the Lincolns' old church in Kentucky, Reverend David Elkin, and asked him to give a proper sermon at his mother's grave. When the Reverend Elkin arrived the following spring, the whole community turned out for the sermon at Nancy's grave. One of the neighbors recalled the scene:

"On a bright Sabbath morning, the settlers of the neighborhood gathered in. Some came in carts of the rudest construction . . . some came on horseback, two or three upon a horse, others came in wagons drawn by oxen, and still others came on foot.

"Taking his stand at the foot of the grave, Parson Elkin lifted his voice in prayer and sacred song and then preached a sermon. He spoke of the precious Christian woman who had gone, with warm praise, which she had deserved, and held her up as an example of true womanhood."[13]

Years later, after President Lincoln was killed, Billy Herndon stood at the grave of Nancy Hanks Lincoln, and those words he heard from her son's lips came to mind. "God bless her," Lincoln said to Herndon that day in the coach. "All that I am or hope ever to be I get from my mother."[14]

Head bowed, Herndon meditated in silence, offering his own tribute to the woman Dennis Hanks called "one of the very best women in the whole race known for kindness, tenderness, charity and love to the world."[15]

CHAPTER 9

"Here's your new mammy."

⸺⟨∞⟩⸺

The winter of 1818–1819 brought loneliness and despair into the Lincoln cabin. A hardened woodsman and carpenter, now forty, a young buck of nineteen, a girl going on twelve, and a ten-year-old boy struggled to hold their family together in that dark season of misery inside the unfinished, windowless, floorless, cheerless hut deep in the woods of Indiana.

Winter had always been a happy time for the Lincolns. They had plenty to celebrate. First Christmas, then the New Year. Tom's birthday came on the sixth of January. And in February they celebrated a whole week of birthdays. Nancy's was February sixth; Sarah's came on the tenth, and Abe's was two days later.

There was no celebrating now. They could only busy themselves with their winter chores, hustling after the simple necessities. They had to survive. "We had to work very hard . . . for to keep soul and body together," Dennis noted. "Every spare time that we had we picked up our rifle and fetched in a fine deer or turkey."[1]

Even the warmth of spring brought little comfort. Without a womanly presence, their home became squalid and depressing. They stopped bathing. Their clothes became tattered and worn. Their meat was barely cooked, and they ate without knives or forks. They slept on piles of twigs, leaves, and skins. Their cabin went untended, reeking from filth and the stale scent of disarray.

Young Sarah did what she could to fill her mother's role, cooking, cleaning, and mending the clothes, but her young shoulders faltered under the weight of her new burdens. Grief hit Sarah harder than the others. Tom, Dennis, and Abe had one another. Every day they went out together to do the things menfolk did. They didn't have to be alone.

"She was the only woman in the cabin that year, an' no neighbors fur miles," recalled Dennis. "Sairy was a little gal, only 'leven, an' she'd git so lonesome, missin' her mother, she'd set by the fire an' cry. Me 'n Abe got 'er a baby coon an' a turtle and tried to git a fawn but we couldn't ketch any."[2]

Abe felt the loss deeply. A neighbor, Arminda Rankin, remembered how he spoke of his mother during one of his frequent visits to her home: "He said he was nine years old when his mother died, that his instruction by her in letters and morals, and especially the Bible stores, and the interest and love he acquired in reading the Bible through this teaching of his mother had been the strongest and most influential experience of his life. He referred with evident sadness to the lonely months after his mother's death, and said that the Bible she had read and had taught him to read was the greatest comfort he and his sister had after their mother was gone."[3]

Tom could not bear to see his children live through another desperate winter. He resolved to change their situation. "He put the corn in the spring an' left us to 'tend to it, an' lit out fur Kaintucky," said Dennis. "Yes, we knowed what he went fur, but we didn't think he'd have any luck, bein' pore as he was, and with two children to raise."[4]

Backtracking through the same forest trails he cut three years before, Tom crossed the Ohio River into Kentucky and headed straight for the old friends he left in Elizabethtown. Isaac Bush still owed him two hundred dollars as part of a land deal they made ten years earlier. Tom may have had another reason to visit the Bush family.

"Old Tom Lincoln had courted Sally Bush before she married Johnston and failed to get her," said Elizabethtown resident John Helm.[5]

Colonel Chapman agreed. "Lincoln had been acquainted with her and proposed marriage to her before either of them had ever married but had been rejected by her," he said.[6]

Sally Bush had married Daniel Johnston on March 13, 1806. Tom married Nancy in June of that year, and the Lincolns and the Johnstons became friends. Nancy and Sally had a lot to talk about. They became pregnant at about the same time and gave birth to two of the prettiest baby girls in Elizabethtown.

Sally's life with Daniel Johnston did not go well. He ran up large debts to merchants in town and was unable to pay his taxes. He had to borrow money from the well-off Bush family. Finally, in 1814, Daniel Johnston found a steady job as jailor of Hardin County. The jailor's family lived in the stone prison, and his wife was expected to serve as caretaker. Sally cooked for the prisoners and cleaned the cells, including the grim basement dungeon. She struggled to make a cheery home for her three young children among whipping posts and criminals. Then, in 1816, her husband died.

"Do you remember Sally Bush who married Daniel Johnston, the jailor who lived on the alley below me?" wrote Samuel Haycraft, then the county clerk. "Johnson died of the cold plague [influenza]," he said.[7]

"She lived an honest poor widow. . . .[8] I knew her well. She was scarce a half mile from myself and I know she was a good woman. When a girl, her mother thought she was too proud, simply because the poor girl tried to make herself look decent and keep in the fashion of that early day."[9]

When Tom Lincoln returned to Elizabethtown he followed the path to the cabin below Haycraft's and came looking for the widow Johnston.

"He made a very short courtship," Haycraft wrote. "He came to see her on the first day of December 1819, and in a straight forward manner told her that they had known each other from childhood."[10]

"Well, Miss Johnston," Tom told her, "I have no wife and you have no husband. I came a-purpose to marry you. I knowed you from a gal and you knowed me from a boy. I've no time to lose, and if you're willing let it be done straight off."

"Tommy," she replied, "I know you well and have no objection to marrying you but I cannot do it straight off as I owe some debts that must first be paid."

"He asked her for a list of them," Haycraft said. "He went and paid them off that same day. . . ."[11] Next morning, I issued the license and they were married within sixty yards of my house."[12]

A few weeks before Christmas, a tough teenage boy and his two young cousins, squeezing out a bare existence for themselves on Little Pigeon Creek, were in for a surprise. They heard a wagon approaching and saw their father jump off to help a sturdy, kindly looking woman and three children, a girl, the same age as Sarah, a boy Abe's age, and a little girl.

"Here's your new mammy," Tom told the family.[13]

"We was all nigh about tickled to death when Tom brung a new wife home," recalled Dennis.[14]

"Lincoln hired his brother-in-law Ralph Croom to take his wagons and horses there to Indiana with their household goods," said Chapman. "Mrs. Johnston having a large supply of household goods for a family in those days. . . . Mrs. Johnston, now Mrs. Lincoln, took with her to Indiana one fine bureau, one table, set of chairs, one large cloth chest, cooking utensils, dishes, knives, forks, spoons, one spinning wheel, clothing, two beds and bedding and other articles."[15]

"Yes, Aunt Sairy was a woman o' propputy, an' coulda' done better, I reckon," said Dennis, "but Tom had a kind o' way with the women, an' maybe it was somethin' she tuk comfort in to have a man that didn't drink an' cuss none."[16]

The most important thing Sarah Lincoln brought with her was a new family. "Mrs. Johnston had three children, all young, a son and two daughters," said Chapman. "They constituted a part of Lincoln's family until grown and married."[17]

"There was now five children in the family," said Dennis, "Sarah and Abe Lincoln—Elizabeth, John D and Matilda Johnston."

"I married Elizabeth," Dennis explained. "I was just 21. She was 15."[18] (Dennis was mistaken about their ages. He was twenty-two and she was fourteen.)

Harriet Hanks Chapman was the daughter of Dennis Hanks and Elizabeth Johnston. She and her husband, Colonel Augustus H. Chapman, lived near the Lincolns. "I spent a great deal of my time with Grand Pa and Grand Ma Lincoln and loved them both dearly," she said.

Harriet Chapman gave us a detailed description of Abraham Lincoln's stepmother. "My grandmother is a very tall woman, straight as an Indian," she recalled. "Very handsome, sprightly, talkative and proud. Wore her hair curled till gray. Is kind hearted and very charitable and also very industrious." [19]

Tom Lincoln's new wife knew nothing of frontier hardships. "Mrs. Lincoln had been raised in Elizabethtown in somewhat a high life," said Dennis. [20] She was used to neighbors down the road, shops nearby, and many travelers passing through. She was in for a rude awakening.

"When we landed in Indiana," Mrs. Lincoln later recalled, "Mr. Lincoln had erected a good log cabin—tolerably comfortable. . . . The country was wild and desolate." [21]

Her son-in-law, Augustus Chapman, later spoke of the shock of her arrival at her new home. "Mrs. Lincoln was astonished to find that there was no floor or door to the house of her husband, no furniture of any kind, no beds or bedding. . . . They used rough stools for chairs. . . . They had no dishes except a few pewter and tin ones, no cooking utensils except a dutch oven and lid and one skillet. . . ." [22]

She brought her feisty, industrious nature to the wilderness and shook things up immediately, remaking that woeful bunch into a respectable family again. Dennis Hanks said: "When she came into Indiana Abe and his sister was wild, ragged and dirty. [23] The fust thing she did was to tell me to tote one o' Tom's carpenter benches to a place outside the door near the hoss-trough. Then she had me 'n Abe n' John Johnston, her boy, fill the trough with spring water. She put out a big gourd full o'soap an' another one to dip water with an' told us boys to wash up fur dinner. . . . [24]

"She soaped, rubbed and washed the children clean so that they looked pretty, neat, well and clean. She sewed and mended their clothes and the children once more looked human as their own good mother left them." [25]

Said Chapman, "She was a woman of great energy, of remarkable good sense, very industrious and saving. Also very neat and tidy in her person and manners. Knew exactly how to manage children." [26]

"You jist naturally had to be somebody when Aunt Sairy was around," said Dennis. [27] "She made a heap more o' Tom, too, than pore Nancy did. Before winter he'd put in a new floor, he'd whipsawed an' planed off so she could scour it, made some good beds an' cheers an' tinkered at the roof so it couldn't snow in on us boys 'at slep' in the loft. Purty soon we had the best house in the kentry." [28]

"The large supply of goods brought by Mrs. Lincoln came in good time," said Chapman. "She at once had a floor laid in the house, doors and windows put in . . . dressed the children up out of the large supply she had brought with her. In fact, in a few weeks, all had changed and where everything was wanting, now all was snug and comfortable." [29]

Dennis marveled at how Aunt Sarah worked her magic. "She had Tom build 'er a loom, an' when she heerd o' some lime burners bein' 'round Gentryville, Tom had to mosey over an' git some lime, an' white-wash the cabin. An' he made 'er an ashhopper fur lye an' a chicken-house nuthin' could git into. Then—te he he he!—she set some kind of a dead fall trap fur him an' got him to jine the Baptist Church! Cracky, but Aunt Sairy was some punkins!" [30]

By spring of 1820, the Lincoln family was reborn. Remnants of three families now shared the one-room cabin. There was Tom Lincoln, forty-two years old, and Sarah Bush Lincoln, thirty-two. Dennis Hanks was twenty-one, Sarah Lincoln and Elizabeth Johnston both thirteen. Abe was eleven, John Johnston was ten, and Matilda Johnston was nine.

"The two sets of children got along finely together as if they had all been the children of the same parents," Chapman said. [31] Somehow, Mrs.

Lincoln made everyone feel at home in their cramped quarters. Abe, Dennis, and John climbed the wall pegs each night and slept in the loft with the rain and snow seeping in through the cracks. Sarah, Elizabeth, and Matilda slept together in a big bed Tom built for them. At bedtime, the men undressed first, then the ladies, and by the frontier code of decency nobody was embarrassed.

"Thar was eight of us then to do fur, but Aunt Sairy had faculty an' didn't appear to be hurried or worried none," observed Dennis. "Little Sairy just chirked right up with a mother an' two sisters fur comp'ny. Abe used to say he was glad Sairy had some good times." [32]

Abe and Sarah, old hands at wilderness living, must have had a grand time showing their city sisters and new brother all the surprises in the woods. The forest was like a store full of delicious treats. Candy bars came from sweet maple sap. Put a mix of sassafras bark and roots in water and you had a tangy, sparkling drink. Sweet juicy berries, picked from patches so thick their clothes would be stained red from the juice, melted on their tongues—juneberries, mulberries, strawberries, dewberries, blackberries, and raspberries. All through summer and fall the children could reach up just about anywhere, pick some sweet fruits or nuts from the trees and pop them into their mouths. The men, hunting all the time, brought back deer, rabbit, squirrels, turkey, quail, pigeons, and wild ducks.

Abe and Sarah taught the Johnston children some games, backwoods style. They made a ball by wrapping some of Mrs. Lincoln's yarn around a pebble and covering it with a piece of buckskin. They played games like "hare and hounds," "wet and dry stones," "prisoner's base," and "hide and seek." They twisted some long hickory saplings and fastened the ends together to make hoops. Grapevines made excellent jump ropes.

Meanwhile, Abraham and his stepmother were forming a close, loving bond. "She took an especial liking to young Abe," said Chapman. "Her love for him was warmly returned and continued to the day of his death. But few children loved their parents as he loved this stepmother." [33]

Mrs. Lincoln spoke of their strong relationship. To her, he was like her own blood-son: "Abe never gave me a cross word or look and never refused in fact or even in appearance to do anything I requested of him. . . . His mind and mine, what little I had, seemed to run together more in the same channel. . . . He was dutiful to me always. He loved me truly, I think. I had a son John who was raised with Abe. Both were good boys, but I must say, both now being dead, that Abe was the best boy I ever saw or ever expect to see." [34]

Tom Lincoln loved his new wife and always remained devoted to her. He had the Lincoln sense of humor, and Sarah played right along. She asked her husband once: "Thomas, you never yet told me who you like best, your first wife or me."

"Sarah," he said, "that reminds me of old John Hardin down in Kentucky who had a fine-looking pair of horses and a neighbor came in one day to look at them and said, 'John, which one of these horses do you like the best?' John said, 'I can't tell. One of them kicks and the other bites and I don't know which is worst.'" [35]

CHAPTER 10

"Land o'Goshen, that boy air a' growin'."

———∞∞∞———

Throughout the 1820s, settlers from Kentucky streamed across the Ohio River to build their homes in the new state of Indiana. The community around Little Pigeon Creek grew—some fifty families lived within five miles of the Lincoln cabin. Not a mile away were nine families with forty-nine children. Yet there was plenty of open space. Farms and cabins were spread too far apart to make a village or a town. This was still frontier land.

The main gathering place was at Gentryville, two miles from the Lincoln home. The Gentrys were the wealthiest family in the county. James Gentry came to Little Pigeon Creek a few years after the Lincolns and bought over a thousand acres of land. He began keeping a small stock of goods to sell at his farmhouse. A blacksmith set up shop nearby, and soon a few more cabins went up. It was the beginning of the town of Gentryville.

The Gentrys had eight children. Abe was friendly with the boys, Matthew, Allen, and Joseph. Abe, Joseph Gentry, and Nat Grigsby went to school together, forming a friendship that lasted until Abe moved to Illinois.

The Grigsby family lived three miles from Abe. They'd been there about a year when Tom Lincoln came to Little Pigeon Creek to build his "half-faced" camp. Reuben Grigsby and his seven sons helped Tom clear the land to build his cabin. They owned a whiskey still. During that first brutal Indiana winter, Reuben Grigsby paid Tom to make wooden casks to hold his liquor.

Both Reuben Grigsby and Tom Lincoln had their own childhood stories to tell about bloody Indian raids. Tom was eight when his father was shot in an Indian ambush. When Reuben Grigsby was about four, a band of Indians massacred his whole family and carried him away. When they tired of his crying, they threw him in a river. An old squaw rescued him. The Indians didn't want him around, so they threw him in again. Again, the squaw swam out to save him. Finally, they decided to let the old woman keep the child. He stayed with the Indians for seven years, learning their language, following their customs, practicing their religion. Even as an old man he was known in the territory as a white man who followed the ways of the Indian.

Now that Abe was entering his teenage years, his glands began churning inside him, stretching his muscles, elongating his bones. He grew tall and lean, strong and hard. He found he could see over the heads of the other boys, and soon he was looking down at their fathers.

"Abe was a long, tall raw-boned boy," said childhood friend David Turnham, "odd and gawky. He had hardly attained 6 feet 4 inches when he left Indiana. Weighed about 160." [1]

The neighbors said, "Land o' Goshen, that boy air a' growin'." [2]

"He was as tall as he was ever goin' to be, I reckon," said Dennis. "He was the ganglin'est, awkwardest feller that ever stepped over a ten-rail snake fence. He had to duck to git through a door an' appeared to be all joints. Tom used to say Abe looked as if he'd been chopped out with an ax an' needed a jackplane took to him." [3]

Abe grew up handling an ax. From the day he set foot in Indiana as a boy of seven, his hands knew the wooden grip of an ax. The skin on his palms was thick with calluses. He learned how to make artful use of his ax. Measuring by eye, he could pinpoint a spot on a log and slice it with precision. Throwing his shoulders, hips swaying behind his swing, he learned how to apply the full weight of his body into each blow. By the time he approached full size, his long, wiry arms could hold the ax straight out in front of him, letting it rest easy in the air as if it were just a twig.

His companions remembered his skill as an axman:

"He was a master woodsman and could size up a tree that would work up well into rails at almost a glance." [4]

"Abe could sink an ax deeper in wood than any man I ever saw." [5]

"My how he could chop. His ax would flash and bite into a sugar tree or sycamore—down it would come. If you heard him felling trees in a clearing, you would say there were three men at work the way the trees fell." [6]

Abe was about sixteen when he accidentally gored his stepsister Matilda with his trusty ax. Tilda was the youngest child in the house.

"My earliest recollection of Abe is playing," she said. "Once when he was going to the field to work I ran—jumped on his back." [7] Without warning she "bounded on his back like a panther." [8] Abe, thrown off balance, fell backward. The ax slipped, slicing Tilda's flesh. Abe tore off part of his shirt to try to soak up the blood.

"Cut my foot on the ax," Matilda remembered. "We said—'What will we tell mother as to how this happened?' I said I would tell her 'I cut my foot on the ax.' That will be no lie."

Abe said: "But it won't all be the truth, the whole truth, will it Tilda?" [9]

Abe gave her some sound brotherly advice. "Tilda, the very best thing you can possibly do is to tell your mother the whole truth and nothing but the truth and risk your mother. This I advise you to do." [10]

Once, Abe was sharpening his ax when it slipped and nearly sliced off his thumb. It left a jagged white scar that became his badge as an ax-man.

Lincoln never forgot how to handle an ax. As commander-in-chief at the height of the war, he visited the Washington Navy Yard some new experimental weapons. A reporter watched as picked up an ax that was hanging on the door. "Here i which I guess I understand better than either of you," he said to the military guards around him. Then, according to the reporter, "he held the ax out at arm's length by the end of the handle . . . a feat not another person of the party could perform." [11]

As folks in Little Pigeon Creek saw Abe take the body of a man, they put him to task doing a man's work. He was hired out as a farmhand, driving teams of horses to plow the fields, cutting down trees to clear the land, and splitting logs to build cabins, pigpens, and fences.

Abe's specialty was building fences. Settlers on the frontier said that a fence had to be "horse high, bull strong, and pig tight." Each fence rail was about ten feet long and four inches wide and Abe could make four hundred of them in a day. For that labor he was paid twenty-five cents.

The grandson of Abe's neighbor Josiah Crawford recalled that "Grandfather employed young Abe to make rails for pens. These rails were longer than the ordinary ten-foot rails and larger. Abe notched the rails at the ends to make them fit closer together." Years later, during the presidential campaign of 1860, there was a great demand for the rails he split as a young man. Crawford returned to the family farm with his grandfather to search for the very rails Lincoln had made. "They were easily identified by their length and size and notches in the ends," he said. [12]

Abe often worked alongside his father, who tried to teach Abe his craft.

"He sometime worked at the cabinet business, his father being a carpenter and cabinet maker," said Nat Grigsby. [13]

As the finest carpenter in the area, Tom Lincoln was chosen by the congregation to supervise the construction of a new meeting house for the Little Pigeon Creek Baptist Church. Abe was his father's right-hand man, working along with the crew. When it was finished, Abe was given the job of sexton of the church, taking care of all church property.

"Thomas Lincoln often and at various times worked for me" recalled family friend William Wood. "Made cupboards and other household furniture for me. He built my house, made floors, run up the stairs, did all the inside work for my house. Abe would come to my house with his father and romp with my children." [14]

Father and son also worked together to build a wagon for James Gentry. It was constructed "entirely out of wood, even to the hickory rims to the wheels."[15]

When the neighborhood boys found some time on their hands, they whooped and frolicked like frisky kittens, holding contests of strength, agility, and endurance. "We used to play Four Corner Bull Pen [a game something like Dodge Ball]," recalled Dennis, "and what we called Cat [short for Catapult which involved throwing a stick and chasing it] . . . and throwing a maul over our shoulders." [16] They ran dashes, wrestled, played "knocking off hats," raced horses, chased foxes, swam, and fished. Abe found that he could beat all the boys his own age, and just about everyone else.

His great strength became legendary. "Lincoln was a powerful man," said neighbor Joseph Richardson. "Could carry what three ordinary men would grunt and swear at. Saw him carry a chicken house made of poles pinned together and carried that weight, at least six hundred (pounds) if not much more." [17]

"He wouldn't take no sass, neither," recalled Dennis. "If a feller was spoilin' fur a fight, an' nothin' else'd do him, Abe'd accomydate him all right. Generally, Abe could lay him out so he wouldn't know nothin' about it fur a spell. . . . When he was fifteen he could bring me down by throwin' his leg over my shoulder. I always was a little runt of a feller." [18]

The boys were always testing one another, backing up their fighting words with fists. Abe and William Grigsby quarreled over a certain spotted pup. Grigsby challenged Lincoln, but Abe only looked down at him and smiled, saying that it would not be a fair fight since Grigsby was too small. If Grigsby really wanted to fight he could take on Abe's stepbrother, John Johnston. The winner could keep the pup.

The day for the big fight was set. Johnston and Grigsby squared off against each other, stripped to the waist, their seconds rooting them on. A crown formed a ring around them, so large and boisterous that one man "climbed a tree that he might see over the heads of the people who gathered around." [19]

The two men lit into each other, punching, mauling, bruising with bloody fists as the crowd yelped and hollered.

"They had a terrible fight," said Green Taylor, whose father was the second for John Johnston. "Wm Grigsby was too much for Lincoln's man Johnston. After they had fought a long time . . . Abe burst through, caught Grigsby, threw him off some feet." [20] "Bodily hurled him over the heads of the crowd," said another witness. [21]

"There he stood," recalled Green Taylor of an angry Lincoln, "proud as Lucifer, and swinging a bottle of liquor over his head, swore he was 'the big buck of the lick. If anyone doubts it,' he shouted, 'he has only to come on and whet his horns.' [22] Being a general invitation for a general fight they all pitched in and had quite a general fight." [23] All the boys jumped in for a wild bone-crushing brawl, and for months they argued about who got the biggest whipping.

Those long legs of Abe's just kept on growing. Nat Grigsby remembered that "between the shoe and sock and his britches made of buckskin, there was bare and naked six or more inches of Abe Lincoln's shin bone." [24] Someone said that "he looked as if he were made for wading in deep water." [25]

"Aunt Sairy often told Abe 'at his feet bein' clean didn't matter so much because she could scour the floor, but he'd better wash his head, or he'd be a rubbin' dirt off on her nice whitewashed rafters," Dennis remarked.

"That put an idy in his head, I reckon . . . thar was always a passel o' youngsters 'round the place. One day Abe put 'em up to wadin' in the mud-puddle by the hoss trough. Then he took 'em one by one, turned 'em upside down, an' walked 'em acrost the ceilin', them ascreamin' fit to kill.

"Aunt Sairy come in, an' it was so blamed funny she set down an' laughed, though she said Abe'd oughter be spanked. I don't know how far he had to go fur more lime, but he whitewashed the ceilin' all over again." [26]

Abe loved to tell stories about life on the frontier, and one day he told Billy Herndon his "coon" story. His father had a little yellow dog named Joe. Whenever Abe and his stepbrother John tried to sneak off into the woods to go coon hunting, Joe would bark and howl and make such a ruckus Tom Lincoln had to chase the boys off.

One night, the boys brought the dog with them. They caught a coon, killed him, and for sport they sewed the coon's hide on little Joe. The dog "struggled vigorously during the operation of sewing on," said Herndon, "and being released from the hands of his captors, made a bee-line for home."

During the night, "other large canines on the way, scenting coon, tracked the little animal home and possibly mistaking him for real coon, speedily demolished him. The next morning old Thomas discovered lying in his yard the lifeless remains of yellow Joe, with strong proof of coon-skin accompaniment."

"Father was much incensed at his death," observed Abe, "but as John and I stood . . . shivering in the doorway, we felt assured little yellow Joe would never be able again to sound the call for another coon hunt."[27]

While his long limbs were abruptly filling out, mysterious changes came over him. While his body was rapidly growing, a simmering burn smoldered in his heart. He spent many quiet moments looking deep within himself. "As he shot up," said David Turnham, "he seemed to change in appearance and action. Although quick witted and ready with an answer, he began to exhibit deep thoughtfulness and was so often lost in studied reflection we could not help noticing the strange turn in his actions. He disclosed rare timidity and sensitiveness, especially in the presence of men and women, and although cheerful enough in presence of boys, he did not appear to seek our company as earnestly as before."[28]

Lincoln's greatest biographer, Carl Sandburg, came to know his subject from the inside and wrote of Lincoln with lyric eloquence that earned him a Pulitzer Prize. Sandburg could almost breathe with Lincoln, follow his heartbeat. He knew the forces that shaped Lincoln's soul as he grew up in backwoods America.

Sandburg wrote of the food that sustained him and made him strong, the nourishment that gave the nation a giant for all generations. He knew the secret of Lincoln's greatness.

"Growing from boy to man, he was alone a good deal of the time. Days came often when he was by himself all the time except at breakfast and supper hours in the cabin home. In some years more of his time was spent in loneliness than in the company of other people. . . .

"It was the wilderness loneliness he became acquainted with. . . . He rested between spells of work in the springtime when the upward push of the coming out of the new grass can be heard, and in autumn weeks when the rustle of a single falling leaf lets go a whisper that a listening ear can catch. . . .

"And so he grew. Silence found him; he met silence," Sandburg noted. "In the making of him as he was, the element of silence was immense." [29]

Chapter 11

"A real eddication."

———◦∞∞◦———

Some Kentucky mornings when Abe was six years old, his mother would get him up early, scrub his face and hands, slick back his hair, and send him off to march two miles down the road with eight year-old Sarah. They were going to school.

"Nancy kep' urging Abe to study," recalls Dennis. "'Abe,' she'd say, 'you l'arn all you kin an' be some account.'" [1]

Tom said he wanted Abe to have "a real eddication. . . . You air-a-goin' to larn readin', writin' and cipherin' [arithmetic]." [2]

"My father," said Abe, "had suffered greatly for the want of an education and he determined that I should be well educated. And what do you think he said his ideas of a good education were? We had an old dog-eared arithmetic in our house and Father determined that somehow or somehow else, I should cipher clear through that book." [3]

A school appeared in a community when a number of parents showed an interest in educating their children. They found a teacher who would open a classroom for a season, and the children were sent there whenever they could be spared from household chores. Families paid the teacher in deer meat, ham, corn, animal skins, or produce, items more valuable than paper money on the frontier.

They were known as "blab schools." Students were called "scholars." Scholars had to recite their lessons aloud and all at once, so the teacher could be sure each student's concentration did not wander from the work. Anyone who happened to pass a school in session would hear a chorus of voices reciting in unison. People said it sounded like "blabbing." Scholars who misbehaved had to wear a dunce cap and sit in the corner. The master only had to wave his whip to fire the seat of ambition in an unruly scholar.

"There were some schools, so called," said Abe. "But no qualification was ever required of a teacher beyond readin', writin' and ciperin' to the Rule of Three. If a straggler supposed to understand Latin happened to sojourn in the neighborhood, he was looked upon as a wizard. There was absolutely nothing to excite ambition for education." [4]

By the time Abe started school at Knob Creek, he knew the alphabet and could read some. "About Abe's early education and his sister's education, let me say this," relates Dennis. "Their mother first learned them ABC's. She learned them out of Webster's old spelling book. It belonged to me and cost in those days 75 cents, it being covered with calfskin. . . . I taught Abe to write with a buzzard's quill which I killed with a rifle, and having made a pen, put Abe's hand in mine and moving his fingers by my hand to give him the idea of how to write. [5]

"I made ink out o' blackberry brier root," said Dennis. "Kind o' ornery ink that was. It et the paper into holes. Got so I could cut good pens out o' turkey-buzzard quills. . . .

"Well, me 'n Abe spelled through Webster's spellin' book twict before he got tired. Then he tuk to writin' on the . . . floor, the fence rails and the wooden fire shovel with a bit o' charcoal.

"When Tom got mad at his markin' the house up, Abe tuk to markin' trees 'at Tom wanted to cut down, with his name, an' writin' it in the sand at the deer-lick. He tried to interest little Sairy in l'arnin' to read, but she never tuk to it. . . .

"It pestered Tom a heap to have Abe writin' all over everything thataway, but Abe was jist wropped up in it.

"'Denny,' he sez to me many a time, 'look at that, will you? ABRAHAM LINCOLN! That stands fur me. Don't look a blamed bit like me!' An' he'd stand an' study it a spell. 'Peared to mean a heap to Abe." [6]

Abe's first teacher at Knob Creek was Zachariah Riney. There Abe learned mostly from a book called Dilworth's Speller. When Mr. Riney left town, the school was taken over by a neighbor, Caleb Hazel.

"Young Abraham commenced trudging his way to school to Caleb Hazel, with whom I was well acquainted and could perhaps teach spelling, reading, and indifferent writing and perhaps could cipher to the rule of three," recounts Samuel Haycraft, who was the town clerk in Elizabethtown. "But he had no other qualification of a teacher except large size and bodily strength to thrash any boy or youth that came to his school." [7]

"With this standard of an education," a friend wrote, "he started to school in a log-house in the neighborhood and began his educational career. He had attended this school but about six weeks, however, when a calamity befell the father. He had endorsed some man's note in the neighborhood for a considerable amount and the prospect was he would have it to pay and that would sweep away all their possessions. His father, therefore, explained to him that he wanted to hire him out and receive the fruits of his labor and his aid in averting his calamity." [8]

When the Lincolns moved to Indiana, word got around that young Abe could read and write, and suddenly his skill was in great demand. Many of their neighbors wanted to write letters to family and friends back in Kentucky. They came to him with personal messages and he listened, writing them down as best he could. Seeing a boy so young reading and writing surprised a lot of people. "He set everybody a wonderin' to see how much he knowed and he not mor'n seven," a neighbor said. [9]

At the time Abe's mother died in his ninth year, he hadn't been to school for three years. "I reckon it was thinkin' o' Nancy an' things she'd done said to him that started Abe to studyin' that next winter," said Dennis. [10]

"Abraham Lincoln and Sally and myself all went to school," recalled Nat Grigsby. "We first went to school to Andy Crawford in the year 1818 in the winter, the same year that Mrs. Lincoln died, she having died in October. Abe went to school nearly a year, say nine months. I was going to school all this time and saw Lincoln there most, if not all, the time." [11]

It was a rough and rugged pioneer school. "There was a school house built two miles south of Thomas Lincoln's farm," recalled Nat, "the first school house that was built in this part of the state. The house was built of round logs just high enough for a man to stand erect under the ruff [roof]. The floor was split logs or what we called puncheons. The chimney was made of poles and clay. The window was constructed by chopping out a part of two logs and placing pieces of split boards at proper distance and then we would take out old copy books and grease them and paste them over the window. This give us light. In this school room Abraham Lincoln and myself entered school. [12]

"When we went to Crawford's," Nat continued, "he tried to learn us manners. . . . He would ask the scholars to retire from the schoolroom, come in, and then some scholar would go around and introduce him to all the scholars, male and female." [13]

His friends remember Abe as a student.

"He was always at school early and attentive to his studies. He was always at the head of his class and progressed rapidly in his studies. He lost no time at home and when he was not at work he was learning his books. He pursued his studies on the Sabbath Day. He also packed books when at work to read when he rested from labor." [14]

"Whilst other boys were idling away their time, Lincoln was studying his books. . . . He read and thoroughly read his books whilst we played." [15]

"He always appeared to be very quiet during playtime, never seemed to be rude, seemed to have a liking for solitude, was the one chosen in almost every case to adjust difficulties between boys of his size and, when appealed to, his decision was an end of the trouble. Was rather noted for keeping his clothes clean longer than any of the others." [16]

Nat Grigsby remembers how one day Abe "came forward with an awkward bow and a deprecative smile to read an essay on the wickedness of being cruel to helpless animals." [17]

Every Friday, Master Crawford had the scholars line up against the wall. "We had spelling matches frequently," said Nat. [18] Kate Roby told of the time she was stuck on a word and Abe gallantly came to her rescue. "Crawford put a word to us to spell," she recalled.

"The word to spell was *DEFIED*. Crawford said that if we did not spell it he would keep us in school all day and night. We all missed the word. Couldn't spell it. We spelled the word every way but the right way. [19]

"Abe stood on the opposite side of the room and was watching me," she continued. "I began *'D-E-F'*—and then I stopped, hesitating whether to proceed with an *'I'* or a *'Y'*. Looking up, I beheld Abe, a grin covering his face and pointing with his index finger to his eye. I took the hint, spelled the word with an *'I'* and it went through all right." [20]

Kate Roby was Abe's special friend. "I knew Mr. L. well," she remembered. "He and I went to school together. I was fifteen years old. Lincoln about the same age. . . ." [21]

"He often and often commented or talked to me about what he read—seemed to read it out of the book as he went along," she confided. "He was the learned boy among us unlearned folks. He took great pains to explain. Could do it so simply."

She recalled a special moment shared by two inquiring teenagers still learning about the world. "One evening, Abe and myself were sitting on the banks of the Ohio. . . . I said to Abe that the sun was going down."

"That's not so," he insisted. "It don't really go down. It seems so. The earth turns from west to east and the revolution of the earth carries us under. We do the sinking, as you call it. The sun, as to us, is comparatively still. The sun's sinking is only an appearance."

Kate was amused. "I said—'Abe, what a fool you are!'"

Years later, Abe's discourse got Kate thinking. "I know now that I was the fool, not Lincoln," she admitted. "I am now thoroughly satisfied that we knew the general laws of astronomy and the movements of the heavenly bodies. He was better read then than the world knows or is likely to know exactly. No man could have talked to me as he did that night unless he had known something of geography as well as astronomy." [22]

Abe liked to tell a story to describe how students in frontier schools learned to read. The teacher required each student to take a turn reading aloud from the Bible. The lesson that stuck in Lincoln's mind was from the third chapter in the Book of Daniel.

The students, including Abe, read:

Nebuchadnezzar the king made an image of gold, whose height was threescore cubit and the breadth thereof six cubits. . . . Thou, O King, hast made a decree that every man . . . shall fall down and worship the golden image. And whoso falleth not down and worshippeth, that he should be cast into the midst of a burning fiery furnace. . . .

There are certain Jews whom thou hast set over the affairs of the province of Babylon, Shadrach, Meshach, and Abednego; these men, O king, have not regarded thee; they serve not thy gods, nor worship the golden image which thou hast set up.[23]

The reading went smoothly until the twelfth verse. A boy named Bud was next to read. "Little Bud stumbled on Shadrach, floundered on Meshach, and went all to pieces on Abednego," recalled Abe. "Instantly the hand of the master dealt him a cuff on the side of the head and left him wailing and blubbering as the next boy in line took up the reading. But before the girl at the end of the line had done reading, he had subsided into sniffles and finally become quiet. His blunder and disgrace were forgotten by the others of the class until his turn was approaching to read again. Then, like a thunderclap out of a clear sky, he set up a wail which even alarmed the master, who with rather unusual gentleness inquired, 'What's the matter now?'

"Pointing with a shaking finger at the verse which a few moments later would fall to him to read, Bud managed to quaver out the answer: 'Look there marster,' he cried. 'There comes them same damn three fellers again.'"[24]

When Abe left Crawford's classroom, he didn't go to school again for two years. He had done plenty of reading on his own when James Swaney opened a school on Hoskins farm. Swaney was just twenty-one and could barely read, write, and cipher himself. Abe's attendance was irregular.

According to John Hoskins, whose family settled in Little Pigeon Creek about the same time as the Lincolns, the young scholar "had to travel four and a half miles—and this going back and forth so great a distance occupied entirely too much of his time. His attendance was therefore only at odd times and was speedily broken off altogether."[25]

Two years later, Abe studied briefly with Azel Dorsey, one of the most prominent citizens in the county who served as tax commissioner, treasurer, and coroner. Dorsey recalled his student: "One of the noblest boys I ever knew. . . . Certain to become noted if he lives. . . . [26] Marked for the diligence and eagerness with which he pursued his studies. . . . Came to the log cabin schoolhouse arrayed in buckskin clothes, a raccoon skin cap and provided with an old arithmetic which had somewhere been found for him to begin his investigation into the higher branches." [27]

That was the end of formal education for Abraham Lincoln. He wrote: "Abraham now thinks that the aggregate of all his schooling did not amount to one year." [28]

By this time, Abe was deeply immersed in the world of books. Books became his passion. His teachers were books. As he passed into his fifteenth year, there was no reason for him to sit in a backwoods classroom. Said Kate Roby: "Could do him no further good. He went to school no more." [29]

CHAPTER 12

"Mighty darned good lies."

———— ✇ ————

"Seems to me now I never seen Abe after he was twelve 'at he didn't have a book some'ers 'round," said Dennis. "He'd put a book inside his shirt an' fill his pants pockets with corn dodgers, an' go off to plow or hoe. When noon come, he'd set down under a tree, an' read an' eat. An' when he come to the house at night, he'd tilt a cheer back by the chimbly, put his feet on the rung, an' set his backbone and read. Aunt Sairy always put a candle on the mantel-piece fur him, if she had one. An' as like as not, Abe'd eat his supper thar, takin' anything she'd give him that he could gnaw at an' read at the same time."[1]

His cousin John Hanks agreed. "When Lincoln, Abe and I, returned to the house from work, he would go to the cupboard, snatch a piece of cornbread, take down a book, sit down on a chair, cock his legs up as high as his head and read."[2]

"His usual way of reading was lying down," remembers Harriet Hanks Chapman. "In warm weather he seemed to prefer the floor. He would turn a chair down on the floor and put a pillow on it and lie there for hours and read."[3]

Said Dennis: "I've seen many a feller come in an' look at him, Abe not knowin' anybody was 'round, an' sneak out agin like a cat, an' say: 'Well, I'll be darned!' It didn't seem natural, nohow, to see a feller read like that."[4]

"He worked for me," recalls neighbor John Romine. "Was always reading and thinking. Used to get mad at him . . . I say Abe was awful lazy. He would laugh and talk and crack jokes and tell stories all the time. Didn't ever work but did dearly love his pay. He worked for me frequently, a few days only at a time . . . Lincoln said to me one day that his father taught him to work but never learned him to love it." [5]

"Abe was not energetic except in one thing—he was active and persistent in learning. Read everything he could," said his stepsister Matilda. [6]

"What Lincoln read," recounts David Turnham, "he read and re-read, read and studied thoroughly. . . . When Lincoln was going about he read everything that he could lay his hands on." [7]

"Lincoln devoured all the books he could get," said John Hanks. "He was a constant and voracious reader. . . . He frequently read the Bible. He read *Robinson Crusoe*, Bunyan's *Pilgrim's Progress*." [8]

"He kept the Bible and Aesop's always within reach, and read them over and over again," added Turnham. [9]

"I feel the need of reading," Abe explained. "It is a loss to a man not to have grown up among books." [10]

He was nine when he read *Aesop's Fables,* wonderstruck at the tales of wise and foolish animals, marveling at the lessons they learned. He read a short biographical sketch of Aesop and discovered this revered sage began life as a humble slave.

Lincoln never forgot the book. Days before he issued the Emancipation Proclamation, President Lincoln told the Senate chaplain how the plight of the American slaves reminded him of a lesson he learned in his childhood reading.

"It made me think of a story I read in one of my first books, *Aesop's Fables,*" Lincoln said. "It was an old edition and had curious, rough wood-cuts, one of which showed four white men scrubbing a Negro in a potash kettle filled with cold water. The text explained that the men thought that by scrubbing the Negro they might make him white. Just about the time they thought they were succeeding, he took cold and died. Now, I am afraid that by the time we get through this war the Negro will catch cold and die." [11]

Pilgrim's Progress by John Bunyan was often found in pioneer homes next to the Bible. Abe lost himself in its pages and was transported to far-off places—the Slough of Despond, Delectable Mountain, Hill Difficulty, Enchanted Ground, the City of Destruction, Celestial Country, Dead-Man's Lane, and Doubting Castle. He met strange improbable characters who had something to teach about life—Mr. Moneylove, Mr. Hold-the-World, Mr. Save-All, Mr. Feeblemind, Mr. Greatheart, Mr. Honest, Mrs. Lightmind, Mr. Lechery, Mrs. Bat-Eyes, Mrs. Inconsiderate, and young Mercy. The hero of the story was a young wandering pilgrim named Christian.

When Abe was buried in a "Slough of Despond" of his own, his profound grief after his mother died, he turned to these books for relief. That dark winter, he lived inside his books. Books lifted him out of his hard, cold world. Books were his refuge.

When he read *Robinson Crusoe* by Daniel Defoe, he found himself suddenly in the midst of a violent shipwreck. He saw a lone survivor thrown onto the beach of a deserted island. He followed the man as he struggled to survive, making his clothes from animal skins, hunting for food, always watching out for wild creatures in the woods.

Abe could follow along as Robinson Crusoe tried to make a home for himself in the jungle wilderness, much as Abe and his family did.

"Abe'd lay on his stummick by the fire an' read out loud to me 'n Aunt Sairy," recalls Dennis. "An' we'd laugh when he did, though I reckon it went in at one ear an' out at the other with her, as it did with me. . . ."[12]

"'Denny,' he'd say, 'the things I want to know is in books. My best friend's the man who'll git me one.' Well, books wasn't as plenty as wildcats, but I got him one by cuttin' a few cords o' wood. It had a lot o' yarns in it. One I ricollect was about a feller that got near some darned fool rocks 'at drawed all the nails out o' his boat an' he got a duckin'. Wasn't a blamed bit o' sense in that yarn.[13]

"'Abe,' sez I, many a time, 'them yarns is all lies.'

"'Mighty darned good lies,' he'd say, an' go on readin' an' chucklin' to hisself, till Tom'd kiver up the fire fur the night an' shoo him off to bed." [14]

Dennis was thinking of an exciting collection of legends from the East called *The Arabian Nights*. Abe could lose himself in far-off lands and adventures in make-believe like "The Seven Voyages of Sinbad the Sailor."

The young man was also intensely curious about the land of his birth, this new nation called the United States and its founding fathers. He grew up hearing their names in awed tones—Washington, Jefferson, Franklin—and he longed to know what made them great. Turning the pages of Franklin's *Autobiography*, he was engrossed by the great man's words. Here was a boy much like himself, inquisitive, hardworking, restless, a boy who loved books as much as Abe did.

Young Benjamin Franklin spoke to a wide-eyed Abe Lincoln.

> *My early readiness in learning to read, which must have been very early, as I do not remember when I could not read....* [15] *From my infancy I was passionately fond of reading and all the money that came into my hands was laid out in the purchasing of books....* [16] *Often I sat up in my chamber reading the greatest part of the night when the book was borrowed in the evening and to be returned in the morning, lest it should be found missing.* [17]

The book that had the greatest impact on Abe caused him the most trouble: *A History of the Life and Death, Virtues and Exploits of General George Washington* by Mason Weems. Abe borrowed the book from Josiah Crawford. "This man Crawford owned Weems' *Life of Washington* in one volume," said Judge John Pitcher. "Crawford was noted for his littleness in all his dealings with his neighbors.... Mr. Lincoln borrowed this from Mr. Crawford and before he had finished reading the book he left it in an open window when a rainstorm wet the book causing the covers to warp and otherwise damage the book." [18]

"Mr. Lincoln felt very much hurt over this misfortune," relates Judge Pitcher. "Took the book to Mr. Crawford." [19]

"I have no money with which to pay you for the damage the book has sustained," Lincoln told him, "but will work it out if you have any work I can do." [20]

Said Judge Pitcher, "Mr. Crawford told Mr. Lincoln to pull fodder two days and they would call it even." [21]

Elizabeth Crawford remembered the entire episode. "Lincoln, in 1829, borrowed this book and by accident got it wet. L. came and told honestly and exactly how it was done. . . . My husband said: 'Abe, as long as it is you, you may finish the book and keep it.' Abe pulled fodder a day or two for it." [22]

Judge Pitcher continued. "Lincoln said to me—'You see, I am tall and long armed. Well, I went to work and there was not a corn blade left on a stalk where I worked during the two days I was paying the damage sustained by the little wetting that book received.'" [23]

Said Abe, "I made a clean sweep." [24]

Lincoln was taught to be honest by his father. In Weems's *Washington*, the boy discovered how his great hero loved the truth. He read how young George came to value honesty.

When George . . . was about six years old, he was made the wealthy master of a hatchet, of which, like most little boys, he was immoderately fond, and was constantly going about chipping every thing that came in his way. One day, in the garden, where he often amused himself hacking his mother's pea-sticks, he unluckily tried the edge of his hatchet on the body of a beautiful young English cherry tree. . . .

The next morning, the old gentleman, finding out what had befallen his tree, which, by the way, was a great favorite, came into the house and with much warmth asked for the mischievous author . . . Nobody could tell him anything about it. Presently, George and his hatchet made their appearance. "George," said his father, "do you know who killed that beautiful little cherry tree yonder in the garden?"

This was a tough question, and George staggered under it for a moment, but quickly recovered himself, and looking at his father

*with the sweet face of a youth brightened with the inexpressible charm
of all-conquering truth, he bravely cried out, "I can't tell a lie, Pa.
You know I can't tell a lie. I did cut it with my hatchet."*

*"Run to my arms, you dearest boy," cried his father in transports,
"run to my arms. Glad am I, George, that you killed my tree. For you
have paid me for it a thousand fold. Such an act of heroism in my son
is more worth than a thousand trees, though blossomed with silver
and their fruits of purest gold."*[25]

Sometime after Abe finished *The Life of Washington*, a book came
into his hands that caught the attention of the American public. It
became something of a best-seller in the 1820s. The exact title was: *An
Authentic Narrative of the Loss of the American Brig Commerce, Wrecked
on the Western Coast of Africa in the Month of August, 1815—With an
Account of the Sufferings of Her Surviving Officers and Crew, Who Were
Enslaved by the Wandering Arabs on the Great African Desert or Zahahrah,
and Observations Historical, Geographical, etc. Made During the Travels of
the Author, While a Slave to the Arabs, and in the Empire of Morocco.* The
author was James Riley.

When Riley was fifteen, he longed to go to sea. With his parents'
consent, he went to work on a ship and learned the fine art of naviga-
tion. Soon, he rose to become a ship's captain. His story was a chilling
tale—his ship was wrecked, and he and his crew were taken into slavery.
Later they were rescued and returned home. It was Abraham Lincoln's
first encounter with the evils of slavery from the viewpoint of a slave.

James Riley, a simple American seaman, wrote to his fellow Americans
of the indignity and humiliation of slavery:

*Unerring wisdom and goodness has since restored me to the comforts
of civilized life, to the bosom of my family, and to the blessing of my
native land, whose political and moral institutions are in themselves
the very best of any that prevail in the civilized portion of the globe,
and ensure to her citizens the greatest share of personal liberty, protec-
tion and happiness. And yet, strange as it must appear . . . my proud-*

spirited and free country-men still hold a million and a half nearly of
the human species in the most cruel bonds of slavery. . . . Adversity
has taught me some noble lessons. I have now learned to look with
compassion on my enslaved and oppressed fellow-creatures. [26]

Abe was most likely the most skilled reader among all his friends. He loved to use his reading talents to entertain anyone who would listen. Nat Grigsby remembers: "There was another book that we boys got a lot of fun out of. Lincoln would read it to us out in the woods on Sundays . . . It was the King's Jester . . . it was a book of funny stories." [27]

Actually, it was a volume of vulgar, bawdy humor called *Quinn's Jests* written by an English actor named James Quinn. It was just the kind of book teenage boys love to read in the woods, hoping their parents never find out.

CHAPTER 13

"Somethin' Peculiarsome."

———⚬⚬⚬———

"Hey! Is that the only way Abe l'arnt things—out o' books?" mused Dennis. "You bet he was too smart to think everything was in books." [1]

Dennis knew how eager the young boy was to learn. "Sometimes Abe was a little rude. When strangers would ride along and up to his father's fence Abe always, through pride and to tease his father, would be sure to ask the stranger the first question, for which his father would sometimes knock him a rod. [2]

"Tom'd have to bang him on the side o' his head with his hat. Abe'd go off a spell an' fire sticks at the snow-birds an' whistle like he didn't keer." [3]

Dennis could see that his father's quick punishment had an effect. "Abe, when whipped by his father, never bawled but dropped a kind of silent unwelcome tear as evidence of his sensations." [4]

Abe complained to Dennis, "Pap thinks it ain't polite to ask folks so many questions. I reckon I wasn't born to be polite, Denny. Thar's so darned many things I want to know. An' how else am I goin' to git to know 'em?" [5]

Dennis described Abe as "a good listener to his superiors—bad to his inferiors. That is, he couldn't endure jabber." [6]

For the curious boy, visitors brought endless fascination. Each caller was an unopened book, filled with amazing stories and captivating new ideas. Mrs. Lincoln watched Abe closely, noticed how he studied their houseguests. "Abe . . . was a silent and attentive observer, never speaking or asking questions till they were gone and then he must understand everything—even to the smallest thing, minutely and exactly. He would then repeat it over to himself again and again, sometimes in one form and then in another and when it was fixed in his mind to suit him, he became easy and he never lost the fact or his understanding of it. Sometimes he seemed pestered to give expression to his views and got mad almost at one who couldn't explain plainly what he wanted to convey." [7]

Shyness did not remain long in Abe Lincoln's personality. Growing more confident and cocky, the boy challenged the adults around him, asking them to explain, clarify, and defend their ideas. "The Baptist preachers always stopped at the house," recalled Dennis. "Once Abe tried to git a preacher to 'count fur them miracles about Jonah an' the whale an' the others an' got him so worked up that when Abe asked him who was the father of Zebedee's children, blamed if he could tell." [8]

Abe loved to make speeches. He would collect the children and made them sit in front of a tree stump. Then, solemnly climbing the stump, he would talk their ears off while they looked on attentively. "I have seen Lincoln—Abraham—make speeches to his step-brother, step-sisters and youngsters that would come to see the family," recalls John Hanks. [9]

Said Colonel Chapman, "When about ten years old Lincoln first showed his talent as a speaker and from that forward would gather the children together, mount a stump or log and harangue his juvenile audience. . . . He would often after returning from church repeat correctly nearly all of the sermon which he had heard, mimicking the style and tone of the Baptist preachers." [10]

"Abe had a powerful good mem'ry," said Dennis. "He'd go to church an' come home an' say over the sermon as good as the preacher. He'd often do it fur Aunt Sairy when she couldn't go an' she said it was jist as good as goin' herself. He'd say over everything from 'beloved brethern' to 'amen' without crackin' a smile, pass a pewter plate fur a collection an then we'd all jine him in singin' the Doxology."[11]

David Turnham remembered how "Abe Lincoln preached the sermon of Jeremiah Cash. Cash had preached a sermon and Abe said he could repeat it. . . . Abe mounted a log and proceeded to give the text and at it he went. He did preach almost the identical sermon. It was done with wonderful accuracy."[12]

"He made other speeches such as interested him and the children," said Mrs. Lincoln.[13]

Abe would talk up a subject in one direction, spin it around, pull on it, scrub it, bounce it, and bring it back to where he began.

"I recollect some of the questions they spoke on," said Elizabeth Crawford. "The Bee and the Ant. Water and Fire. Another was—which was the strongest, wind or water."[14]

His mother said that "His father had to make him quit sometimes as he quit his own work to speak and made the other children as well as the men quit their work."[15]

"He was a tricky man," said Dennis. "Sometimes when he went to a log house raising, corn shucking and such like things, he would say to himself and sometimes to others—'I don't want these fellows to work any more'—and instantly he would commence his pranks, tricks, jokes, stories and sure enough, all would stop, gather round Abe and listen, sometimes crying, and sometimes bursting their sides with laughter."[16]

"Abe was one day bothering the girls," remembered Elizabeth Crawford. "His sister and others playing yonder and his sister scolded him, saying—'Abe, you ought to be ashamed of yourself. What do you expect will become of you?'"

Abe quickly responded: "Be President of the U.S."[17]

Dennis always said there was "somethin' peculiarsome" about Abe.[18] In a place where "books wasn't as plenty as wildcats" and where there was "absolutely nothing to excite ambition for education," a guiding angel found Abe and noticed his peculiar ambitions. Offering unfailing support and gentle encouragement, she pushed him along his chosen path, doing her level best to clear away the obstacles. Abe Lincoln's best education mentor was his stepmother.

"She didn't haven no eddication herself but she knowed what l'arnin' could do fur folks," said Dennis. "She wasn't thar very long before she found out how Abe hankered after books.[19] Aunt Sairy'd never let the children pester him. She always said Abe was goin' to be a great man some day. An' she wasn't goin' to have him hindered."[20]

The most important help Mrs. Lincoln could provide for her book-happy stepson was persuading Tom Lincoln to allow Abe to set aside his chores in order to read. "I induced my husband to permit Abe to read and study at home as well as at school," she recalled. "At first he was not easily reconciled to it but finally he, too, seemed willing to encourage him to a certain extent. . . ."[21] Mr. Lincoln never made Abe quit reading to do anything if he could avoid it. He would do it himself first."[22]

Said Mrs. Lincoln: "When Abe was reading my husband took particular care not to disturb him. Would let him read on and on till Abe quit of his own accord."[23]

Abe's young friend Joseph Richardson remembers it the same way: "When Abe was reading his father made it a rule never to ask him to lay down his book. No difference what was to do but let him read until he saw fit to lay it by himself."[24]

Tom Lincoln was a practical man. To his mind, the only education a man needed was knowing what could help him in his daily life. He saw no sense in dwelling on fanciful things like history, poetry, science, and philosophy. Years later, after Abe had left home, Tom complained about his son's misspent youth: "I suppose Abe is still fooling hisself with eddication. . . . I tried to stop it but he has got that fool idea in his head and can't be got out. Now I hain't got no eddication but I get along far better than if I had." [25]

Yet Tom had an inkling that his son was blessed with an uncommon gift. "Old Tom couldn't read himself," remarked a family friend, "but he wuz proud that Abe could and many a time he'd brag about how smart Abe wuz to the folks around about." [26]

Abe's love for reading and his thirst for knowledge were unstoppable. "Abe read all the books he could lay his hands on," his stepmother said.[27] "He would ask my opinion of what he had read and often explained things to me in his plain and simple language." [28]

Sarah Bush Lincoln gave us the clearest description we have of Abraham Lincoln's self-made education. "When he came across a passage that struck him he would write it down on boards if he had no paper and keep it there till he did get paper. Then he would rewrite it, look at it, repeat it," she said. [29] "Frequently he had no paper to write his pieces down on. Then he would put them with chalk on a board or plank, sometimes only making a few signs of what he intended to write. . . . .[30] When the board would get too black he would shave it off with a drawing knife and go on again." [31]

"He had a copybook," revealed Mrs. Lincoln, "a kind of scrapbook in which he put down all things and then preserved them." [32] Ten badly worn pages survived the years, providing the earliest samples of writing by the hand of Abraham Lincoln.

The book turned up during Herndon's visit to Lincoln's beloved stepmother on September 8, 1865. "She gave me . . . a few leaves from a book made and bound by Abe, in which he had entered, in a large bold hand, the tables of weights and measures and the sums to be worked out in illustration of each table." [33]

"This book he made in Indiana," said Dennis. "I bought the paper. Gave it to Abe." [34]

Said Herndon: "On one of the pages which the old lady gave me, just underneath the table which tells how many pints there are in a bushel, the facetious young student had scrawled these four lines of schoolboy doggerel:

Abraham Lincoln
his hand and pen.
He will be good
but God knows when.

On top of one page is written: *Long Division 1824.*
At the bottom left: *Abraham Lincoln's Book.*
In the lower right-hand corner:

Abraham Lincoln is my name
And with my pen I wrote the same
I wrote in both haste and speed
And left it here for fools to read. [35]

Abe's "peculiarsome" gift, his facility with language, set him apart from his neighbors. Abe was hungry. The more he learned about the world, the greater his appetite grew. He wanted to know about everything. Like a starving man, he looked everywhere for his nourishment.

"I can say this," observed Abe. "That among my earliest recollections I remember how when a mere child I used to get irritated when anybody talked to me in a way I could not understand. I don't think I ever got angry at anything else in my life. But that always disturbed my temper and has ever since.

"I can remember going to my little bedroom after hearing the neighbors talk . . . with my father and spending no small part of the night walking up and down and trying to make out what was the exact meaning of some of their—to me—dark sayings. I could not sleep though I often tried to when I got on such a hunt after an idea until I had caught it. And when I thought I had got it, I was not satisfied until I had repeated it over and over, until I knew to comprehend. This was a kind of passion with me and it has stuck by me. For I am never easy now when I am handling a thought till I have bounded it north and bounded it south and bounded it east and bounded it west." [36]

Lifelong friend Joshua Speed admired Lincoln's keen intellect and memory as a grown man. "I once remarked to him that his mind was a wonder to me," said Speed. "Impressions were easily made upon his mind."

"No," Lincoln said, "you are mistaken. I am slow to learn and slow to forget that which I have learned. My mind is like a piece of steel, very hard to scratch anything on it and almost impossible after you get it there to rub it out." [37]

Observing. Listening. Discussing. Questioning. Dennis Hanks described the only high school and college available in the backwoods country when the nation was young. "We learned by sight, scent and hearing," he said. "We heard all that was said and talked over and over the questions heard—wore them slick, greasy and threadbare."[38]

CHAPTER 14

"Chronicles of Reuben."

———— ❧ ————

As Abraham Lincoln turned into his teens, the flower of romance was in full bloom. In 1821, Cousin Dennis, now a man of twenty-two, was making sweet eyes at Sarah Bush Lincoln's oldest daughter.

Abe watched them marry in the cabin. "I was married there to Abe's step-sister, Miss Elizabeth Johnston," said Dennis.[1] The bride, then fourteen, was barely older than Abe.

The new Mr. and Mrs. Dennis Hanks didn't go very far. They built their cabin about a mile away, close enough to keep coming around.

Abe was seventeen during the summer of 1826 when he saw two more weddings in his cabin. His stepsister, the mischievous Matilda, married Squire Hall. Then, on August 2, Abe witnessed the most important marriage of his young life. His beloved sister Sarah (Sally) exchanged vows with Aaron Grigsby.

"I knew Abraham's own sister Sarah," offered John Hanks. "She was a short-built woman, eyes dark gray, hair dark brown. She was a good woman—kind, tender and good natured and is said to have been a smart woman. That is my opinion."[2]

Sarah Lincoln Grigsby was nineteen years old. "Sally Lincoln was older than Abe," said Nat Grigsby. "Sally married Aaron Grigsby, my brother, in August 1826."[3]

Abe's pal Nat became Sarah's brother-in-law. He knew Sally well. "Sally was a quick-minded woman and of extraordinary mind. She was industrious, more so than Abraham. . . . Her good humored laugh, I can see now, is as fresh in my mind as if it were yesterday. She could, like her brother Abe, meet and greet a person with the very kindest greeting in the world. Make you easy at the touch and word." [4]

Like many youngsters growing up in frontier communities, Aaron Grigsby and Sarah Lincoln knew each other since they were children. Sarah Lincoln grew to be a fine, hardworking young lady. She took a job working for the Crawfords, and one time, her young friend Aaron came calling on her. The Crawfords' young son Samuel sneaked a peek at the young lovers and caught them smooching. "One day I ran in, calling out 'Mother! Mother! Aaron Grigsby is sparking Sally Lincoln! I saw him kiss her!" he revealed years later. "Mother scolded me and told me I must stop watching Sally or I wouldn't get to the wedding."[5]

Abe composed a song in honor of the new bride and groom. It was a lighthearted romp, all in fun, a clever way to celebrate the joy of his sister's wedding. Yet he may have had another purpose—to remind Aaron Grigsby to take proper care of his new wife.

"This song was sung at Abraham's sister's wedding," wrote Elizabeth Crawford. "The first that I ever heard of it was the Lincoln family sung it. I rather think that A.L. composed it himself, but I am not certain. I know that he was in the habit of making songs and singing them."[6]

ADAM AND EVE'S WEDDING SONG

When Adam was created, he dwelt in Eden's shade,
As Moses has recorded; and soon an Eve was made.
Ten thousand times ten thousand
Of creatures swarmed around
Before a bride was formed,
And yet no mate was found.
The Lord then was not willing
The man should be alone

But caused a sleep upon him
And took from him a bone.
And closed the flesh in that place
And then he took the same
And of it made a woman
And brought her to the man.
Then Adam, he rejoiced
To see his loving bride,
A part of his own body,
The product of his side.
This woman was not taken
From Adam's feet we see,
So he must not abuse her
The meaning seems to be.
This woman was not taken
From Adam's head, we know,
To show she must not rule him,
'Tis evidently so.
This woman, she was taken
From under Adam's arm,
So she must be protected
From injuries and harm.[7]

Now that the boys and girls his own age were beginning to notice each other, there were plenty of social gatherings where they could meet. Abe went right along with the rest of the boys. "Always attended house raisings, log rolling, corn shucking and workings of all kinds," said Nat Grigsby.[8]

Abe was impossible to miss in any crowd. He towered over the other boys. His great strength and athletic prowess gave him special status among his peers. But it was his warmth, his wit, and sense of fun that drew people around him. "When he appeared in company, the boys would gather and cluster around him to hear him talk," said Grigsby. "He made fun and cracked his jokes making all happy. But the jokes and fun were at no man's expense. He wounded no man's feelings. . . . He naturally assumed the leadership of the boys."[9]

"He was so odd, original and humorous and witty that all the people in town would gather around him," remarked Dennis. "He would keep them there till midnight or longer, telling stories, cracking jokes . . . I would get tired, want to go home—cuss Abe and most heartily. Lincoln was a great talker."[10]

Yet Abe was not popular with the girls his age. He was certainly no handsome specimen. Kate Roby gave a careful account of his appearance: "His skin was shriveled and yellow. His shoes, when he had any, were low. He wore buckskin breeches, linsey-woolsey shirt and a cap made from the skin of a squirrel or coon. His breeches were baggy and lacked by several inches meeting the tops of his shoes, thereby exposing his shin-bone, sharp, blue and narrow."[11]

"All the young girls of my age made fun of Abe," one of the local women remembers.[12] Another explained that she stayed away from him because of "his awkwardness and large feet."[13]

Abe was good-natured and he didn't seem to mind. Said stepbrother John Johnston, "Abe didn't take much truck with girls."[14]

Kate Roby agreed. "Abe did not go much with the girls . . . didn't like girls much. Too frivolous."[15]

His friend David Turnham remembered that "He did not seem to seek the company of the girls and when about them was rather backward."[16]

Abe usually laughed off his shyness with women. "A woman is the only thing I am afraid of that I know can't hurt me."[17]

As a young man, Abraham Lincoln's relationships with women were mostly in his dreams. The image of one special woman—he called it his first love—played in his mind. Typical of boys his age, rampant adolescent fancy wove a great romantic tale. Years later, he confided his daydream to a Springfield journalist. "Did you ever write out a story in your mind? I did when I was a little codger."

Abe went on to explain: "One day, a wagon with a lady and two girls and a man broke down near us, and while they were fixing up, they cooked in our kitchen. The woman had books and read us stories, and they were the first I ever heard.

"I took a great fancy to one of the girls and when they were gone I thought of her a great deal. One day when I was sitting out in the sun by the house, I wrote out a story in my mind. I thought I took my father's horse and followed the wagon and finally found it, and they were surprised to see me. I talked with the girl and persuaded her to elope with me. And that night I put her on my horse and we started off across the prairie.

"After several hours we came to a camp. And when we rode up we found it was the one we had left a few hours before—and we went. The next night, we tried again and the same thing happened. The horse came back to the same place. And then we concluded that we ought not to elope. I stayed until I had persuaded her father to give her to me.

"I always meant to write that story out and publish it, and I began once. But I concluded it was not much of a story. But I think that was the beginning of love with me."[10]

There were more Indiana weddings. On April 16, 1829, two Grigsby boys, Reuben Jr. and Charles, took brides. The entire frontier community came to the Grigsby place for a grand reception to honor the two brides and two grooms.

"All the neighbors excepting the Lincoln family were invited," recalled Joseph Richardson. "The Lincoln and Grigsby family had a kind of quarrel and hence for some time did not like each other. . . . Abe Lincoln undoubtedly felt miffed, insulted, pride wounded. . . . He declared that he would have revenge."[19]

The old-timers still living around Gentryville after President Lincoln died remembered the Grigsby wedding well. The occasion was notorious, and not only for the wedding. Billy Herndon unearthed the curious story of a grand revenge scheme against the Grigsbys, a plot hatched by none other than Abraham Lincoln.

Billy Herndon set the scene. "Two Grigsby boys were subsequently married on the same night . . . Old Man Grigsby, for the two boys, held an infair, as was the custom at the time, at his house. The neighbors were invited except Abraham, and all went along as merry as a Christmas bell.

"Abraham got the ears of some of his chums who were in the house and at the infair. Abraham was not invited and so he felt huffy and insulted. He therefore told the boys inside this: 'Let's have some fun.'

"It was arranged between the insides and outsides that the two married couples should be put to bed all changed around and in the wrong places."[20]

Joseph Richardson was one of the witnesses who recalled the story for Herndon. "After the infair was ended," he said, "the two women were put to bed. The candles were blown out upstairs. The gentlemen, the two husbands, were invited and shown to bed. Charles Grigsby got into bed with, by accident as it were, Reuben Grigsby's wife, and Reuben got into bed with Charles' wife."[21]

Herndon went on: "Both husbands got in the wrong bed by direction made between Abraham and the invited insiders. . . . Soon, however, a scream and a rattling of boards aloft were heard and all was confusion worse confounded. A candle was lit and things found out and explained to the satisfaction of the women and men.

"Probably," Herndon guessed, "the women knew the voices of their loved ones and by that means the terrible mistake was found out. But who caused it and what for were not found out for some time. Here is Abraham, who was joyous and revenged that night—the good saint at one of his jokes."[22]

That wasn't the end of Abe's prank. A short narrative, written in mock reverent Old Testament style, mysteriously turned up by the roadside near the Grigsby home. The title was "The Chronicles of Reuben." Included with the story was a crude little poem.

"Chronicles" was a biting satire of the Grigsby wedding, barbs aimed at the entire Grigsby clan and their neighbors, especially Josiah Crawford, who shortly before the wedding made Abe work to pay for his damaged book. The grand climax of the story featured the hilarious mix-up of husbands and wives in the wrong bed.

"Lincoln was by nature witty, and here was his chance," said Richardson. "So he got up a witty poem called the 'Book of Chronicles' in which the infair, the mistake in partners, Crawford and his blue nose came in each for his share. . . . This called the attention of the people to Abe intellectually.

"Abe dropped the poem in the road carelessly—lost it, as it were. It was found by one of the Grigsby boys."[23]

"Chronicles" became an immediate hit throughout the countryside. The Grigsby misadventure was on people's lips everywhere. Folks loved it and committed the entire text to memory, repeating it again and again with gusto. Some, like Elizabeth Crawford, remembered it into old age.

"This poem is remembered here in Indiana in scraps better than the Bible, better than Watts' hymns," Richardson claimed.[24]

Samuel Crawford remembered reading it. "I took the 'Reuben's Chronicles' to Gentryville and read them in public. R. D. Grigsby, being present, got very mad over it." [25]

Betsy Grigsby was one of the unlucky brides. She had her own version of the double wedding and the high jinks afterward. "Yes, they have a joke on us," Betsy Grigsby recalled. "They said my man got into the wrong room and Charles got into my room but it wasn't so. Lincoln just wrote that for mischief. Natty Grigsby told us it was all written down, all put on record. Abe and my man often laughed about that."[26]

"Lincoln did write what is called the 'Book of Chronicles,' a satire on the Grigsbys and Josiah Crawford," Nat Grigsby admitted to Herndon after Lincoln died. "The satire was good, sharp, cutting and showed the genius of the boy. It hurt us then, but it's all over now."[27]

Years later, it was Nat Grigsby who took Billy Herndon to the Crawford home. On September 16, 1865, Herndon met Elizabeth Crawford, now old and blind, who remembered the "Chronicles" well. "The poem is smutty," the old woman remembered. "I can't tell it to you. Will tell it to my daughter-in-law. She will tell her husband. He shall send it to you."[28]

Several months later, Herndon received a copy of the "smutty" poem and the entire "Chronicles of Reuben" from Elizabeth Crawford's son Samuel. Nat Grigsby read it and confirmed that it was accurate. "I think they are correctly written," said Grigsby.[29]

THE POEM

I will tell you a joke about Josiah and Mary.
It is neither a joke or a story.
For Reuben and Charles had married two girls
But Billy has married a boy.
The girls he had tried on every side
But none could he get to agree.
All was in vain, he went home again
And since that, he is married to Natty.
So Billy and Natty agreed very well.
And mamma's well pleased at the match.
The egg it is laid, but Natty's afraid
The shell is so soft that it never will hatch.
But Betsy, she said: "You cursed baldhead,
My suitor you can never be.
Besides, your low crotch proclaims you a botch
And that never can answer for me." [30]

CHRONICLES OF REUBEN

Now there was a man whose name was Reuben, and the same was very great in substance, in horses and cattle and swine and a very great household. It came to pass when the sons of Reuben grew up that they were desirous of taking to themselves wives, and being too well know as to honor in their own country, they took a journey into a far country and there procured for themselves wives.

It came to pass also that when they were about to make the return home they sent a messenger before them to bear the tidings to their parents. These, inquiring of the messengers what time their sons would come, made a great feast and called all their kinsmen and neighbors in and made great preparations.

When the time drew nigh, they sent out two men to meet the grooms and their brides with a trumpet to welcome them and accompany them. When they came near unto the house of Reuben, the father, the messenger came on before them and gave a shout, and the whole multitude ran out with shouts of joy and music playing on all kinds of instruments. Some were playing on harps, some on viols, and some blowing on ram's horns. Some were also casting dust and ashes towards heaven, and chief among them was Josiah, blowing his bugle and making sound so great the neighboring hills and valleys echoed with the resounding acclamation. When they had played and their harps had sounded till the grooms and brides approached the gates, Reuben, the father, met them and welcomed them to his house.

The wedding feast now being ready, they were all invited to sit down to eat, placing the bridegrooms and their wives at each end of the table. Waiters were then appointed to serve and wait on the guests. When all had eaten and were full and merry, they all went out again and played and sung till night, and when they had made an end of feasting and rejoicing, the multitude dispersed, each going to his own home.

The family then took seats with their waiters to converse while preparations were being made in an upper chamber for the brides and grooms to be conveyed to their beds. This being done, the waiters took the two brides upstairs, placing one in a room at the right hand of the stairs and the other on the left. The waiters then came down and Nancy, the mother, then gave directions to the waiters of the bridegrooms, and they took them upstairs and placed them in the wrong rooms. The waiters then all came downstairs. But the mother, being fearful of a mistake, made enquiry of the waiters and learning the true facts, took the light and sprang upstairs.

It came to pass that she ran to one of the rooms and exclaimed, 'O, Lord, Reuben, you are in bed with the wrong wife!' The young men, alarmed at this, ran out with such violence against each other they came near knocking each other down. The tumult gave evidence to those below that the mistake was certain. At last, they all came down and had a long conversation about who made the mistake, but it could not be decided. So endeth the chapter.[31]

CHAPTER 15

"Why dost thou tear more blest ones hence?"

———— ⊕⊖⊕ ————

Young Abraham was always in love with words. Since he was a child learning the ABCs from his mother, and later shaping letters on planks with charcoal, Abe used words as playthings.

"Abe was always troubled about words, what they meant," said Dennis.[1]

When he discovered a rhyme, he reveled in the silly ways he could put sounds together. He found fun in the name of a local Indian named Johnny Kongapod.

Here lies poor Johnny Kongapod.
Have mercy on him gracious God,
As he would do if he was God
And you were Johnny Kongapod.[2]

Abe dashed off clever little verses like this one for Joseph Richardson.

Good boys who to their books apply
Will all be great men by and by.[3]

The mind of the young man was opening to the world. He began to look beyond the surface of things, searching for deeper causes. "There was more in Abe's head than wit and fun," observed his good friend R. B. Rutledge.[4]

"He dwelt altogether in the land of thought," wrote Herndon. "His deep meditation and abstraction easily induced the belief among his horny-handed companions that he was lazy."[5]

Joseph Richardson noticed that he "was witty and sad and thoughtful by turns."[6]

In Abe's 1824 copybook, Herndon discovered a verse that opened a window to the subtle questions turning in the boy's mind. In these lines, young Lincoln peers beyond time to muse on the fleeting nature of a moment.

"Nothing indicates that they were borrowed," said Herndon, "and I have always, therefore, believed that they were original with him. Although a little irregular in meter, the sentiment would, I think, do credit to an older head."[7]

> *Time, what an empty vapor 'tis,*
> *And days, how swift they are;*
> *Swift as an Indian arrow—*
> *Fly on like a shooting star.*
> *The present moment just is here,*
> *Then slides away in haste;*
> *That we can never say they're ours,*
> *But only say they're past.*[8]

As a young lawyer in Springfield, Lincoln found others who loved poetry, including Billy Herndon. "About 1837, 8 and 9, a parcel of young men in the city formed a kind of Poetical Society, association or what not," recalled one member, James Matheny. "Lincoln once or twice wrote short poems. . . . One verse, on seduction by Lincoln, runs thus:

Whatever spiteful fools may say,
Each jealous, ranting yelper,
No woman ever played the whore
*Unless she had a man to help her.*⁹"

Lincoln explained how the urge to put his thoughts and feelings in poetry came to him. "In the fall of 1844, thinking I might aid some to carry the State of Indiana for Mr. Clay, I went into the neighborhood in that state in which I was raised where my mother and only sister were buried, and from which I had been absent about fifteen years.

"That part of the country is, within itself, as unpoetical as any spot of the earth. But still, seeing it and its objects and inhabitants aroused feeling in me which were certainly poetry—though whether my expression of those feelings is poetry is quite another question."[10]

MY CHILDHOOD'S HOME I SEE AGAIN

My childhood's home I see again,
And sadden with the view;
And still, as memory crowds my brain,
There's pleasure in it too.

O Memory! Thou midway world
'Twixt earth and paradise,
Where things decayed and loved ones lost
In dreamy shadows rise,

And, freed from all that's earthly vile,
Seem hallowed, pure and bright,
Like scenes in some enchanted isle
All bathed in liquid light.

As dusky mountains please the eye

When twilight chases day;
As bugle-notes that, passing by,
In distance die away;

As leaving some grand waterfall,
We, lingering list its roar—
So memory will hallow all
We've known, but know no more.

Near twenty years have passed away
Since here I bid farewell
To woods and fields and scenes of play
And playmates loved so well.

Where many were but few remain
Of old familiar things;
But seeing them to mind again
The lost and absent brings.

The friends I left that parting day,
How changed, as time has sped!
Young childhood grown, strong manhood gray,
And half of all are dead.

I hear the loved survivors tell
How naught from death could save,
Till every sound appears a knell,
And every spot a grave.

I range the fields with pensive tread,
And pace the hollow rooms,
And feel companion of the dead;
I'm living in the tombs.

And now away to seek some scene
Less painful than the last—
With less of horror mingled in
The present and the past.

The very spot where grew the bread
That formed my bones, I see.
How strange, old field, on thee to tread,
And feel I'm part of thee! [11]

Pain deepens wisdom. Abraham knew the agony of loss. As a small boy, he saw the tiny blue lifeless body of his newborn brother. He watched the living breath leave his own mother. As a young man, he had to face the death of his only sister.

Sarah Lincoln Grigsby was married less than a year when she became pregnant. Tom and Sarah Lincoln were looking forward to their new grandchild. Abe was excited about being an uncle. Sally and Aaron Grigsby had "a very bright future before them," said Nancy Grigsby, Aaron's niece. "And Sally was much thought of and loved by all her husband's people." [12]

On January 20, 1828, Sally went into labor. The baby was coming. Before the night was over, both mother and baby were gone.

"I remember the night she died," recalled Mrs. J. W. Lamar, one of the neighbors. "My mother was there at the time. She had a strong voice and I heard her calling father. . . . He went after a doctor but it was too late. They let her lay too long." [13]

That night, Abe was doing a job for Old Man Grigsby, "at our house doing a little carpenter work," one of the Grigsbys remembered. "Aaron, Sarah's husband, came running up from his house a quarter of a mile away and said that Sarah had just died. We went out and told Abe. I will never forget that scene. He sat down in the door of the smoke house and buried his face in his hands. The tears slowly trickled from between his bony fingers and his gaunt frame shook with sobs. We turned away." [14]

"This was a hard blow to Abe, who always thought her death was due to neglect," one of his friends said. "From then on he was alone in the world, you might say."[15]

The Little Pigeon Creek Baptist Church had just opened a new cemetery near the meetinghouse. Sarah Lincoln Grigsby was laid to rest there, her nameless baby in her arms. They were one of the first to be buried in the new churchyard cemetery. Even into his adult years, Abraham pondered long over the mystery of life and death. One episode still perplexed him. His childhood friend Matthew Gentry was born into the wealthiest family in town. His father was the founder of Gentryville, Indiana. Abe knew him as a "bright lad." One day, without warning, he went mad, howling, begging, swearing, weeping, praying. He fought with his father, tried to kill his mother. In his frenzy he maimed himself. Neighbors rushed to subdue him, binding his arms and legs. They watched in horror as the troubled young man they once knew glared at them with "burning eyeballs," railing with "maniac laughter."

When Lincoln returned to Gentryville in 1844, fifteen years after witnessing his friend's mental breakdown, he saw Matthew Gentry. He had grown old, still locked in a kind of "mental night." Shocked at the sight of a man he remembered with affection, Lincoln was inspired to write a poem.

"The subject of the present one is an insane man," Lincoln explained. "His name is Matthew Gentry. He is three years older than I and when we were boys we went to school together. He was rather a bright lad and the son of the rich man of our very poor neighborhood.

"At the age of nineteen, he unaccountably became furiously mad, from which condition he gradually settled down into harmless insanity. When . . . I visited my old home in the fall of 1844, I found him still lingering in this wretched condition. In my poetizing mood I could not forget the impressions his case made upon me."[16]

The verses end with a question, a plea to the "awe inspiring prince," the power of Death itself. It is a heartfelt prayer, a desperate cry for understanding the laws of life and death. Young Abraham tasted life and had seen too much of death. He carried a powerful sense of dread, knowing that the overwhelming forces of darkness could come to claim those in the world he loved most—his brother, mother, sister, all devoured by death.

A few years later, a beautiful young woman, someone he cared for deeply—his friends said they planned to marry—would be taken away suddenly. He would bury two of his own sons. As president, with the stench of death permeating the nation, he would see a generation of healthy young Americans destroyed. Finally, before he could grow old, on a night that found him laughing at the theater, death came to claim him as well.

"He always had a conviction, more or less, of ruin," wrote Billy Herndon.[17]

"Billy," Lincoln confided ominously, "I feel as if I shall meet with some terrible end."[18]

So the poet yearned to know—why would death take so many of God's good and gentle souls and let a howling madman live?

WHY DOST THOU TEAR MORE BLEST ONES HENCE?

But here's an object more of dread
Than ought the grave contains—
A human form with reason fled,
While wretched life remains.
Poor Matthew! Once of genius bright,
A fortune-favored child—
Now locked for aye in mental night,
A haggard mad-man wild.
Poor Matthew! I have ne'er forgot,
When first, with maddened will,
Yourself you maimed, your father fought,
And mother strove to kill.
When terror spread, and neighbors ran,

Your dangerous strength to bind;
And soon a howling crazyman
Your limbs were fast confined.
How then you strove and shrieked aloud,
Your bones and sinews bared;
And fiendish on the gazing crowd,
With burning eyeballs glared—
And begged and swore and swept and prayed,
With maniac laughter joined;
How fearful were those signs displayed
By pangs that killed thy mind!
And when at length, tho' drear and long,
Time soothed thy fiercer woes,
How plaintively thy mournful song
Upon the still night rose.
I've heard it oft, as if I dreamed,
Far distant, sweet and lone,
The funeral dirge, it ever seemed
Of reason dead and gone.
To drink its strains, I've stole away,
All stealthily and still,
Ere yet the rising God of day
Had streaked the Eastern hill.
Air held his breath; trees, with the spell,
Seemed sorrowing angels round,
Whose swelling tears in dew-drops fell
Upon the listening ground.
But this is past, and naught remains
That raised thee o'er the brute.
Thy piercing shrieks and soothing strains
Are like, forever mute.
Now fare thee well—more thou the cause
Than subject now of woe.
All mental pangs, by time's kind laws

Hast lost the power to know.
O Death! Thou awe-inspiring prince,
That keepest the world in fear;
Why dost thou tear more blest ones hence,
And leave him ling'ring here? [19]

CHAPTER 16

"I can see the quivering and shining of that half-dollar yet."

———— ✦ ————

The great Ohio River was a natural highway for travelers in the new America. From its beginning in Pittsburgh, the Western Waters connected cities, towns, and villages north to south almost the full length of the nation, merging in the Mother Mississippi and flowing into the Gulf of Mexico at New Orleans.

Newfangled steamboats, belching smoke, made the water routes possible. The first steamboat appeared on the Ohio River in 1811. By 1826, 160 steamboats were crossing the waters. Travel by steamboat was risky business. Accidents or mechanical failure cut the fleet in half. The bottom of the river was littered with steamboats.

An infamous Ohio River disaster stranded one of America's great Revolutionary War heroes. In May 1825, Marquis de Lafayette cruised the river for his triumphal tour of the United States. His steamer hit a snag and sank, dumping all the passengers into the river, including the illustrious old general. No one was lost, and the Marquis paddled safely to the Kentucky shore in a lifeboat. A proud Kentuckian opened his home to Lafayette, and by next morning the whole town showed up to greet him.

The river swallowed many good men. If swirling currents didn't get you, the river gangs did. Bandits like Mike Fink, claiming to be "half horse and half alligator," hid along the rugged banks to ambush passenger ships and cargo boats.

Traders and travelers knew the dangers of the river and went anyway. A parade of steamboats passed one another up and down the river on the three-week voyage from Pittsburgh to New Orleans. Houseboats carried whole families while flatboats were loaded with fruits, vegetables, meats, grains, furniture, plows, wagons, and livestock—all America was passing along the water highway.

Abe was sixteen when he got a job on James Taylor's farm along the riverbank where Anderson Creek joined the great Ohio River. "Abe lived with my father in the year 1825 and worked about six or nine months," recalled Green Taylor. "He plowed, ferried, ground corn on the hand mill."[1]

Taylor owned the ferry that connected settlements on both sides of the Ohio River. "I knew Abe Lincoln well," Green Taylor said. "Run the ferry for my father from the Kentucky shore to the Indiana shore."[2] For his labor as farm boy and ferryman, Abe was paid six dollars a month.

Many people had business on the other side of the river, so Abe was constantly busy. For foot passengers without any cargo, Abe would leave his large flatboat tied up and scull across in a small rowboat. The price of a round trip was 6¼ cents.

One ferry passenger remembered the tall boatman. "I can see now, how with one sweep of the oars, he could send his boat from shore to shore at low water."[3]

Abe was living at the Taylor farmhouse, sharing a room with the owner's son. Green Taylor described how the two spirited young men got along. "It was during the season that Abe was operating the ferry . . . we were told to go to the crib and husk corn. Abe taunted me about a certain girl in Troy that I did not like and kept it up until I tore the husk off a big ear of corn and threw it at him. It struck him just above the eye. . . . This blow left a scar that Lincoln carried to his grave."[4]

Whenever they could, Abe and his buddies, Dennis Hanks and Squire Hall, Matilda's husband, went down to the river to drum up some business for themselves. "All went to Posey's Landing on the Ohio River to cut cord wood, supposing they could get the money," Colonel

Chapman explained. "They found they would have to take the pay for any wood they might cut in store goods. They cut 9 cords and received for it 9 yards of white domestic [cloth]."

Abe made good use of his pay. "Of this, Abe had a shirt made and this is positively the first white shirt he ever had in his life," said Chapman.[5]

By the time he was eighteen, Abe learned enough about the ways of the river to go into business for himself. Wielding an ax, a saw, and a carving knife, Abe designed and built a boat. He cut down trees, planed them into planks, and pegged the pieces together so that the boat would float. He made his own ferry, fashioned from the forest.

He set the craft into the Ohio River at Bates Landing, about a mile and a half from Anderson Creek. Customers came. Lincoln earned a steady income ferrying passengers out to waiting steamships and picking them up from the ships and carrying them to shore.

Once, when he was president, he reminisced about his days as a ferryman. "Seward," he asked his Secretary of State, "did you ever hear how I earned my first dollar?

"Well," said Abe, "I was about eighteen years of age . . . I was contemplating my new boat and wondering whether I could make it stronger or improve it. . . . Two men with trunks came down to the shore in carriages and looking at the different boats, singled out mine and asked, 'Who owns this?'

"I answered modestly, 'I do.'

"'Will you,' said one of them, 'take us and our trunks out to the steamer?'

"'Certainly,' said I.

"I was very glad to have the chance of earning something, and supposed that each of them would give me a couple of bits.

"The trunks were put in my boat, the passengers seated themselves on them and I sculled them out to the steamer. They got on board and I lifted the trunks and put them on the deck. The steamer was about to put on steam again when I called out, 'You have forgotten to pay me.' Each of them took from his pocket a silver half-dollar and threw it on the bottom of my boat. I could scarcely believe my eyes as I picked up the money.

"You may think it was a very little thing," said Abe, "and in these days, it seems to me like a trifle, but it was a most important incident in my life. I could scarcely credit that I—the poor boy—had earned a dollar in less than a day; that by honest work I had earned a dollar."[6]

Abe confided the rest of the story to Leonard Swett, a fellow lawyer and friend from his Illinois circuit riding days. Swett recalls, "Afterwards, playing upon a flatboat which was fastened so as to reach out into the stream, he dropped his half dollar from the farthest end of the boat. . . ."

"I can see the quivering and shining of that half-dollar yet," moaned Abe. "In the quick current it went down the stream and sunk from my sight forever."[7]

One day someone called to him from the Kentucky shore. When Abe rowed out to find him, no one was there. He stepped out of the boat to have a look around when two men jumped out of the bushes, grabbed hold of him, and threatened to "duck" him in the river. They warned him—he had no right operating a ferry on the river and he'd better stop.

The two angry men were the Dill brothers. They owned the exclusive license granted by the state of Kentucky to operate a ferry across the Ohio River. They were out to make sure that nobody interfered with their business.

There was no river "ducking." One look at the giant ferryman's muscular arms probably persuaded the Dill brothers to settle their dispute peaceably. They demanded that Abe come with them to appear before a judge.

The three men marched a few hundred yards to the home of Squire Samuel Pate, the local justice of the peace. A warrant was sworn by John T. Dill for the arrest of one Abraham Lincoln of the state of Indiana. The case of "The commonwealth of Kentucky versus Abraham Lincoln" began.

Abe was charged with violating the law on the operation of ferries. This was a statute based on the original act that admitted Kentucky to the Union, granting Kentucky jurisdiction over the Ohio River. The Kentucky law stated that "if any person whatsoever shall, for reward, set any person over any river or creek whereupon public ferries are appointed, he or she so offending shall forfeit and pay five pounds current money for every such offence."[8]

Squire Pate gaveled the trial into session. The plaintiffs introduced their evidence. The defendant, they claimed, transported passengers from the Indiana shore to steamboats on the Ohio River without a license to operate a ferry. The only party with a license to carry passengers across the Ohio River from the Kentucky shore to the Indiana shore was John T. Dill, himself.

The defendant admitted the facts as alleged. But he contended that he did not violate the statute and therefore did not infringe on the rights of the authorized ferry operator.

He told the judge that he was not claiming the right to "set a person over any river or creek." He took them only part way across. The Dill's ferry, based on the Kentucky shore, could not be on the Indiana side when a steamer approached, he reasoned. Passengers who came to the Indiana shore should have the right to hire a boat to carry them to the steamer.

Squire Pate announced his ruling. Since there was no evidence the defendant "set any person over any river or creek," the case was dismissed.

The judge was impressed by the young man's sincerity, poise, and sharp reasoning. After the trial, the squire invited Abe to come home with him, where they sat on the porch and talked about the law. Squire Pate warned Abe about the difficulties that arise because people are not informed about the law. Every man should know the law, the squire told him.

They shook hands and left as friends. This was not the last time Squire Pate would see Abe. Whenever the court was in session, Abe rowed across the river and sat at the back of the courtroom, observing the law at work, listening to statements of witnesses, following arguments of lawyers, watching Squire Pate direct the whole show.

Abraham Lincoln's first encounter with the law inspired him to learn more. Soon afterward he found a copy of the *Revised Statutes of Indiana* in a friend's library. He devoured the pages with the same appetite he had earlier showed for *Aesop's Fables* and *Pilgrim's Progress*. This became his first class at law school.

CHAPTER 17

"River Man."

———⊗⊗⊗———

In the fall of 1828, James Gentry needed a hired hand. The founder and main shopkeeper in the town of Gentryville was looking for a skilled boatman to take his merchandise, flour, pork, livestock, and produce down the Mississippi River to New Orleans to sell for profit.

He knew he could trust Abe Lincoln. Abe had already demonstrated that he could handle the tricky currents and snags on the river. Gentry was certain that this rawboned giant would frighten away any river pirates who had an idea of looting the boat.

In pioneer days, most business was done by barter and trade. When you went to shop at a local store you could take soap, cloth, pots and pans, or any item off the shelf in return for your farm produce. Storekeepers could then sell the produce and earn a profit.

For his latest venture to New Orleans, Gentry hired a crew of two. His son Allen went to look after the business while Abe piloted the boat. For designing and constructing a flatboat, loading the cargo, navigating a thousand miles of treacherous river, negotiating business deals, and returning with a handsome profit, Abe was paid eight dollars a month.

Abe and Allen started working near the water's edge, cutting down giant oaks and poplars and hewing them into planks. They assembled the hull, bottom-side up. When it was ready, they hitched a team of oxen to a rope and turned the hull over. The boat was about sixty-five feet long and eighteen feet wide with a cabin for shelter and pairs of long oars at the bow and stern.

While the boat was under construction, Abe lived at the home of Alfred Grass, near the riverbank. He worked all day and would come home tired. Still he kept his evenings free for his favorite pastime. One member of the family remembered how Abe "would sit in the evening near the table with the rest of the family until the tallow dip [candles] had burned out. Then he would lie down on his back with his head toward the open fireplace so as to get the light upon the pages of the book, and there he would often read until after midnight. . . . He would bake the top of his head or wear himself out for want of rest, but he was always up in the morning ready for work."[1]

The flatboat was finished in December, but the crew was not yet ready to leave. There was a hitch in their plans. Mrs. Allen Gentry, the former Kate Roby, Abe's school friend, was due to have a baby any day. So they had to wait. Then on December 18, 1828, the second James Gentry was born. Two weeks later the boys were off to New Orleans.

They paddled and poled through clear still waters and windblown whitecaps. At night they pulled ashore, and when they spotted other craft approaching, they waved a lantern or a piece of burning firewood to greet them.

Along the Ohio they passed the "Cave-in-Rock," a huge cavern on the Illinois shore with its notorious advertising sign: *Wilson's Liquor Vault and House of Entertainment.* A few years later, explorers would find sixty human skeletons in the cave, the remains of boatmen and travelers robbed and killed by the Wilson gang.

One river traveler, a member of the British Parliament, happened to make the journey downriver shortly before Abraham and Allen. He noted his impressions in a diary in which he described scenes the boys would soon see:

> *During the whole day we had no view save the interminable forest and dull ragged banks on both sides. . . . Very few settlements have yet been*

attempted and these generally on high bluffs. . . . We passed only one today where I observed something like the appearance of a village. . . . We saw several flocks of wild turkeys on the shore. One of our party killed a bird from the boat with his rifle. Most of the Americans in this part of the country are excellent shots. . . . The number of steamboats here is almost incredible. Went on board several that were lying below us. The largest, called the "Washington," is built like a three story house and with every accommodation that could be found in a good hotel.

When the Englishman's boat crossed the Ohio into the Mississippi, he noted that "you soon discover the difference in the character of the two rivers. The Ohio moving slow and placid whilst the Mississippi sweeps along with a fierce and tempestuous current."[2]

Every day the nineteen-year-old boatman gained more mastery over the tricks of the great "Father of Waters." He could handle the bends and sweeps of the river with a sure tug on the oars. He could steer a steady course through violent storms and shifting winds.

Yet the river had its tricks and illusions. Abe had to keep his wits about him. He would hear the loud rumbling, a growing roar coming from downriver. Were dangerous rapids looming ahead? Or was it the swift current beating against a downed tree trunk? In the dark morning mists he'd see a huge black form slowly approaching. A steamer going off course? Did the boatman fall asleep? Or maybe the dim light and thick drizzle were playing pranks on his eyes.

When they reached Baton Rouge, about 150 miles above New Orleans, the boys tied their boat for the night near the plantation of Madame Duchesne and expected to stay a few days. Here was a ripe market, and the boys hoped to do a brisk business selling Gentry's goods. This was the Louisiana "sugar coast," rows of prosperous sugar plantations side by side along the shore. "The nature of part of the cargo load . . . made it necessary . . . to linger and trade along the Sugar Coast," Abe said.[3]

They slept on the boat while the mortal dangers of the river were silently creeping up on them. "One night," relates Abe, "(We) were attacked by seven Negroes with intent to kill and rob."[4]

The raiders spied their merchandise and leaped into the boat, ready to kill the boys and take their goods.

"The Negroes had hickory clubs," said Kate. "My husband said—'Lincoln! Get the guns and shoot!'"

Only they had no firearms. "Pretended to have guns," Kate said. "Had none."

The trick worked. "The Negroes took alarm and left," said Kate.[5]

"(We) were hurt some in the melee," said Abe, "but succeeded in driving the Negroes from the boat. Then cut cable, weighed anchor, and left."[6]

As the boat pulled away, Abe dabbed his bloody face with a bandana. The incident left its mark, said Lincoln's lawyer friend Leonard Swett, "making a scar which he wore always and which he showed me at the time of telling this story."[7]

In a few days the boys were steering their flatboat into the crescent-shaped harbor of exotic New Orleans. Abe had never seen such a large city. Nothing in Kentucky or Indiana could prepare him for the experience.

The English scribe who visited New Orleans a few weeks before Allen and Abe saw a city "built like an old French provincial town—the same narrow streets, old fashioned houses and lamps suspended by a chain across the road."

He saw "bogs, swamps, morasses in every direction. . . . Mosquitoes are, of course, abundant. Even now they swarm in myriads as bad as in the worst places in the West Indies.

"I should suppose that New Orleans . . . is not famous for its morality or religious feeling. Those who come here on account of trade think only of making money as fast as they can and trouble themselves very little about other matters."[8]

Miles and miles of water-going craft of all sorts lay at anchor outside the city—steamers, flatboats, arks, rafts, schooners, and sloops from all over the world. These ships would soon be off for such faraway places as Hamburg, Gibraltar, Bremen, Havana, Veracruz, New York, and Philadelphia.

There were sailors and deckhands from many nations jabbering in strange tongues. He heard conversations in French, Dutch, Creole, Swedish, Italian, Spanish, and Russian. He heard a sort of English spoken with a curious twang ("Ow, blimey mates!") when he met some British sailors. The mix of languages in the air seemed like the clucking and chattering of animals at dawn.

He passed saloons by the dozen, where beautiful women sipping French wine or Jamaican rum laughed with the sailors. He saw posters around town advertising a public showing of an Egyptian mummy over three thousand years old.

They saw gangs of slaves by the hundreds, handcuffed and chained, heading for work in the cotton fields. "We stood and watched the slaves sold in New Orleans and Abraham was very angry," said Allen Gentry.[9]

The boys remained for a few days until they sold everything, all their cargo and the boat. Then they booked passage on a steamer heading north.

It was Abe's first trip on a steamship. They passed dozens of steamers on the river, boats with names like *DeWitt Clinton, Isabella, Patriot, Lady Washington, Montezuma, Amazon, Crusader, Daniel Boone,* and *Lady of the Lake.*

Abe passed his twentieth birthday away from home. By spring of 1829 he was back home in Indiana working on his father's farm and hiring out to neighbors, felling trees, splitting rails, plowing fields, grinding meal, or feeding livestock. Whatever Abe had left of the twenty-four dollars he earned on his three-month trip to New Orleans he turned over to his father. This was the law and the custom for a boy under twenty-one years of age. Said Dennis: "Tom owned Abe's time."[10]

Abe was a changed man. Gentryville could no longer satisfy him. He had tasted the great world beyond his small frontier village. The river called to him. He longed to be a steamboat captain piloting his craft up and down the "Father of Waters." "He was all fur bein' a river man fur a while," remarked Dennis.[11]

Lincoln's neighbor William Wood knew the boat business. He recalled the day in 1829 when Abe appeared at his door. "Abe came to my house one day and stood round about timid and shy. I knew he wanted something. I said to him—'Abe, what is your care?'

"Abe replied—'I want you to go to the river and give me some recommendation to some boat.'

"I remarked—'Abe, your age is against you. You are not twenty-one yet.'

"'I know that' said Abe, 'but I want a start.'"

Wood knew that Abe was big, strong, and capable and could probably handle a boat as well as any man. But he would not go against the custom. Explained Wood: "I concluded not to go for the boy's good."[12]

CHAPTER 18

"Snowbirds."

———— ∞∞∞ ————

Fall 1829. Abe was looking ahead to February 12, 1830, when he would turn twenty-one years old. In the eyes of the community, he would be his own man, free to leave home to find his way in the world.

Before leaving, he wanted to be sure his mother and father could manage without him. The log cabin home they built twelve years earlier was worn and weathered and needed repair. As a going-away present, Abe began working on a new and better log cabin for his parents.

"Saw him cutting down a large tree one day," said William Wood. "I asked him what he was going to do with it. He said he was going to saw it into planks for his father's new house."[1]

Then suddenly the Lincolns changed their plans. They never built the house. "Abe sold his plank to Crawford, the book man," said Wood. "Josiah Crawford put the lumber in his house where it is now to be seen in the south east room. I sat on this plank myself."[2]

The remaining lumber Abe used to build a wagon, fashioning a carriage with wheels and axles. The entire family—Lincolns, Johnstons, Hankses, and Halls and their wives, children, and grandchildren—all packed up to move to Illinois.

"I reckon it was John Hanks 'at got restless fust an' lit out fur Illinois an' wrote fur us all to come an' he'd get land fur us," said Dennis.[3]

"I moved from Kentucky to Illinois in the fall of 1828," John Hanks explained. "I wrote to Thomas Lincoln what kind of a country it was."[4] The Indians called it *Sangamo*—"land of plenty to eat." Billy Herndon, who lived there as a boy, noted that "the final syllable of this name was pronounced to rhyme with 'raw.'"[5]

Dennis Hanks was the one who pushed for the move. The dreaded milk sickness was back. Dennis lost four cows and eleven calves in a week. He took to bed with the sickness and nearly died. "I'm goin' to git out o' here and hunt a country where the milk-sick is not," resolved Dennis. "It's like to ruin me. . . .[6] This was reason enough, ain't it, for leaving!"[7]

When Dennis visited his cousin John in Illinois, he liked what he saw. He came back and sold his brother-in-law Squire Hall on the idea. Their wives, Elizabeth Johnston Hanks and Matilda Johnston Hall, made plans to go. Their mother, Sarah Lincoln, "could not think of parting with them,"[8] according to Dennis, and "the proposition . . . met with the general consent of the Lincoln family."[9]

The Lincoln farm on Little Pigeon Creek did not prove to be a wise investment. After buying his eighty acres at two dollars an acre and tending the land for fourteen years, Tom sold it for a loss. Charles Grigsby paid him $125 for the land.

The family joke was how moving was in Tom's blood. "Tom was always ready to move . . . always lookin' fur the land o' Canaan," said Dennis.[10] They said the family packed up and moved so often the chickens knew it and would lie belly-up, feet in the air, waiting to be tied and loaded on the wagon.

Of the family that endured their first brutal Indiana winter fourteen years earlier, only Abe and his father were left. The Lincolns had grown. They were three families now. "There was thirteen in the three families," recounted Dennis. "Thomas Lincoln, wife, Abe, J.D. Johnston, Squire Hall, wife (Matilda Johnston Hall), son, Dennis F. Hanks, wife (Elizabeth Johnston Hanks), three daughters, one son."[11]

The night before he left, Abe visited the Gentrys' store. James Gentry, the owner's son, recalled how his father helped Abe choose merchandise for a new business venture. "He and Lincoln spent considerable time on that last night making selection of notions."[12] Abe bought thirty dollars' worth of pins, needles, buttons, thread, tinware, and assorted household items. He planned to peddle his stock along the route to earn a few extra dollars. Now, at twenty-one, he could keep every penny.

Before they left Indiana for good, the family held a silent vigil at the grave of Nancy Hanks Lincoln. They paid a last visit to Abe's sister, Sarah, buried in the churchyard cemetery, just as they had stopped at the grave of baby Thomas Lincoln in Kentucky fourteen years before.

When a family left their village for good, it was traditional for friends and neighbors to gather round them as they pulled away to wish them well. "I well remember the day when the Lincolns started for Illinois," said James Gentry. "Nearly all the neighbors was there to see them leave."[13]

"Piled everything into ox-wagons an' we all went—Linkhorns, an' Hankses an' Johnstons, all hangin' together," said Dennis. "I reckon we was like one o' them tribes o' Israel that you kain't break up nohow."[14]

"March 1, 1830," Lincoln wrote in his autobiographical sketch, "Abraham, having just completed his twenty-first year, his father and family with the families of the two daughters and sons-in-law of his step-mother left the old homestead in Indiana and came to Illinois. Their mode of conveyance was wagons drawn by ox-teams and Abraham drove one of the teams."[15]

Bellowing "Heah!" and "Git up!" the men whipped the animals into action, and the wagons pulled away.

"I helped to hitch the two yoke of oxen to the wagon and went with them half a mile," remembered Redmond Grigsby.[16]

"Thomas Lincoln moved from Indiana to Illinois in a large four horse wagon drawn by two yoke of oxen," said Colonel Chapman. "He brought to Illinois with him some stock cattle, one horse, three beds and bedding, one bureau, one table, one clothes chest, one set of chairs, cooking utensils, clothing and so forth."[17]

"It took us two weeks to git thar," said Dennis, "raftin' over the Wabash, cuttin' our way through the woods, fordin' rivers, pryin' wagons an' steers out o' sloughs with fence rails, an' makin' camp.

"Abe cracked a joke every time he cracked a whip an' he found a way out o' every tight place while the rest of us was standin' 'round scratchin' our fool heads."[18]

"Mr. Lincoln once described this journey to me," Herndon remembered. "He said the ground had not yet yielded up the frosts of winter, that during the day the road would thaw out on the surface and at night freeze over again, thus making traveling, especially with oxen, painfully slow and tiresome.

"There were, of course, no bridges and the party were consequently driven to ford the streams unless by a circuitous route they could avoid them. In the early part of the day [they] were also frozen slightly and the oxen would break through a square yard of thin ice at every step.

"Among other things which the party brought with them was a pet dog which trotted along after the wagon. One day the little fellow fell behind and failed to catch up till after they had crossed the stream. Missing him, they looked back and there, on the opposite bank he stood, whining and jumping about in great distress. The water was running over the broken edges of the ice and the poor animal was afraid to cross. It would not pay to turn the oxen and wagon back and ford the stream again in order to recover a dog and so the majority, in their anxiety to move forward, decided to go on without him."

"I could not endure the idea of abandoning even a dog," said Abe. "Pulling off shoes and socks, I waded across the stream and triumphantly returned with the shivering animal under my arm. His frantic leaps of joy and other evidences of a dog's gratitude amply repaid me for all the exposure I had undergone."[19]

Meanwhile, Abe was doing brisk business as a salesman. Said the son of William Jones, who clerked at Gentry's store, "When the Lincolns reached their new home near Decatur, Illinois, Abraham wrote back to my father stating that he had doubled his money on his purchases by selling them along the road."[20]

Traveling salesmen were not always welcome, Abe discovered. One day, he brought his needles, notions, and knickknacks to the door of a farmhouse. He heard loud wailing and whimpering coming from inside, and when he peeked in he saw an assortment of youngsters, boys and girls from seventeen months to seventeen years. Every child was crying, moaning, and carrying on. Their mother, red-haired, red-faced, and harried, was hollering and waving a whip over her head when she saw the tall stranger at her doorway.

The woman demanded to know what he was doing there.

Abe figured there wasn't much use in asking the woman if she wanted some pots and pans just then. "Nothing, madam," he answered. "I merely dropped in as I came along to see how things were going."

"Well, you needn't wait," the woman screeched. "There's trouble here and lots of it too. But I kin manage my own affairs without the help of outsiders. This is jest a family row. But I'll teach these brats their places if I have to lick the hide off every one of 'em. I run this house so I don't want no one sneakin' round tryin' to find out how I do it, either."[21]

Soon the traveling party crossed into Illinois. "Reached the county of Macon and stopped there sometime within the same month of March," said Abe.[22]

They passed through the town of Decatur on their way to John Hanks's place. Years later Abraham Lincoln returned to Decatur as one of Illinois's most prominent lawyers. One of his colleagues remembered walking past the courthouse with him. "Lincoln walked out a few feet in front and after shifting his position two or three times said as he looked up at the building, partly to himself and partly to me—'Here is the exact spot where I stood by our wagon when we moved from Indiana twenty-six years ago. This isn't six feet from the exact spot.'

"I asked him if he, at that time, had expected to be a lawyer and practice law in that courthouse, to which he replied: 'No, I didn't know I had sense enough to be a lawyer then.'"[23]

They spent the night in the Hanks cabin, four miles outside Decatur. The next morning, John Hanks led them to the land that would be their new home, "ten miles west of Decatur and about a hundred steps from the north fork of the Sangamon River and on the north side of it on a kind of bluff," he said.[24]

"It was a purty kentry up on the Sangamon," observed Dennis.[25]

"Here [we] built a log cabin," said Abe. "Made sufficient rails to fence ten acres of ground. Fenced and broke the ground and raised a crop of sown corn upon it the same year."[26]

"The house—the logs of it, I cut myself in 1829," said John Hanks. "Gave them to old man Lincoln."[27]

Said Dennis: "Abe helped put up a cabin fur Tom on the Sangamon."[28]

"Lincoln broke up fifteen acres of land," said John Hanks. "Abraham and myself split the rails."[29]

They barely settled into their new home when nature came with a vengeance to warn them that she was a force to be reckoned with. "In the autumn," said Abe, "all hands were greatly afflicted with ague and fever."[30]

"They were greatly discouraged," admitted Abe, "so much so that they determined on leaving the county. They remained, however, through the succeeding winter."[31]

The winter of 1830 nearly killed them. It was "the winter of the very celebrated 'deep snow' of Illinois," Abe said.[32] It was Christmas week. Snowstorms blasted them, leaving blankets of white two and a half feet deep. The blizzard raged for two days. When it stopped, the white cover was frozen solid. Another storm hit, burying the prairie in snow four feet deep.

If you were caught outside during the storm, your clothing would freeze to your skin. The feet of geese and chickens stuck fast to the ice. Cows, hogs, and horses froze to death or starved. Men traveling on horseback who became trapped on the prairie killed their mounts and gutted them so they could crawl inside the carcass for warmth. A rider who barely made it to town alive had to be taken down off his horse and carried indoors to thaw, still stuck to his saddle.

Neighbors and whole villages were cut off for weeks. Travel was impossible. Families with no food reserve died of starvation in their cabins. Those with no wood to burn froze.

By February, the Lincolns were running out of food. Abe made a desperate run to the nearest neighbor, the Warnicks, three miles away. When he reached their house, his feet were nearly frozen. Mrs. Warnick packed his feet in snow to take out the frostbite, then rubbed them in grease. He was laid up for days.

Spring came. The snow melted and the prairies swelled with rivers of water and mud. The Illinois settlers who survived the ordeal always referred to the winter of 1830–1831 as the year of the "deep snow." They called themselves "Snowbirds."[33] They were happy to be alive.

CHAPTER 19

"I found him no green horn."

————∞————

As the deep snows melted in the spring, a fresh new breeze blew in off the Sangamon River. He was loud and windy, a fast-talking, hard-drinking maker of schemes, a chaser of dreams. Denton Offutt was a visionary businessman, a hopeful hustler.

"He was certainly an odd character," said Herndon.[1] Some folks said he was "a clear-headed, brisk man of affairs." Others thought differently. "Wild, noisy, reckless," they said, "rattlebrained, unsteady and improvident."[2] James Short of New Salem described him as a "wild harumscarum kind of a man."[3]

Denton Offutt came to Decatur with a plan. He had a newly acquired stock of goods and was looking to make a handsome profit by selling them down in New Orleans. He needed some hired help to get it there, so he went looking for John Hanks.

"Offutt came to my house in February 1831," said Hanks. "Wanted to hire me to run a flatboat for him, saying that he had heard that I was quite a flatboat man in Kentucky. He wanted me to go badly."[4]

John Hanks knew that if he was going to make the trip he'd need a good crew of experienced, reliable men. "I went and saw Abe and John Johnston," he said. "Introduced Offutt to them. We made an engagement with Offutt at 50 cents per day and $60 to make the trip to New Orleans."[5]

Said Abe: "[We] were to join him—Offutt—at Springfield, Illinois as soon as the snow should go off. When it did go off, which was about the first of March 1831, the county was so flooded as to make traveling by land impracticable. . . . Purchased a large canoe and came down the Sangamon River in it." [6]

"Abe and I came down the Sangamon River in a canoe in March 1831," recalled John Hanks. "Landed at what is now called . . . Jamestown, five miles east of Springfield. . . . We left our canoe . . . walked afoot to Springfield and found Offutt. He was at a tavern. Probably Elliot's. It was Elliot's." [7]

Andrew Elliot kept the finest tavern in Springfield, the Buckhorn Inn. A painted head of a big buck hung above the front door. When the boys met Denton Offutt, he was cheerfully enjoying Mr. Elliot's fine spirits.

As part of the deal, Offutt had promised the boys that he would have a boat ready for them. "Learned from him that he had failed in getting a boat," said Abe. [8]

The crew was undaunted. They would build their own boat for pay. Offutt agreed to hire them to build a flatboat at twelve dollars a month.

"Abe, Johnston and myself went down to the mouth of Spring Creek and there cut the timbers to make the boat," recalled John Hanks.

"We were about two weeks cutting our timber," he said. "We then rafted the logs down to the Sangamon River, to what is called Sangamontown, seven miles northwest of Springfield.

"When we got to Sangamontown we made a shanty shed. Abe was elected cook. We sawed our lumber at Kirkpatrick's Mill. . . . We finished making and launching the boat in about four weeks."[9]

Sangamontown was a small flourishing frontier settlement on the Sangamon River. Newcomers were watched closely. When three men suddenly appeared on the river bank building a boat, they drew notice. One villager, Caleb Carman, stopped by to talk to the men. The tall one impressed him greatly. "When I first saw him I thought him a green horn, though after half hour's conversation with him I found him no green horn."[10]

Abe called himself "chief cook and bottle-washer." [11] His appearance was so striking that he naturally attracted attention. John Roll helped the boys with their boat. He was struck by Lincoln: "He was a tall, gaunt young man, dressed in a suit of blue homespun jeans, consisting of a round-about jacket, waistcoat and breeches which came to within about four inches of his feet. The latter were encased in rawhide boots, into the tops of which—most of the time—his pantaloons were stuffed. He wore a soft felt hat which had at one time been black, but now, as its owner dryly remarked, 'was sunburned until it was a combine of colors.'" [12]

At night when they could no longer work, the men gathered near the mill to "shoot the breeze," tell stories, joke, whittle, and talk. Abe quickly won everyone over with his endless tales and yarns. The men peeled a log for a bench so they could sit and listen to the entertainment. "Whenever he'd end up in his unexpected way, the boys on the log would whoop and roll off," said John Roll. [13]

With the men falling off time after time, the log was transformed. It became shiny and smooth, polished like a mirror. Good-naturedly, they blamed Abe. They called the seat "Abe's log."

"Abe was full of jokes during all this time," recalled John Hanks. "Kept us all alive." [14]

"He was funny," said Caleb Carman, "jokey, humorous, full of yarns, stories." [15]

"I saw Abe at a show one night at Sangamontown," Carman remembered. "The showman cooked eggs in Abe's hat. . . . Abe, when the man called for his hat, said—'Mister, the reason why I didn't give you my hat before was out of respect to your eggs, not care for my hat.'" [16]

"It caused a great laugh," said Carman. "But Lincoln turned the joke over well, as he always did on any occasion." [17]

It was early April, and the river was swollen from the melting snow. The men working on the boat suddenly found themselves in a dangerous predicament. John Roll was there and witnessed the excitement:

"It was the spring following the winter of the deep snow. Walter Carman, John Seamon and myself, and at times others of the Carman boys, had helped Abe in building the boat. . . . When we had finished we went to work to make a dugout or canoe to be used as a small boat with the flat. We found a suitable log about an eighth of a mile up the river and with our axes went to work under Lincoln's direction.

"The river was very high, fairly booming. After the dugout was ready to launch we took it to the edge of the water and made ready to let her go. Walter Carman and John Seamon jumped in as the boat struck water, each one anxious to be the first to get a ride. As they shot out from the shore they found they were unable to make any headway against the strong current. Carman had the paddle and Seamon was in the stern of the boat.

"Lincoln shouted to them to 'head up stream' and 'work back to shore' but they found themselves powerless against the stream. At last they began to pull for the wreck of an old flatboat, the first ever built on the Sangamon, which had sunk and gone to pieces leaving one of the stanchions sticking above the water. Just as they reached it, Seamon made a grab and caught hold of the stanchion when the canoe capsized, leaving Seamon clinging to the old timber and throwing Carman into the stream. It carried him down with the speed of a mill-race. Lincoln raised his voice above the road of the flood and yelled to Carman to swim for an old tree which stood almost in the channel. . . .

"Carman, being a good swimmer, succeeded in catching a branch and pulled himself up out of the water, which was very cold and had almost chilled him to death. There he sat shivering and chattering in the tree.

"Lincoln, seeing Carman safe, called out to Seamon to let go of the stanchion and swim for the tree. With some hesitation he obeyed . . . while Lincoln cheered and directed him from the bank. As Seamon neared the tree he made one grab for a branch and missing it, went under the water. Another desperate lunge was successful and he climbed up beside Carman."

The trip was pretty exciting now, for there were two men in the tree and the canoe was gone.

"It was a cold, raw April day and there was great danger of the men becoming benumbed and falling back into the water. Lincoln called out to them to keep their spirits up and he would save them. The village had been alarmed by this time and many people had come down to the bank.

"Lincoln procured a rope and tied it to a log. He called all hands to come and help roll the log into the water and after this had been done, he, with the assistance of several others, towed it some distance up the stream. A daring young fellow by the name of Jim Dorrell then took his seat on the end of the log and it was pushed out into the current with the expectation that it would be carried downstream against the tree where Seamon and Carman were.

"The log was well directed and went straight to the tree. But Jim, in his impatience to help his friends, fell a victim to his good intentions. Making a frantic grab at a branch, he raised himself off the log which was swept from under him by the raging water and he soon joined the other two victims upon their forlorn perch.

"The excitement on shore increased and almost the whole population of the village gathered on the river bank. Lincoln had the log pulled up the stream and securing another piece of rope called to the men in the tree to catch it if they could when he should reach the tree. He then straddled the log himself and gave the word to push out into the stream.

"When he dashed into the tree he threw the rope over the stump of a broken limb and let it play until it broke the speed of the log and gradually drew it back to the tree, holding it there until the three now nearly frozen men had climbed down and seated themselves astride. He then gave orders to the people on the shore to hold fast to the end of the rope which was tied to the log and leaving his rope in the tree he turned the log adrift. The force of the current acting against the taut rope swung the log around against the bank and all on board were saved.

"The excited people, who had watched the dangerous experiment with alternate hope and fear, now broke into cheers for Abe Lincoln and praises for his brave act. The adventure made quite a hero of him along the Sangamon and the people never tired telling of the exploit." [18]

CHAPTER 20

"I'll hit it hard."

⸺❦⸺

"It was in connection with this boat that occurred the ludicrous incident of sewing up the hogs eyes," Abe recalled. "Offutt bought thirty-odd large fat live hogs but found difficulty in driving them from where he purchased them to the boat and thereupon conceived the whim that he could sew up their eyes and drive them where he pleased."[1]

"We tried to drive them aboard but could not," said John Hanks. "They would run back past us. Lincoln then suggested that we sew their eyes shut."[2]

Here is where conflicting claims obscure our understanding of what happened. Sometimes history becomes a blur. Lincoln attributed the idea to Offutt. John Hanks said Lincoln thought of it first. Wherever the idea originated, it was something Lincoln was not willing to do.

"Abe said: 'I can't sew the eyes up,'" remembers Hanks.[3] "We caught them, Abe holding their heads and I their tails while Offutt sewed up their eyes."[4]

"It proved to be no benefit," said Coleman Smoot, "for the hogs scattered in every direction causing much trouble."[5]

Said Abe, "In their blind condition, they could not be driven out of the lot."[6]

"At last," Hanks said, "becoming tired, we carried them to the boat."[7]

Finally the boys were ready to go. Their boat, packed tight with barrels of meat, produce, and squealing hogs, began to float downriver toward New Orleans. Their adventures were just beginning.

"We landed at the New Salem mill about April 19th and got fast [stuck] on Rutledge's mill dam," said John Hanks. "On the dam part of a day and one night."[8]

Their journey of a thousand miles had barely begun, and already they were at a dead stop. For twenty-four hours the bow of the boat hung in the air, helplessly leaning over the dam's edge. The cargo was slipping astern, dangerously unbalancing the boat. Crowds of New Salem residents gathered atop the bluff overlooking the river to watch the befuddled boatmen. They called to the boys, shouting advice and encouragement.

Denton Offutt watched from the shore as his financial empire was slowly sinking toward disaster.

Ignoring catcalls and comments from bystanders, the tall boatman moved quickly to save his plunging craft. His friend Bill Greene remembered the moment well. "The boat coming down the Sangamon River grounded and lodged on the New Salem Mill dam. . . . I saw the boat soon after it landed—on the same hour or day. Then and there for the first time I saw Abraham Lincoln. . . .

"When I first saw him he was endeavoring to pry the boat over the dam. While straining every nerve to push the boat off the dam, Mr. Lincoln having noticed by his quick river eye that the river was falling, remarked to Offutt: 'We will have to get the boat to the shore and unload it or it will sink.'"[9]

"We unloaded the boat," said Hanks. "That is, we transferred the goods from our boat to a borrowed one. We then rolled the barrels forward. Lincoln bored a hole in the end over the dam. The water which had leaked in ran out and we slid over."[10]

The New Salem crowd greatly admired the quick-thinking boatman. They gave him a rousing cheer. Offutt was beside himself with glee. He swore to the aroused New Salemites that he would be back, promising to bring a steamboat down the Sangamon. If so, it would be the first. So what if the Sangamon River ran dangerously low in summer and froze in winter? He would figure a way to tame the river.

"Offutt said he intended to build it with rollers underneath so that when it came to a sand bar it would roll right over and runners underneath for to run on the ice," explained Coleman Smoot. "Offutt seemed to think that with Lincoln as pilot or captain there was no such thing as fail."

"By thunder!" Offutt bellowed. "She would have to go!"[11]

"We then proceeded," said John Hanks, "Offutt, John Johnston, Abe Lincoln and myself down the Sangamon River. . . . We kept our victuals and, in fact, slept down in the boat at one end. Went down by a kind of ladder through a scuttle hole. . . . Rushed through Beardstown in a hurry. People came out and laughed at us. Passed Alton, Cairo and stopped at Memphis, Vicksburg, Natchez.

"I can say we soon—say in May—landed in New Orleans," Hanks said.[12] They tied their flatboat beside thousands of others and stepped out, walking nearly a mile over boats at anchor until they reached the shore.

The boys lingered in New Orleans for a month, exploring this strange and exotic city like world travelers. "For the first time," wrote Herndon, "Lincoln beheld the true horrors of human slavery."[13]

New Orleans was a major center of the slave trade. Signs everywhere showed the nefarious business of buying and selling humans as merchandise. Bills and posters advertised slave markets and sales, offering "the highest prices in cash for good and likely Negroes."[14]

One trading company sent out this notice: "We have now on hand and intend to keep through the entire year a large and well-selected stock of Negroes, consisting of field hands, house servants, mechanics, cooks, seamstresses, washers, ironers, etc., which we can sell and will sell as low or lower than any other house here or in New Orleans. Persons wishing to purchase would do well to call on us before making purchases elsewhere as our fresh and regular arrivals will keep us supplied with a good and general assortment. Our terms are liberal. Give us a call."[15]

A business man advertised that he was looking to acquire some merchandise: "I will at all times pay the highest cash prices for Negroes of every description and will also attend to the sale of Negroes on commission, having a jail and yard fitted up expressly for boarding them."[16]

Another was looking for profit: "Forty-five Negroes now on hand, having this day received a lot of twenty-five direct from Virginia—two or three good cooks, a carriage driver, a good house boy, a fiddler, a fine seamstress, and a likely lot of field men and women—all of whom will sell at a small profit."[17]

There were buyers: "Wanted—I want to purchase twenty-five likely Negroes between the ages of 18 and 25 years, male and female, for which I will pay the highest prices in cash."[18]

And sellers: "For sale—several likely girls from 10 to 18 years old, a woman 24, a very valuable woman 25, with three very likely children."[19]

"We saw Negroes chained, maltreated, whipped and scourged," said Hanks. "Lincoln saw it. His heart bled. Said nothing much. Was silent from feeling. Was sad. Looked bad. Felt bad. Was thoughtful and abstracted."[20]

"One morning," wrote Herndon, "in their rambles over the city, the trio passed a slave auction. A vigorous and comely mulatto girl was being sold. She underwent a thorough examination at the hands of the bidders. They pinched her flesh and made her trot up and down the room like a horse to show how she moved and in order, as the auctioneer said, that 'bidders might satisfy themselves' whether the article they were offering to buy was sound or not. The whole thing was so revolting that Lincoln moved away from the scene with a deep feeling of 'unconquerable hate.' Bidding his companions follow him he said: 'By God, boys! Let's get away from this. If ever I get a chance to hit that thing [slavery], I'll hit it hard.'"[21]

According to John Hanks, twenty-two-year-old Abraham Lincoln saw something that changed him, left its mark. "I can say knowingly," Hanks declared, "that it was on this trip that he formed his opinions of slavery. It ran its iron in him then and there—May 1831. I have heard him say often and often."[22]

Years later, Lincoln wrote about a steamboat journey he took as a young man. It haunted him, preyed on his conscience. The experience forced him to come face to face with the American abomination that was slavery.

"There were on board ten or a dozen slaves shackled together with iron," he said.[23] "They were chained six and six together. A small iron clevis was around the left wrist of each and this was fastened to the main chain by a shorter one, at a convenient distance from the others so that the Negroes were strung together precisely like so many fish upon a trot-line.

"In this condition they were being separated forever from the scenes of their childhood, their friends, their fathers and mothers and brothers and sisters, many of them from their wives and children and going into perpetual slavery where the lash of the master is proverbially more ruthless and unrelenting than any other."[24]

"That sight was a continued torment to me," Lincoln said, "and continually exercises the power of making me miserable."[25]

Those who knew Lincoln as a young man heard him express his hatred of slavery. Caleb Carman, who first laid eyes on Abe the day he appeared on the banks of the Sangamon River to build a flatboat, said he was not shy about speaking his mind. "He was opposed to slavery," said Carman, "He thought it a curse to the land."[26]

Said Lincoln, with simple and devastating logic and the moral authority of biblical wisdom, "Whenever I hear anyone arguing for slavery I feel a strong impulse to see it tried on him personally."[27]

When the boys had had enough of New Orleans, they headed for home. "Offutt, Johnston, Abe and myself left New Orleans in June 1831," Hanks recalled. "We came to St. Louis on the steamboat together, walked to Edwardsville, twenty-five miles east of St. Louis—Abe, Johnston and myself. Abe and Johnston went to Coles County and I to Springfield, Sangamon County. Thomas Lincoln had moved to Coles County in 1831, in, say, June."[28]

Soon after Abe returned to Illinois, he found himself facing his next test. "Lincoln was a great wrestler," Colonel Chapman said. "His fame for this was widespread."[29]

The undisputed wrestling champion in Coles County was a giant named Dan Needham. The champ heard all about this tall new boy.

"Came to see Lincoln," said Chapman. "Lincoln and Needham met at Wabash Point in Coles County and Needham challenged Lincoln."[30]

A big crowd was there for a house-raising. Abe and Big Dan eyed each other, and a war of nerves was on. The two giants stood face-to-face, each man a mountain of muscle, six feet four and bull tough.

They set up a ring, and the crowd egged them on. "Lincoln threw Needham twice. Needham said: 'Lincoln—you have thrown me twice but you can't whip me.' Lincoln replied: 'Needham, are you satisfied that I can throw you? If you are not and must be convinced through a thrashing I will do that too. For your sake.'"[31]

Needham backed down. Now everyone knew Abe could beat all comers with his fists and brawn. Soon he would show he could win with words as well.

Lincoln was in Decatur with John Hanks one day. It was election time, and one of the candidates was there making a speech. "It was a bad one," Hanks remembered. "I said Abe could beat it. I turned down a box or keg and Abe made his speech. The other man was a candidate. Abe wasn't. Abe beat him to death . . .

"The man, after the speech was through, took Abe aside and asked him where he had learned so much—Abe explained, stating his manner and method of reading and what he had read. The man encouraged Lincoln to persevere."[32]

"It must 'a ben about that time 'at Abe left home fur good," said Dennis Hanks.[33]

So Abe said good-bye to his father, his stepmother, stepsisters, and cousin Dennis and all his little nieces and nephews. Many years would pass before he would see them again. He collected his belongings, which didn't amount to much, and wrapped them all in a bandanna tied to the end of a stick. Slinging the bundle over his shoulder, Abe started on the long walk down the road to make his mark on history.

CHAPTER 21

"A kind of driftwood."

———⊗⊗⊗———

"Abraham stopped indefinitely and for the first time, as it were, by himself, at New Salem," Lincoln wrote of himself. "This was in July 1831."[1]

New Salem resident Nult Greene remembered when he came. "He used to say to the boys and young men that they might always know when he came to New Salem by the high water the spring after the Deep Snow, that he came down with it as a kind of 'driftwood.'"[2]

New Salem, Illinois (population 100), was one of many villages to spring up along the Sangamon River about the same time as another village about the same size was growing to the north. That village was called Chicago.

For a thousand years, wild horses, shaggy buffalo, and Indians roamed the high bluffs overlooking the Sangamon River where the village of New Salem appeared. "To reach it," said Herndon, "the traveler must ascend a bluff a hundred feet above the general level of the surrounding country. . . . Skirting the base of the bluff is the Sangamon River, which, coming around a sudden bend from the southeast, strikes the rocky hill and is turned abruptly north. Here is an old mill driven by water-power and reaching across the river is the mill-dam on which Offutt's vessel hung stranded in April 1831. . . . The roar of water, like low, continuous, distant thunder, could be distinctly heard through the village day and night."[3]

William Herndon knew well the frontier town of New Salem and its colorful inhabitants. His father, Archer Herndon, settled in Sangamon County. Later, he represented that county, along with Abraham Lincoln, in the Illinois State Legislature. Billy Herndon's cousins, James and Rowan Herndon, lived in New Salem and owned a general store there.

New Salem began as a commercial enterprise, and the whole community was involved. "My father moved to and laid out the town of New Salem in the summer of 1829," said R. B. Rutledge.[4] James Rutledge and John Cameron bought the land high on the bluff as well as the rights to the river below. Here they built a milldam. A thousand wagon loads of gravel and stones were laid in the river and packed solid.

"At times," recalled Rutledge, "when it was necessary to construct a dam to afford the proper water power, word would be sent through the neighborhood and the people would come ten and fifteen miles en masse and assist gratuitously in the work. On such occasions Mr. Lincoln was ever ready to work with his stalwart hand and to assist in constructing or repairing the dams or mill, raising houses in the village etc. . . . an illustration of the generosity and nobleness of the settlers at that early day. It also shows an element of the character of the people. . . .

"The mill was a saw and grist mill. Was the first one built on the Sangamon River and supplied a large section of country with its meal, flour and lumber. . . .

"At that period, New Salem was a small village of not more than ten or fifteen families who lived in log cabins and who were as social and familiar as persons are who find themselves thus isolated from the great world outside."[5]

Farmers came from fifty miles around to have their grain mashed into flour at the mill and to buy salt, sugar, coffee, hardware, and cloth at the Rutledge store. The stage coach, called a "mud wagon" by the settlers, came once a week carrying mail to the New Salem Post Office. At its peak New Salem had two mills, two doctors, a school, a church, a saloon, a blacksmith, and four stores.

Many settlers came from Kentucky and Virginia. There were Yankees from New England and New York, some Pennsylvania Dutch, and recent immigrants from Britain, Germany, and France.

They worked hard and played hard. Every Saturday, farmhands from around the countryside came into town. It was their day off, and they were looking for a good time. They drank, wrestled, and fought. There were horse races and footraces.

One of their favorite sports was gander pulling. They hung a live goose by his feet from the limb of a tree. His long slender neck was greased till it was too slippery to hold. The boys paid ten cents for a chance to get the gander. On horseback they would charge at full gallop toward the struggling goose, then lunge out to grab the unfortunate bird by the neck. The rider who managed to pull the head clean off won the goose and the money.

On the frontier, disputes were settled with fists. Once, two men exchanged angry words and agreed to work out their differences on the other side of the river. The whole town watched them paddle across to the other shore, where they stripped and fought like wolves. When they didn't come back, their friends sent over a search party. They found the two men down, exhausted and bleeding. They made them shake hands and brought them home. One man nursed his wounds for a year before he died.

In these rough frontier towns, you tussled with your friends as quickly as your enemies. One New Salem old-timer remembered what happened when a group of revelers mounted their horses to go home after a night of carousing.

"They were on their horses and trying to pull each other off when Little John Wiseman said to Greasy George Miller: 'George, you have torn my shirt.' 'Yes,' said George 'and I can tear your hide too.'

"That was enough. They all got down and hitched their horses and formed a ring and the crowd all stopped to see fair play. The two com-batants shook hands and then stepped back eight or ten feet and at the word 'go' rushed at each other. . . . . Old Salem battles had no rules. They were strike, gouge, bite, kick, any way to win."[6]

There was another New Salem, a more civilized segment of the population. Decent, hardworking men and women strove to live productive and God-fearing lives. "Many . . . citizens never had to contend with its barbaric customs," said one resident. "Only those who trained in that school were subject to its conditions."[7]

There were barbecues, dances, house-raisings, wolf hunts, and camp meetings. At quilting bees each guest would "take his or her needle as the case may be for any man can quilt as well as the woman."[8]

One popular pastime was shooting for beef. Men came with their rifles at the appointed hour and wrote their names on a list alongside the number of shots they planned to take. The fee was twenty-five cents a shot. A board with a painted cross served as the target. Judges graded the shots, and the five best shooters won a part of the beef. The best shot got the hide. The next best had his choice of hindquarters, and the third took the other hindquarters. The fourth took his choice of forequarters, and the fifth got the remaining forequarter. The sixth best shot won all the lead bullets left in the target.

The respectable folks in town tried to boost the forces for virtue in the community. The church kept growing. One Sunday, fifty men, women, and children were baptized in the Sangamon River. Dr. John Allen, a Presbyterian elder who organized the first Sunday school in the village, founded a spirited Temperance Society, which met regularly to find ways to discourage the general use of liquor. Members were required to make a lifelong pledge to drink no intoxicating liquors.

Whiskey was everywhere on the frontier. Good and decent folks who worked hard during the day looked for good times when their work was done. Wherever people gathered to sing, laugh, or dance at weddings, sporting events, and meetings of all kinds, the flow of whiskey helped them to optimize their fun.

Even church members would not give up their spirits. When Mentor Graham, New Salem's only schoolmaster, joined Dr. Allen's Temperance Society, the church trustees showed their displeasure by voting to suspend him. Then, to make sure their gesture would not be taken to mean an unqualified support of intoxication, they suspended another member of the congregation who had gone blind drunk.

One church member, puzzled by these actions, brought a bottle of whiskey to the next meeting. "Brethering," he announced, waving his whiskey bottle. "You have turned one member out because he would not drink and another because he got drunk. And now I wants to ask a question." He held the bottle over his head. "How much of this here critter does a man have to drink to remain in full fellership in this church?"[9]

When Abe arrived in New Salem it was alive and busy, a typical pioneer community on the edge of the frontier. "In the days of land offices and stage coaches it was a sprightly village with a busy market," Herndon wrote.[10] Lincoln came there looking for opportunity. He wanted to make his own way in the world. He came looking for Denton Offutt.

"During this boat enterprise acquaintance with Offutt, who was previously an entire stranger, he conceived a liking for Abraham," Abe explained in his autobiography. "Believing he could turn him to account, he [Offutt] contracted with him to act as clerk for him on his return from New Orleans, in charge of a store and mill at New Salem."[11]

When Abraham Lincoln ambled down the main street of New Salem, he saw some men gathered outside a log cabin and joined them. This time he was no stranger. They recognized him immediately as the quick-thinking boatman who saved his craft at the milldam several months earlier.

It was Election Day in Illinois. All over the state, men would be voting for their government. The clerk spotted the tall newcomer and asked if he wanted to vote. So, for the first time in his life, Abe voted. According to the election returns dated August 1, 1831, Abraham Lincoln voted for a congressman, two justices of the peace, and two constables.[12]

The clerk for the election was the town schoolmaster, Mentor Graham. He remembered the day Abraham Lincoln came to New Salem. "The first time I saw him was an election day. We were deficient a clerk for the polls. Mr. Lincoln was about the street looking around and was asked by some of us if he could write."

"Yes, a little," replied Abe.

"Will you act as clerk of elections today?" Graham asked.

Said Abe: "I will try and do the best I can if you so request."

"He was then sworn in," said Graham, "and acted as clerk of the August election."[13]

Voting in those days was done by word of mouth. Each voter came before the election judge to say which candidates he wanted to vote for. The judge would announce the voter's name and his candidates, and all the names would be duly recorded by the clerks. All of New Salem voted. That was how Abe got to know the names and faces of almost all the men in town on his first day there.

"Rapidly made acquaintances and friends," he observed.[14] The folks at New Salem were drawn to this tall giant by his pleasant spirits and his knack for making people laugh. As that first New Salem afternoon wore on, the new clerk passed the long moments between ballots by telling stories, delighting the crowd.

"My cousin, J. R. Herndon, was present and enjoyed this feature of the election with the keenest relish," said Billy Herndon. "He never forgot some of Lincoln's yarns and was fond of repeating them in after years."

Rowan Herndon recalled, "In the afternoon, as things were dragging a little, Lincoln, the new man, began to spin out a stock of Indiana yarns," he remembered. "One that amused me more than any other he called the Lizard Story."

Lincoln recalled the tale: "The meeting house was in the woods and quite a distance from any other house. It was only used once a month. The preacher, an old line Baptist, was dressed in coarse linen pantaloons and shirt of the same material. The pants, manufactured after the old fashion, with baggy legs and a flap in front, were made to attach to his frame without the aid of suspenders. A single button held his shirt in position and that was at the collar.

"He rose up in the pulpit and with a loud voice announced his text thus: 'I am the Christ whom I shall represent today.' About this time a little blue lizard ran up his roomy pantaloons. The old preacher, not wishing to interrupt the steady flow of his sermon, slapped away on his legs expecting to arrest the intruder. But his efforts were unavailing and the little fellow kept on ascending higher and higher.

"Continuing the sermon, the preacher slyly loosened the central button which graced the waist-band of his pantaloons and with a kick, off came that easy-fitting garment. But meanwhile, Mr. Lizard had passed the equatorial line of waist-band and was calmly exploring that part of the preacher's anatomy which lay underneath the back of his shirt.

"Things were now growing interesting but the sermon was still grinding on. The next movement on the preacher's part was for the collar button and with one sweep of his arm off came the tow linen shirt.

"The congregation sat for an instant as if dazed. At length, one old lady in the rear of the room rose up and glancing at the excited object in the pulpit shouted at the top of her voice: 'If you represent Christ then I'm done with the Bible!'"[15]

CHAPTER 22

"The best feller that ever broke into this settlement."

⸺⸺

A s the people of New Salem got to know their new resident, the tall young man made quite an impression, quickly winning their respect and affection. Four decades later they eagerly recalled young Lincoln's wild introduction to their community.

R. B. RUTLEDGE:"You ask, first: 'When did you first become acquainted with Lincoln?' 'Where was it and what was he doing?' I answer: In the year 1830 or 1831 in the town of New Salem, Illinois. He was at that time a clerk in the store of Denton Offutt, having just returned with Offutt from New Orleans, with whom he had gone on a flatboat as a hand. . . . At that time he boarded with John Cameron, a partner of my father in laying out the town of New Salem."[1]

BILLY HERNDON:"In the meantime Offutt's long expected goods had arrived and Lincoln was placed in charge. . . . In keeping with his widely known spirit of enterprise Offutt rented the Rutledge and Cameron mill which stood at the foot of the hill and thus added another iron to keep company with the half-dozen already in the fire. As a further test of his business ability Lincoln was placed in charge of this also." [2]

BILL GREENE: "Lincoln was made Offutt's chief and head clerk within a few days after the goods were put up in the store at New Salem. I went down there and was employed by Offutt as clerk to keep the store."[3]

BILLY HERNDON:"William G. Greene was hired to assist him and between the two a lifelong friendship sprang up." [4]

BILL GREENE: "Mr. Lincoln and I clerked together for Offutt about 18 months and slept in the same cot. When one turned over the other had to do likewise."[5]

BILLY HERNDON:"At the head of these varied enterprises was Offutt. . . . Offutt relied in no slight degree on the business capacity of his clerk. In his effusive way he praised him beyond reason. He boasted of his skill as a businessman and his wonderful intellectual acquirements. As for physical strength and fearlessness of danger, he challenged New Salem and the entire world to produce his equal."[6]

DENTON OFFUTT:"He knows more than any man in the United States. Some day he will be President. . . . He can outrun, outlift, outwrestle and throw down any man in Sangamon County." [7]

BILLY HERNDON:"Honors such as Offutt accorded to Abe were to be won before they were worn at New Salem."[8]

DR. JASON DUNCAN: "There was a clan in that vicinity who prided themselves on their manhood and ready to measure steel with anyone who could be induced to enter the contest or trial of manhood."[9]

JAMES SHORT: "New Salem and the surrounding country was settled by roughs and bullies who were in the habit of winning all the money of strangers at cards and then whipping them in the bargain."[10]

BILLY HERNDON:"In the neighborhood of the village . . . lay a strip of timber called Clary's Grove. The boys who lived there were a terror to the entire region. They were friendly and good-natured. They could trench a pond, dig a bog, build a house; they could pray and fight, make a village or create a state . . . Though rude and rough, though life's forces ran over the edge of the bowl, foaming and sparkling in pure deviltry for deviltry's sake . . . there was never under the sun a more generous parcel of rowdies. . . . A stranger's introduction was likely to be the most unpleasant part of his acquaintance with them." [11]

JOHN STUART: "Took it upon themselves to try the mettle of every newcomer and ascertain what sort of stuff he was made of." [12]

MENTOR GRAHAM: "It was an ordeal through which all comers had to pass." [13]

BILLY HERNDON: "They conceded leadership to one Jack Armstrong, a hardy, strong and well-developed specimen of physical manhood. Under him they were in the habit of 'cleaning out' New Salem whenever his order went forth to do so." [14]

R. B. RUTLEDGE: "Armstrong was a man in the prime of life, square-built, muscular and strong as an ox." [15]

JAMES SHORT: "Armstrong was a regular bully, very stout and tricky in wrestling." [16]

HENRY McHENRY: "Jack Armstrong was a powerful twister." [17]

J. G. GREENE: "Jack Armstrong was as strong as two men." [18]

BILLY HERNDON: "Offutt and Bill Clary, the latter skeptical of Lincoln's strength and agility, ended a heated discussion in the store one day over the new clerk's ability to meet the tactics of Clary's Grove." [19]

R. B. RUTLEDGE: "Offutt made a bet with William Clary that Abe could throw down in a wrestle any man in the county." [20]

JAMES SHORT: "Offutt, in '31, made bet of five dollars that L could throw Jack Armstrong."[21]

HENRY McHENRY: "We tried to get Lincoln to tussle and scuffle with Armstrong. L. refused." [22]

ABE LINCOLN: "I never tussled and scuffled and will not. Don't like this wooling and pulling." [23]

JUDGE JAMES HARRIOT:"L [says] that when he came to Salem that the Clary Boys intended to whip L and run him off."[24]

HENRY McHENRY:"I was present at the wrestle of Lincoln and Armstrong."[25]

R. B. RUTLEDGE:"The match took place in front of Offutt's store. All the men of the village and quite a number from the surrounding country were assembled."[26]

HENRY McHENRY: "We bet knives and whiskey."[27]

ABE LINCOLN: "I am sorry that you bet the money. I do not believe that there is a man on earth that can throw me now."[28]

R. B. RUTLEDGE: "Trials of strength were very common among the pioneers. Lifting weights, as heavy timbers piled one upon another, was a favorite pastime and no workman in the neighborhood could at all cope with Mr. Lincoln in this direction."[29]

ROWAN HERNDON: "I saw him lift between 1000 and 1300 pounds of rock weighed in a box. . . . He was by far the stoutest man that I ever took hold of. I was a mere child in his hands and I considered myself as good a man as there was in the country until he came about."[30]

JIMMY SHORT: "Lincoln was a scientific wrestler."[31]

R. B. RUTLEDGE: "The contest began and Jack soon found so worthy an antagonist."[32]

JOHN STUART: "He had got hold of the wrong customer."[33]

JIMMY SHORT: "They wrestled for a long time without either being able to throw the other until Armstrong broke holds and caught L. by the leg and floored him."[34]

J. M. RUTLEDGE: "Caught Lincoln rather by the legs and partly threw him. I did not think it fairly done."[35]

ROYAL CLARY: "Jack Armstrong legged Lincoln. Jack said before his death that he threw L but did not do it fairly."[36]

R. B. RUTLEDGE: "Would have brought him to the ground had not Mr. Lincoln seized him by the throat and thrust him at arm's length from him."[37]

HENRY McHENRY: "L. at last picked up Armstrong. Swung him around."[38]

R. B. RUTLEDGE: "Jack, having played foul, there was every prospect of a general fight." [39]

J. M. RUTLEDGE: "There was like to be a fuss."[40]

NULT GREENE: "Clary claimed the money and said he would have it or whip Offutt and Lincoln both. Offutt was inclined to yield as there was a score or more of the Clary Grove Boys against him and Mr. Lincoln and my brother W. G. Greene. But Lincoln said they had not won the money and they should not have it and although he was opposed to fighting, if nothing else would do them he would fight Armstrong, Clary or any of the set."[41]

J. M. RUTLEDGE: "I noticed Lincoln standing with his back against a storehouse nearby where they wrestled, and a crowd of men standing around him. He seemed to be undaunted and fearless."[42]

HENRY McHENRY: "Lincoln would have fought any or all of them if necessary."[43]

R. B. RUTLEDGE: "At this time James Rutledge, having heard of the difficulty, ran into the crowd and through the influence which he exerted over all parties, succeeded in quieting the disturbance and preventing a fight."[44]

NULT GREENE: "So the money was drawn and from that day forward the Clary Grove Boys were always his firm friends."[45]

R. B. RUTLEDGE: "After this wrestling match Jack Armstrong and his crowd became the warmest friends and staunchest supporters of Mr. Lincoln."[46]

JAMES SHORT: "L took the matter in such good part and laughed the matter off so pleasantly that he gained the good will of the roughs and was never disturbed by them." [47]

ROYAL CLARY: "He won us by his bravery and boldness."[48]

JACK ARMSTRONG: "He's the best feller that ever broke into this settlement."[49]

HANNAH ARMSTRONG: "Am the wife of Jack Armstrong. . . . Knew Abraham Lincoln in July or August 1831. Know this by the birth of one of my children. Lincoln was clerking for Offutt at the time. I was living four miles from New Salem. Our acquaintance began then. Abe would come to our house; drink milk and mush, corn bread, butter; bring the children candy. Would rock the cradle of my baby . . . . He would nurse babies, do anything to accommodate anybody . . . I fixed his pants, and made his shirts . . . Jack Armstrong and Lincoln never had a word. They did wrestle—no foul play—all in good humor. Commenced in fun and ended in sport."[50]

JACK ARMSTRONG JR.: "Uncle Johnny, tell him about the wrestling match with father. You remember all about that."

UNCLE JOHNNY POTTER: "I remember it. Your father was considered the best man in all this country for a scuffle. . . . When Lincoln came to this country there was a crowd called the Clary Grove Boys who pretty much had their own way. And Jack Armstrong was the leader among them. Most every new man who came into the neighborhood had to be tried. Lincoln was pretty stout and the boys made it up to see what there was in him. . . .

"Bill Clary kept at Lincoln until he got him into a bet of five dollars. Then he put Jack Armstrong against him. They were pretty well matched but Abe was a good deal taller and could bend over Jack. They wrestled a good while, and I think Abe had thrown Jack two points and was likely to get him down. Clary, I expect, thought he was in danger of losing his money, for he called out: 'Throw him any way, Jack'. At that, Jack loosed his back hold and grabbed Abe by the thigh and threw him in a second.

"Abe got up pretty mad. He didn't say much but he told somebody that if it ever came right he would give Bill Clary a good licking. You see, the hold Jack took was fair in a scuffle but not in a wrestle. And they were wrestling. After that Abe was considered one of the Clary's Grove boys."[51]

DR. JASON DUNCAN: "He so managed with that pugilistic class as to obtain complete control over them."[52]

JOHN STUART: "This was the turning point in Lincoln's life." [53]

R. B. RUTLEDGE: "In all matters of dispute about horse racing or any of the popular pastimes of the day, Mr. Lincoln's judgment was final to all. . . . People relied implicitly upon his honesty, integrity and impartiality. . .

"Two neighbors, Henry Clark and Ben Wilcox had a law suit. The defeated [Clark] declared that although he was beaten in the suit he could whip his opponent. This was a formal challenge and was at once carried to the ears of the victor [Wilcox] and was promptly accepted.

"The time, place and second were chosen . . . Mr. Lincoln being Clark's and John Brewer, Wilcox's second. The parties met, stripped themselves, all but their brecches, went in, and Mr. Lincoln's principal was beautifully whipped. . . . During this performance, the second of the party opposed to Mr. Lincoln remarked: 'Well, Abe. My man has whipped yours and I can whip you!'

"Now this challenge came from a man who was very small in size. Mr. Lincoln agreed to fight provided he would chalk out his size on Mr. Lincoln's person and every blow struck outside of that mark should be counted foul. After this sally there was the best possible humor and all parties were as orderly as if they had been engaged in the most harmless amusement."[54]

RUSSELL GODBEY: "When a fight was on hand Abe used to say to me—'Let's go and stop it. Tell a joke. A story. Say something humorous and end the fight in a good laugh.' We never failed to accomplish the end."[55]

CHAPTER 23

"Something that was knotty."

————∞∞————

Storekeepers were citizens of great importance in small country hamlets like New Salem. Everyone stopped by to pick up their necessary supplies. It was the place to go for camaraderie and community and to hear the latest news. Storekeepers always knew what was going on. When folks came around to share their latest doings, the storekeepers were at the center of it all.

"Our store was a kind of meeting, social gathering place," said Parthena Hill, who, with husband Samuel Hill, owned and operated one of the main stores in New Salem. [1]

Evenings and Saturdays when farmwork was light, they came to the stores in town. "Men met here and talked politics, told stories," said Mrs. Hill. [2]

On the frontier social scene, the storekeeper had an important role to play. He was the master-of-ceremonies; the host, moderator, and referee. Theories, rumors, and disputes were referred to him for judgment. Folks wanted his opinion. The words of a storekeeper mattered.

Through the fall and winter of 1831–1832, Offutt's clerk reveled in his new career. "He was a good obliging clerk and an honest one," recalled Henry McHenry. "Everybody loved him." [3]

"He was among the best clerks I ever saw," said Mentor Graham. "He was attentive to his business, was kind and considerate to his customers and friends and always treated them with great tenderness, kindness and honesty."[4]

For the first time in his life, Lincoln could earn money without hard labor. "He used to unload sacks of wheat from farmer's wagons, measure out and settle with them," recalled Jason Duncan.[5]

When ladies asked for a dozen yards of calico, he would measure and cut. Some men wanted whiskey, so he tipped the barrel and poured it out. His long arms could reach the high shelves for pots, pans, buttons, hides, furs, and tools of all kinds. He counted Offutt's money and kept his books. Said McHenry, "He increased Offutt's business much by his simplicity."[6]

Once, when he counted the store's earnings, he realized that he had taken six cents too much from a customer. He walked three miles to her home to return the money.

Another time he sold a half pound of tea just before the store closed. Next morning he found the weight he used to measure the tea still on the scale. He realized that he had used the wrong weight and accidentally shortchanged his customer. Immediately he weighed the rest of the tea the customer had paid for and ran off to deliver it.

Stories like that passed among the villagers. "You ask what gave him the title of Honest Abe?" mused Mentor Graham. "That is answered in these few words. He was strictly honest, truthful and industrious. And in addition to this he was one of the most companionable persons you will ever see in this world."[7]

Young Lincoln was making a name for himself—boatman, storekeeper, wrestler, humbler of ruffians. "Lincoln's influence with the men of New Salem can be attributed to his extraordinary feats of strength," said Herndon.[8] He could show off his superior powers even behind the counter at the store. "He lifted a barrel of whiskey from the ground and drank from the bung [spout]," Herndon said. "But in performing this latter almost incredible feat he did not stand erect and elevate the barrel but squatted down and lifted it to his knees, rolling it over until his mouth came opposite the bung."[9]

But he found his greatest fame as an entertainer. "He was known as a storyteller before he was heard of either as a lawyer or politician," related Herndon. "He loved a story, however extravagant or vulgar, if it had a good point. . . . If it was merely a ribald recital and had no sting in the end, if it exposed no weakness or pointed no moral, he had no use for it. . . . As a mimic he was unequalled and with his characteristic gestures he built up a reputation for storytelling—although fully as many of his narratives were borrowed as original."[10]

"Mr. Lincoln took great delight in amusing others," said A. Y. Ellis, a great friend of Abe's who clerked at the store with him. "His way of laughing too was really funny."[11]

"Mr. Lincoln was all life and animation," R. B. Rutledge remembered. "He seemed to see the bright side of every picture."[12]

Robert Wilson, who was elected to the Illinois House of Representatives with Lincoln, gave us a vivid portrait of the future president in his most joyous, lighthearted moments. "When enlivened in conversation or engaged in telling or hearing some mirth-inspiring story, his countenance would brighten up," he said. "Rapidly, the muscles of his face would begin to contract. Several wrinkles would diverge from the inner corners of his eyes and extend down and diagonally across his nose. His eyes would sparkle, all terminating in an unrestrained laugh in which everyone present, willing or unwilling, was compelled to take part."[13]

He had crowds rolling and rollicking to his amusing stories, jokes, and ballads. Said Herndon, "Listen to one—'How St. Patrick Came to be Born on the 17th of March.' Who composed it or where Lincoln obtained it I have never been able to learn. Ellis says he often inflicted it on the crowds who collected in his store on winter evenings."

The first factional fight in old Ireland, they say,
Was all on account of St. Patrick's birthday.

It was somewhere about midnight, without any doubt,
And certain it is, it made a great rout.

On the eighth day of March, as some people say,
St. Patrick at midnight he first saw the day;
While others assert 'twas the ninth he was born—
'Twas all a mistake—between midnight and morn.

Some blamed the baby, some blamed the clock.
Some blamed the doctor, some the crowing cock.
With all these close questions sure no one could know,
Whether the babe was too fast or the clock was too slow.

Some fought for the eighth, for the ninth some would die;
He who wouldn't see right would have a black eye.
At length these two factions so positive grew,
They each had a birthday, and Pat, he had two.

Till Father Mulcahy who showed them their sins,
He said none could have two birthdays but as twins.
"Now boys, don't be fighting for the eight or the nine;
Don't quarrel so always—now why not combine?"

Combine eight with nine. It is the mark.
Let that be the birthday. Amen! said the clerk.
So all got blind drunk, which completed their bliss,
And they've kept up the practice from that day to this.[14]

A. Y. Ellis tried to reconstruct one of Lincoln's many stories. "I once heard Mr. Lincoln tell an anecdote on Colonel Ethan Allen of Revolutionary War notoriety which I have never heard from any one besides him. . . .

"It appears that shortly after we had peace with England Mr. Allen had occasion to visit England and while there the English took great pleasure in teasing him and trying to make fun of the Americans and General Washington in particular. . . .

"One day they got a picture of General Washington and hung it up the Back House [outhouse] where Mr. Allen could see it. They finally asked Mr. Allen if he saw that picture of his friend in the Back House. Mr. Allen said no. But said he thought that it was very appropriate for Englishman to keep it.

"Why, they asked. 'For' said Mr. Allen, 'there is nothing that will make an Englishman shit so quick as the sight of General Washington.'

"And after that they let Mr. Allen's Washington alone."[15]

"There is many others that I could mention," admitted Rowan Herndon, "but they are on the vulgar order."[16]

Years later, law colleague H. E. Dummer remembered not only Lincoln's gift as a raconteur but that the man himself did not think very much his talents. "Lincoln had been telling his yarns," he said. "A man, a kind of lick spittle, a farmer, said—'Lincoln, why do you not write out your stories and put them in a book?'

"Lincoln drew himself up, fixed his face, as if a thousand dead carcasses and a million privies were shooting all their stench into his nostrils, and said—'Such a book would stink like a thousand privies.'"[17]

Customers flocked to the store and stayed a while, swapping stories, news, gossip, and sharing laughs. But in cold or rainy weather, people stayed home. Then, for long hours, the storekeeper would find himself alone.

"Silence found him," Sandburg said. "He met silence. In the making of him as he was, the element of silence was immense."[18]

Silent and alone. In the presence of only himself and his deepest wonderings and longings, he felt an emptiness, a hunger. There was so much he wanted to know. He could remember as a boy, lying alone in his loft at night, replaying the words he heard from grown-ups. "I could not sleep," he would say, "trying to make out what was the exact meaning of some of their—to me—dark sayings."[19]

Something was missing. There was a deep hole in his life, and he began finding ways to fill it. "Wanted to get hold of something that was knotty," said Bill Greene.[20]

"Lincoln had long before realized the deficiencies of his education," said Herndon. "Resolved—now that the conditions were favorable—to atone for early neglect by a course of study."[21]

He wanted to make his mark in the world. But how? What could he do? Who would bother listening to his uneducated, half-baked notions? "Nothing was more apparent to him than his limited knowledge of language and the proper way of expressing his idea," said Herndon.[22]

Lincoln approached New Salem's most accomplished teacher, Mentor Graham. "Spoke to me one day and said: 'I had a notion of studying grammar,'" recalled Graham. "I replied to him: 'If you ever expect to go before the public in any capacity I think it the best thing you can do.'

"He said to me: 'If I had a grammar [book] I would commence now.'

"There was none in the village and I said to him: 'I know of a grammar at one Vance's [a man named John Vance], about six miles'—which I thought he could get.

"He was then at breakfast. Ate, got up and went on foot to Vance's and got the book. He soon came back and told me he had it. He then turned his immediate and almost undivided attention to English grammar. The book was Kirkham's Grammar, an old [1826] volume."[23]

"He, at once, applied himself to the book," said Herndon. "Sometimes he would stretch out at full length on the counter, his head propped up on a stack of calico prints, studying it. Or he would steal away to the shade of some inviting tree and there spend hours at a time in a determined effort to fix in his mind the arbitrary rule that 'adverbs qualify verbs, adjectives, and other adverbs.'"[24]

"Abraham requested me to assist him in the study of English grammar," recalled Jason Duncan. "His application through the winter was assiduous and untiring. His intuitive faculties were surprising. He seemed to master the construction of the English language and apply the rules for the same in a most astonishing manner."[25]

"He could be seen usually when in pursuit of his ordinary avocations with his book under his arm," remembered R. B. Rutledge. "At a moment of leisure, he would open it.[26]

"If it was but five minutes time, would open his book, which he always kept at hand, and study, close it, recite to himself—then entertain company or wait on a customer in the store or post office, apparently without any interruption.[27]

"Have seen him reading, walking the streets, occasionally become absorbed with his book, would stop and stand for a few moments, then walk on."[28]

"Would walk down to the river reading," said Rowan Herndon. "Would return the same way." [29]

Recalled R. B. Rutledge, "In summer season he frequently retired to the woods to read and study.[30] Cannot tell you how he read in the woods as I never intruded on his retirement. Simply know he read in the woods by seeing him return and having heard him say he had been reading in the brush."[31]

Rowan Herndon remembered the same thing. "He often took a stroll to the country, as he said, for refreshment. He generally took a book with him or brought one back. I think his object was to study and be by himself."[32]

"He read aloud very often," said Jimmy Short. "Frequently assumed a lounging position when reading."[33]

"He was sometimes sitting, sometimes standing and sometimes on his back," said Rowan Herndon. "If [he] commenced reading anything very interesting he generally put it through and he always remembered what he read."[34]

Jimmy Short agreed. "He read very thoroughly and had a most wonderful memory. Would distinctly remember almost everything he read. Used to sit up late nights reading and would recommence in the morning when he got up."[35]

"He had access to any books that was in and around the town of Salem," said Rowan Herndon, "for all knew that he was fond of reading."[36]

When long afternoons dragged on in the store, he would call his fellow clerk Billy Greene over, hand him his book and say: here, ask me some questions. Some thirty years later, when Bill Greene visited his old friend at the White House, Lincoln introduced him to the secretary of state as the man who taught him grammar. Later, an embarrassed Greene turned to the president. "Abe," he said, "What did you mean by telling Mr. Seward that I taught you grammar? Lord knows I don't know any grammar myself, much less could I teach you."

Abe replied, "Bill, don't you recollect when we stayed in Offutt's store at New Salem and you would hold the book and see if I could give the correct definitions and answers to the questions?"

"Yes," said Billy, "but that was not teaching you grammar."

"Well," responded the president, "that was all the teaching of grammar I ever had."[37]

CHAPTER 24

"I am young and unknown."

———⊶∞⊷———

During the winter of 1832, the young storekeeper got his first taste of public speaking. "A debating club of which James Rutledge was President was organized and held regular meetings," said his son, R. B. Rutledge. "Mr. Lincoln made his first effort at public speaking."[1]

Jason Duncan was there. "The first time I ever heard him attempt to speak in public was at a polemic Society meeting in an underground room of a rude log cabin."[2]

R. B. Rutledge described the moment. "As he rose to speak, his tall form towered above the little assembly. Both hands were thrust down deep in the pockets of his pantaloons.

"A perceptible smile at once lit up the faces of the audience, for all anticipated the relation of some humorous story. But he opened up the discussion in splendid style to the infinite astonishment of his friends. As he warmed with his subject, his hands would forsake his pockets and would enforce his ideas by awkward gestures, but would very soon seek their resting place. He pursued the questions with reason and argument so pithy and forcible that all were amazed."[3]

James Rutledge was impressed. The founder of the Debating Society, a man who owned a personal library of nearly thirty books, was widely respected as one of New Salem's leading citizens. R. B. Rutledge recalled his father's reaction to the storekeeper's maiden speech. "Remarked to his wife that there was more in Abe's head than wit and fun; that he was already a fine speaker. All he lacked was culture. . . .

"From that time," he continued, "Mr. Rutledge took a deeper interest in him. Soon after, Mr. Rutledge urged him to announce himself as a candidate for the legislature. This he—at first—declined to do, [saying] that it was impossible to be elected. It was suggested that a canvass of the county would bring him prominently before the people and in time would do him good."[4]

In 1832, politics was on everyone's mind. President Andrew Jackson was campaigning for reelection against his rival Henry Clay. At saloons, stores, mills, or wherever men gathered to talk politics, you were either a Jackson man or a Clay man. When they weren't arguing over the merits of their favorite candidates, they debated government policies and political issues such as the national bank, protective tariffs, and internal improvements such as building roads and canals and widening rivers.

"Lincoln was a Clay man," said James Gourley.[5]

"He loved and adored Clay. I know this," said Judge David Davis, who rode the Illinois Circuit with Lincoln when they were young lawyers and later was appointed by President Lincoln to the United States Supreme Court.[6]

Jason Duncan agreed. "Mr. Lincoln was in favor of Henry Clay in 1832. Voted for him during that memorable campaign, though the New Salem precinct was largely for Jackson."[7]

Anyone could become a candidate. All a person had to do was to make a public announcement to inform people where the candidate stood on the pressing issues of the day. Supporters of the candidate distributed posters and leaflets stating their policies and showed up to cheer for the candidate at public speeches.

Lincoln's friends began pushing him to run. Jason Duncan recognized his great ability. "His external appearance was not prepossessing but on cultivating an acquaintance with him found something about the young man very attractive, evincing intelligence far beyond the generality of youth of his age and opportunities."[8]

"Encouraged by his great popularity among his immediate neighbors," wrote Lincoln in his autobiography, "he ran for the legislature."[9]

Lincoln and his friends worked carefully on his first public announcement. James Rutledge and Mentor Graham helped him compose it. "I corrected, at his request, some of the grammatical errors in his first address to the voters of Sangamon County," recalled John McNeil,[10] who would always consider himself Lincoln's friend despite the whispers around town that Abe fell in love with McNeil's bride-to-be, the beautiful Miss Ann Rutledge.

On March 15, 1832, the campaign began. An announcement appeared in local newspapers: Abraham Lincoln was now a candidate for the Illinois State Legislature.

To the people of Sangamon County: Having become a candidate for the honorable office of one of your Representatives in the next General Assembly of this state, in accordance with an established custom and the principles of true Republicanism, it becomes my duty to make known to you, the people whom I propose to represent, my sentiments with regard to local affairs.

The candidate supported a plan for improving the transportation system in Sangamon County.

No other improvement that reason can justify us in hoping for can equal in utility the railroad. It is a never-failing source of communication between places of business remotely situated from each other.

The candidate railed against an overextended treasury.

There is always a heart-appalling shock accompanying the account of its cost . . . $290,000 . . .

Lincoln proposed government-sponsored improvements to the Sangamon River to encourage river commerce. Lincoln reminded his friends and neighbors that he was one of the most experienced river men around and knew what he was talking about.

> *The improvement of the Sangamon River is an object much better suited to our infant resources. From my peculiar circumstances, it is probable that for the last twelve months I have given as particular attention to the stage of the water in this river as any other person in the country. I think I may say, without the fear of being contradicted, that its navigation may be rendered completely practicable.*

The candidate came out strongly in favor of education.

> *Upon the subject of education—I can only say that I view it as the most important subject which we as a people can be engaged in. That every man may receive at least a moderate education and thereby be enabled to read the histories of his own and other countries, by which he may duly appreciate the value of our free institutions, appears to be an object of vital importance . . . to say nothing of the advantages and satisfaction to be derived from all being able to read the Scriptures.*

Lincoln assured voters that he would be an independent and open-minded officeholder and would always be ready to do what was right.

> *I have spoken as I have thought. I may be wrong. . . . But holding it a sound maxim that it is better to be only sometimes right than at all times to be wrong, so soon as I discover my opinions to be erroneous, I shall be ready to renounce them.*

The candidate concluded his campaign manifesto with a personal note.

> *Every man is said to have his peculiar ambition. . . . I have no other so great as that of being truly esteemed of my fellow-men, by rendering myself worthy of their esteem. . . . I am young and unknown to*

many of you. I was born and have ever remained in the most humble walks of life. I have no wealthy or popular relations or friends to recommend me. My case is thrown exclusively upon the independent voters of this county. If elected, they will have conferred a favor upon me for which I shall be unremitting in my labors to compensate. But if the good people, in their wisdom, shall see fit to keep me in the background, I have been too familiar with disappointments to be very much chagrined.
Your friend and fellow citizen,
A. Lincoln.[11]

CHAPTER 25

"They surely thought it was a dream."

———— ∞∞∞ ————

April 1832. New Salem was buzzing with the news. All those who built their homes in settlements along the Sangamon River grew excited about the future. A steamer was coming down the river, the first ever to brave the narrow forbidding waters of the Sangamon.

If a steamship from Cincinnati could make its way west on the Ohio River, head north on the Mississippi past St. Louis, and continue on to the Illinois River to the Sangamon, it would end up in Springfield, the capital of Illinois. This new route would open up worlds of opportunity for business in the state of Illinois. Money and goods would change hands, commerce would grow, and all sorts of merchandise from all over the young nation would become available, particularly items from ports along the Atlantic coast.

"In the spring of '32, very early that spring, there was a company from Springfield that chartered the steamboat *Talisman* to navigate the Sangamon," said Rowan Herndon.[1] Captain Vincent Bogue hired the *Talisman* in Cincinnati and announced his intention to carry merchandise along the waterways to Springfield, Illinois. Up and down the Sangamon River business was booming. Newspapers ran advertisements for merchandise from the east. Posters promised cheap goods, easy travel, new opportunities. Along the riverbank landowners subdivided their real estate and sold it in lots. Plans were drawn up for new towns. The whole countryside was glowing with optimism, with everyone anticipating a new era of prosperity.

Captain Bogue sent word to the communities along the river: a giant steamer was coming. Clear the way. Move the boulders. Cut overhanging limbs. Clean out the weeds and driftwood. The Sangamon River, raw and wild, would be tamed.

A small army of men armed with long-handled axes met the boat at Beardstown, where the Illinois River joined the Sangamon. They went to work, hacking away at the woods along the riverbank. Among them was a tall man from New Salem, a young storekeeper known along the Sangamon as a skilled boatman who was also a candidate for the state legislature. The man was Abraham Lincoln.

The *Talisman* pushed upriver, smoking and chugging past waving and cheering crowds. The whole town of Springfield turned out at the courthouse for a grand reception and dance to honor the arrival of the captain and crew. One homespun poet celebrated the gala event in a verse that appeared in the *Sangamon Journal*, April 5, 1832:

> *O, Captain Bogue, he gave the load,*
> *And Captain Bogue, he showed the road;*
> *And we came up with a right good will,*
> *And tied our boat up to his mill.*
> *Now we are up the Sangamo,*
> *And here we'll all have a grand hurrah,*
> *So fill your glasses to the brim,*
> *Of whiskey, brandy, wine and gin.*
> *Illinois suckers, young and raw,*
> *We're strung along the Sangamo,*
> *To see a boat come up by steam,*
> *They surely thought it was a dream.*[2]

The *Talisman* never reached Springfield. The boat pulled in at Bogue's Mill about five miles away, and that would be the end of their journey.

Billy Herndon was there. He was fourteen and he never saw anything like it. "I and other boys on horseback followed the boat along the river bank as far as Bogue's Mill where she tied up," he remembered. "There we went aboard and, lost in boyish wonder, feasted our eyes on the splendor of her interior decorations. . . .

"I remember the occasion well for two reasons," said Herndon. "It was my first sight of a steamboat and also the first time I ever saw Mr. Lincoln."[3]

Captain Bogue hired two local boatmen to pilot the steamer, two men who knew the tricky snags and currents of the Sangamon better than anyone. He hired Rowan Herndon and Abraham Lincoln.

"I was sent for, being an old boatman, and I met her some 12 or 15 miles above Salem," said Rowan Herndon. "Mr. Lincoln was one of the company that met her at the mouth of the river and helped pilot her up when she came to Salem."[4]

The *Talisman* anchored at Bogue's Mill for a week. Experienced boatmen were saying that the rest of the trip would not be easy. Up to Bogue's Mill, passage on the river had been aided by swift spring currents, swollen by the runoff of melting snow. Now that the water was receding, the river might be too shallow for the steamer to pass.

The two navigators turned the boat back toward Beardstown. It was a difficult trek. Said Boatman Herndon, "When she left Bogue's Mill the river was falling fast. The boat only made about three or four miles a day on account of the high wind."[5]

The river was so shallow they could hear the sound of the hull scraping bottom. When they reached New Salem, the steamer could not pass the milldam owned by Cameron and Rutledge, the same dam that caught Lincoln and his flatboat the year before.

Captain Bogue wanted the dam removed so his boat could go through. Cameron and Rutledge protested vehemently. While the debate raged back and forth, crowds watched from the shore, calling out to them, shouting advice and encouragement, lending their interested voices to the ruckus. The boat went nowhere.

The poets sang:

And when we came to Salem dam
Up we went against it jam!
We tried to cross with all our might,
But found we couldn't and staid all night.[6]

A cooler head pointed to a law stating that no one had the right to erect a dam or in any way obstruct a navigable stream. Since Bogue had demonstrated that the Sangamon was navigable, he claimed the right to remove the dam. Cameron and Rutledge looked on disconsolately as the crew began to demolish the dam.

"When we struck the dam she hung," Rowan Herndon recalled. "We then backed off and threw the anchor over. We tore away part of the dam and raised steam. Run her over on the first trial."[7]

Herndon and Lincoln piloted the vessel down the Sangamon to the Illinois River. "I think the Captain gave Mr. Lincoln $40 to run her down to Beardstown. I am sure I got $40," said Herndon.[8]

The *Talisman* made it back to Cincinnati and then went on to oblivion. "As soon as she was over, the company that chartered her was done with her," said Rowan Herndon.[9] Captain Bogue realized that his expedition on the Sangamon only proved how treacherous steamboat travel was on the river, and he swore never to do it again. The *Talisman* was the first and last steamboat to navigate the waters of the Sangamon. A few months later, the *Talisman* met a fiery end while docked at the wharf in St. Louis.

Meanwhile, Abe's promising career as a merchant was in danger of coming to an abrupt end. "In less than a year, Offutt's business was failing," recalled Abe.[10] Offutt could no longer put off his creditors, who were demanding money for their merchandise. One day men appeared at the store waving some legal papers. They loaded up all the stock and carted it away.

According to Lincoln, Offutt just "petered out."[11] Nobody in New Salem was surprised when his business failed. Folks were just as happy when he left town. "He talked too much with his mouth," remarked one New Salem resident.[12] And that summed up the career of Denton Offutt.

However, wild characters like Offutt do not remain out of sight for long. In 1873, Herndon received a letter from a Baltimore physician. "I fished up from memory that some twenty-five years ago one Denton Offutt appeared in Baltimore, hailing from Kentucky, advertising himself in the city papers as a veterinary surgeon and horse tamer, proposing to have a secret to whisper in the horse's ear . . . by which the most . . . vicious horse could be gentled and controlled. For this secret he charged five dollars, binding the recipient by oath not to divulge it. I know several persons, young fancy horsemen, who paid for the trick.

"Offutt advertised himself not only through the press. . . . He appeared in the streets on horseback and on foot, in plain citizen's dress of black but with a broad sash across his right shoulder of various colored ribbons, crossed on his left hip under a large rosetta of the same material, rendering his appearance most ludicrously conspicuous."[13]

In 1860, the same year his former clerk was elected president of the United States, Denton Offutt published a book. It was titled: *The Educated Horse: Instructions for Educating Horses and Other Animals to Obey a Word, Sign, or Signal and to Work or Ride, Also Showing How Children May Be Taught to be Quiet and Obedient by Kindness and Without Punishment.*[14]

Lincoln did hear from Offutt again. Years later, when he was a prominent Springfield attorney, a former New Salem resident told him how he bumped into Offutt in a small town in Mississippi. He watched Offutt's exhibition of animal obedience and training. He approached Offutt after the show, and they spoke about old times. Offutt asked about his protégé Lincoln and was pleased to hear that he was now a famous man.

"Mr. Offutt gave me a message to deliver to you," the New Salem man said to Abe.

"Tell it to me," said Lincoln. "Tell it just as Offutt said it."

"He told me to say to you—'Tell Lincoln to get out of his rascally business of politics and law and do something honest, like taming horses.'"

Lincoln rolled with delight. "That's Offutt," he chuckled. "That's just like Offutt."[15]

CHAPTER 26

"Captain Abraham Lincoln's Company of the First Regiment of the Brigade of Volunteers."

───── ∞∞∞ ─────

It was a quiet April morning in 1832 when a mud-soaked rider came galloping through the streets of New Salem. He passed out handbills signed by the governor of Illinois. The call was going out—they needed fighting men.

Chief Black Hawk had led his Sauk tribe off their reservation and crossed the Mississippi, heading toward Illinois. Terrified settlers appealed for help, and the governor promptly signed a proclamation calling for volunteers to drive the Indians back across the Mississippi.

Every able-bodied male between eighteen and forty-five was required by law to join the Army Reserve. The men met twice a year to practice military drills. The penalty for missing these drills was one dollar. "As a dollar was hard to raise," said one old-timer, "everybody drilled."[1]

Lincoln was a member of the Sangamon County Militia. Since Offutt's store closed, he was out of work. When the call came for volunteers, he stepped forward. As a candidate for the state legislature, a thirty-day stint as an Indian fighter would show voters that he was the kind of man who would stand with them in time of need. Said Rowan Herndon,

"He volunteered to serve his country with the balance of the patriotic boys to defend the frontier settlers of his state from the savage's tomahawk and scalping knife."[2]

The Sauk tribe had been living peacefully in northwestern Illinois for hundreds of years. They planted corn, hunted, fished, and buried their dead at the mouth of the Rock River. Then settlers came and leveled the forest, built cabins, forts, and roads, and chased away the wild game animals. The Sauks were forced to move north and west to hunt for food. Soon they found themselves encroaching on Sioux territory and fighting war parties of angry Sioux braves.

In 1804, Sauk tribesmen sold the rights to their ancient homeland to the United States government. A key stipulation in the treaty allowed them to return to hunt, fish, and raise corn.

For the next twenty-eight years, the Sauk nation and American pioneers lived uneasily along the river in mutual suspicion. Anger and violence flared up on both sides. During the War of 1812, when Britain made an ill-fated effort to recapture the American colonies, Black Hawk and the Sauks joined the British side hoping an American defeat would bring a return of their homeland. This made the settlers ever more distrustful. They called Black Hawk and his tribe "that British Band."

The old chief ached to see his homeland desecrated. White settlers lived there now. His people longed to see the graves of their loved ones. Black Hawk's own daughter was buried there. Spring was coming. His people were hungry. They needed to grow their corn. They needed to be back on their land.

Black Hawk never recognized the authority of the tribesmen who signed away the land. "My reason teaches me that land cannot be sold," he wrote. "The Great Spirit gave it to his children to live upon and cultivate, as far as is necessary, for their subsistence; and so long as they occupy and cultivate it they have the right to the soil. But if they voluntarily leave it, then any other people have a right to settle upon it. Nothing can be sold but such things as can be carried away."[3]

He did not trust the white settlers or their government. He believed they had tricked his people out of their land. "The white people brought whiskey to our village," he explained. "They made our people drunk and cheated them out of the horses, guns and traps. I visited all the whites and begged them not to sell my people whiskey. One of them continued the practice openly. I took a party of my young men, went to his house, broke in the head of the barrel and poured out the whiskey. I did this for fear some of the whites might get killed by my people when they were drunk."[4]

In 1831, Black Hawk gathered his braves and crossed the Mississippi to drive the white settlers out. He was met by a large force of US Army troops. In the negotiations, General Atkinson persuaded Black Hawk to return west of the Mississippi. The US government would provide his people with 60,000 bushels of corn in exchange for the promise not to cross the river again. Black Hawk accepted the terms, and the Sauks moved on. "I touched the goose quill to the treaty and was determined to live in peace," he said.[5]

But the Sauk homeland was never far from his mind. That winter, Black Hawk believed that his Indian neighbors—the Ottawas, Chippewas, Winnebagoes, Pottowottomies, and the Fox—would join the fight against their common enemy, the white man. He hoped that his friends, the British, would come to his aid with guns, ammunition, and provisions. The Great Spirit and the Voices of the Fathers seemed to be commanding the noble Sauk chief to move back home and once and for all drive the settlers from Indian land.

At sunup on April 6, 1832, Black Hawk painted his face and tied a string of eagle feathers around his head. Leading five hundred warriors, he crossed the Mississippi, burning farms, murdering families, and taking scalps.

News of the massacres traveled fast. All over northwest Illinois, settlers fled their homes and took refuge in forts protected by the US Army. General Atkinson sent word to the governor that he needed reinforcements. On April 16, Governor Reynolds dispatched riders throughout the state to call for help. Volunteers were ordered to assemble at Beardstown on April 22.

Lincoln later told his lawyer friend Leonard Swett how he came to be chosen as captain. "A line of two was formed by the company," explained Swett, "with the parties who intended to be candidates for officers standing in front. The candidate for captain then made a speech to the men, telling them what a gallant man he was, in what wars he had fought, bled and died and how he was ready again, for the glory of his country, to lead them. . . . When the speechmaking was ended, they commanded those who would vote for this man or that to form a line behind their favorite. . . . They counted back and the fellow who had the longest tail to his kite was the real captain."[6]

"Lincoln beat Bill Kirkpatrick for Captain," said Bill Greene.[7]

Kirkpatrick owned a sawmill outside New Salem. The mill owner hired Abe to haul logs and said he would buy him a cant hook to help move the logs. Forget the cant hook, Abe told him. He would move the logs without it if Kirkpatrick gave him the two dollars the tool would cost. Kirkpatrick agreed.

"He never settled for my toil," said Abe. "He used me badly."[8]

When Bill Kirkpatrick stepped forward as a candidate for captain, Lincoln leaned over to Greene and said, "Bill, I believe I can make Kirkpatrick pay me that two dollars he owes me on the cant hook. I'll run against him for captain."[9]

The boys from Clary's Grove huddled with Abe and made a pact among themselves. "We'll fix Kirkpatrick," they told one another.[10]

"The boys seized Lincoln," Swett continued, "and pushed him out of the line and began to form behind him and cried—'Form behind Abe!' In a moment of irresolution, he marched ahead and when they counted back he had two more than the other captain."[11]

"I was elected Captain of the volunteers," said Abe, "a success which gave me more pleasure than any I have had since."[12]

"I cannot tell you," Abe told Swett, "how much the idea of being captain of that company pleased me."[13]

Now he was Captain Lincoln of the First Regiment of the Brigade of Mounted Volunteers. He made Jack Armstrong his first sergeant. Bill Kirkpatrick became the quartermaster.

The volunteers were a special breed of soldier. There were no uniforms. They wore homemade buckskin breeches and coonskin caps.

Everyone had a flintlock rifle and a powder horn. Every man carried his own blanket.

"They were a hard looking set of men, unkempt and unshaved," wrote one newspaper reporter.[14] Hardy and weathered, the men could wrestle wildcats, outlast bears, and fight the fiercest Indian warrior who ever swung a tomahawk. But they had no use for military discipline. They liked Captain Lincoln. But no one could tell them what to do. Said Herndon, "I heard Mr. Lincoln say once . . . to the first order given one of them, he received the response—'Go to the devil, sir!'"[15]

Military tactics and precision exercises were something new to the captain. "I remember his narrating his first experience in drilling his company," reported a newspaperman. "He was marching with a front of over twenty men across a field when he desired to pass through a gateway into the next enclosure."

Said Captain Lincoln: "I could not for the life of me remember the proper word of command for getting my company endwise so that it could get through the gate. So as we came near the gate I shouted—'This company is dismissed for two minutes when it will fall in again on the other side of the gate!'"[16]

The new captain, unfamiliar with army rules and regulations, often found himself in trouble with his superior officers.

"I was a private in Captain Lincoln's Company," said David Pantier. "While in camp there a general order was issued prohibiting the discharge of firearms within fifty steps of the camp. Captain L disobeyed the order by firing his pistol within ten steps of the camp. For this violation of orders was put under arrest for that day and his sword taken from him."[17]

According to Private Pantier, the captain's military career survived this violation of military discipline. "The next day his sword was restored and nothing more was done in the matter."[18]

Another scandal put Captain Lincoln in the brig for a second time. Private Pantier's testimony offers the names, dates, and details that led to the imprisonment of Abraham Lincoln.

"About the 15th of April we reached the mouth of Rock River. Three or four nights afterwards, a man named Rial P. Greene, commonly called

Pot Greene . . . came to our Company and waked up the men and proposed to them that if they would furnish him with a tomahawk and four buckets, he would get into the officer's liquors and supply the men with wines and brandies.

"The desired articles were furnished him and with the assistance of one of our company, he procured the liquors. All this was entirely unknown to Captain Lincoln.

"In the morning, Captain L ordered his men to form the company for parade. But when the orderly called the men to parade, they called 'parade' too but wouldn't fall into line. Most of the men were unmistakably drunk.

"The rest of the forces marched off and left Captain L's company behind. The Company didn't make a start till about ten o'clock and then, after marching about two miles, the drunken ones laid down and slept their drunk off. . . .

"Captain L was again put under arrest and was obliged to carry a wooden sword for two days. And this, although Captain L was entirely blameless in the matter."[19]

The captain's troubles with military authorities only increased Lincoln's popularity with the men. They knew he would stand up for them. When his volunteers complained, he took their grievances to the brass. Bill Greene remembered Captain Lincoln challenging a regular army officer on behalf of his men. "Sir," he scolded, "you forget that we are not under the rules and regulations of the War Department at Washington. We are only volunteers under the order and regulations of Illinois. Keep in your own sphere and there will be no difficulty. But resistance will hereafter be made to unjust orders. My men must be equal in all particulars—in rations, arms, camps—to the regular army."[20]

The men learned that Captain Lincoln was a man of honor who meant what he said. When an old Indian strayed into camp, he was quickly surrounded. "Our boys thought he was a spy," said Royal Clary. "Sprang to our feet. Was going to shoot the man." [21]

Trembling with fear, the old warrior produced a safe-conduct pass. It was, said Billy Greene, "written by [General] Lewis Cass stating that the Indian was a good and true man."[22]

This was not good enough. These were ornery men primed for battle. They wanted blood. "We have come out to fight the Indians," they said, "and by God we intend to do so."[23]

"The letter is a forgery," one voice claimed.[24]

"Make an example of him," bellowed another.[25]

"The Indian is a damned spy," they railed.[26]

The captain did not like what was happening. He knew it was wrong. Suddenly, Clary saw him move in. "Lincoln jumped between our men and the Indian."[27]

Said Lincoln, "Men, this must not be done. He must not be shot and killed by us.[28] We must not shed his blood."[29]

It was a tense moment. "Lincoln stood between the Indian and the vengeance of the soldiers," said Bill Greene. "Some of the men said to Mr. Lincoln—'This is cowardly on your part Lincoln.'"[30]

Greene saw Lincoln "rising to an unusual height." The captain faced down his angry men. "If any man thinks I am a coward, let him test it," he growled.

Said Greene, "This soon put to silence quickly all charges of the cowardice of Lincoln."[31]

The men left the old Indian alone.

William Miller of Sangamon County was a volunteer in the Black Hawk War. "During this short Indian campaign we had some hard times," he said. "Often hungry. But we had a great deal of sport, especially nights, foot racing, some horse racing, jumping, telling anecdotes, in which Lincoln beat all, keeping up a constant laughter and good humor."[32]

The number one sport was wrestling. The men knew his reputation. Few wanted to try him. Lincoln was ready for any challenge. "While in the army he kept a handkerchief tied around him very near all the time for wrestling purposes, said Miller. "Loved the sport as well as any man could."[33]

"He was the strongest man in our regiment and one of the very best wrestlers," said Bill Greene. "Speaking of Lincoln's physical strength, let me say I saw him lift one thousand and twenty four pounds." [34]

"One man in the army alone could throw him," said Greene, "and that man's name was Thompson." [35]

"Told my boys I could throw him," said Lincoln, "and they could bet what they pleased. You see, I had never been thrown or dusted, as the phrase then was. . . . You may think a wrestle, or 'wrastle' as we called such contests of skill and strength, was a small matter but I tell you the whole army was out to see it." [36]

Bill Greene described the fight. "The Company to which I belonged knew that Mr. Lincoln was physically powerful and artful and skilled in wrestling. The Company bet their knives, blankets, tomahawks etc. on Mr. Lincoln's wrestling.

"The men, Lincoln and Thompson walked out and fixed for the match," said Greene. [37]

"We took holds," said Lincoln. "His choice first, a side hold. I then realized from his grip for the first time that he was a powerful man and that I would have no easy job." [38]

Greene remembered: "Lincoln remarked to his friends—'This man is the most powerful man I ever had hold of.'"

It was a tough battle. "Mr. Lincoln caught Mr. Thompson and held him off some time," related Greene. "At last the man got the crotch lock on Mr. Lincoln. Lincoln slid off but the man caught him and partially threw Mr. Lincoln." [39]

Said Lincoln, "The struggle was a severe one but after many passes and efforts he threw me." [40]

"We were taken by surprise," Greene said. "Got up a kind of an excuse as to the result in order to avoid giving up our bets. We declared that the fall was a kind of a 'dog fall.'" [41]

"My boys yelled out 'a dog fall' which meant then a drawn battle. But I told my boys it was fair," Lincoln said. [42]

Greene agreed. "Lincoln rose up and said—'Boys, the man actually threw me once fair.'" [43]

Lincoln wasn't done yet. He described the second fall. "Said to Thompson—'Now it's your turn to go down . . . .' We took our holds again and after the fiercest struggle of the kind I ever had, he threw me again. . . . My men raised another protest but I again told them it was fair down."

When it was all over, Lincoln said, "Why gentlemen, that man could throw a grizzly bear."[44]

CHAPTER 27

"Charges upon the wild onions . . . Bloody struggles with the mosquitoes."

⸺ ⚬⚬⚬ ⸺

On April 27, 1832, sixteen hundred men set out from Beardstown to find Black Hawk and his "British Band" of warriors. They trudged through swamps, forded streams, slept in mud, and ate in the rain. They marched to the Mississippi and reached Dixon on the Rock River by May 12. Here they saw their first battle of the war. It became known as Stillman's Defeat.

"We stopped at Dixon about five days," said Royal Clary. "Waited for provisions to come up Rock River in boats. . . . Here we met Stillman with his squad."[1]

On the night of May 14, Major Isaiah Stillman led a detachment of 340 men to scout the area for signs of Black Hawk. They set up camp about twelve miles from the main camp in Dixon. Indian lookouts spotted them and reported the news to Black Hawk.

By now the old warrior realized there would be no aid from other Indian tribes and no supplies from the British. He decided to end the hostilities and bring his people back across the Mississippi. He sent a party of three braves to the army camp waving a white flag to ask for a peace conference with General Henry Atkinson, commander of the US troops. Five braves watched their comrades from a distant hill.

Meanwhile, Stillman's men were busy drinking the company's stock of whiskey. When they saw three Indians approaching, they quickly remembered they were supposed to be fighting Indians. They jumped them, beat them, and left them for dead. When they saw the other five braves "spying" in the distance, they started after them, killing two.

Three surviving braves reached Black Hawk with the story of how his peace emissaries were brutally murdered. The old warrior grew enraged and raised a war whoop. He took all the remaining braves with him, numbering about forty, and charged after his tormentors, too angry to consider that he was outnumbered eight to one.

Black Hawk and his braves attacked, storming the soldier's camp, whooping and hollering. Stillman's men ran. Whoever could grab a horse galloped away frantically. Most of the men lit out on foot. "They fled in all directions," said William Miller.[2]

That night the first of the terrified squadron found their way back to the main garrison at Dixon. "About twelve o'clock that night they commenced coming into our camp," Miller recalled, "and kept coming in all the remainder of that night and next day. . . . Came in, some on foot and some on horseback, leaving the killed and missing about sixty in number."[3]

Now Black Hawk was convinced more than ever that the white man could not be trusted. He charged onto the warpath in earnest. Signs of Indian wrath appeared all over the countryside—deserted homes, some in smoldering ashes, corpses of cattle and hogs, scalps of whole families dangling from tree limbs. Scenes of horror were left behind to taunt arriving army troops.

The Indians roamed the land at will. No army could find them. They were masters at warfare by ambush, striking suddenly, setting false trails, appearing here and there, then vanishing like ghosts. The volunteer soldiers seethed in frustration. Tired and hungry, angry at the slow progress of the campaign, they were ready to go home. One company under the command of Colonel Zachary Taylor (soon to become president of the

United States) refused to cross the Rock River into Indian territory, claiming that they had only signed up to protect the state of Illinois and should not leave its borders.

Colonel Taylor listened to their complaints. Then he coolly showed them the backbone of a soldier. "I feel that all gentlemen here are my equals," he told the rebellious crowd. Trying some strategic flattery, the colonel assured his ornery troops that in a few years many of them would "be my superiors and perhaps in the capacity of members of the Congress . . . I expect to obey them as interpreters of the will of the people. And the best proof that I will obey them is now to observe the orders of those whom the people have already put in the place of authority. . . . In plain English, Gentlemen and fellow citizens, the word has been passed on to me from Washington to follow Black Hawk and to take you with me as soldiers. I mean to do both."[4]

The reluctant warriors saw the boats in front of them, ready to carry them to battle. Behind them stood a wall of Uncle Sam's infantry, rifles ready, waiting for the order to escort every last one of the Illinois volunteers aboard. The mutineers grumbled that fighting Indians was better than fighting the army, so they headed for the boats.

Meanwhile, Captain Lincoln and his men kept marching in the general area, twenty-five miles one day, twenty miles another day. Tired of walking, starving for a decent meal, sleepless, exhausted, the men cursed the army and talked about going home. Sick of camp food, the men outraged local farmers by raiding their livestock, which they cooked and ate on the spot, broiled, fried, or toasted. "Some of the settlers complained that they made war upon the pigs and chickens," reported a news correspondent.[5]

"We had been very hungry for about two days" said George Harrison, who served with Lincoln. The men "came upon a new cabin at the edge of a prairie that the pioneer . . . family had vacated and skedaddled for fear they would lose their scalps. There were plenty of chickens about . . . so they went to shooting, clubbing and running them as long as any could be found. . . . By this time many of the chickens were broiling for want of grease or gravy to fry them."[6]

Said Captain Lincoln, "It is much like eating saddlebags."[7]

On May 21, the men came upon a gruesome discovery—the remains of three families brutally murdered and scalped. Fifteen mutilated bodies were strewn around their homes. Neighbors told the army that two young girls were missing and probably kidnapped. News like that rattled the men and filled them with a sense of doom.

The army camped near the Fox River at night. The men slept in tents or in the open air. Suddenly the quiet was broken. Men were shouting and cursing. They grabbed their hats and guns. The horses ran wild, trampling over half-asleep bodies. Tents sagged and toppled. A groggy bugle blared. Bewildered men formed a desperate battle line, ready to fire on an unseen enemy. There was no enemy. The horses, spooked by some unnamed fear, broke into a furious, snorting gallop. For the rest of the night, the men had to gather and calm the horses, all the time grumbling about lost sleep.

By this time, the military high command had seen enough of the Illinois fighting man. "The more I see of the militia the less confidence I have of their affecting anything of importance," reported Colonel Taylor to his superiors.[8] Governor Reynolds called a conference of captains and asked for a vote—stay and fight the enemy or go home. Captain Lincoln cast his vote along with the others. When they counted the votes, it was a tie. The Illinois Militia had voted itself into paralysis.

The show of ineptitude so enraged General Samuel Whiteside that he swore he would lead these men only to their discharge papers. Four days later, Captain Lincoln's company was officially disbanded.

With the Indian fighters staying out of sight, darting out only for surprise attacks, the men thought the serious fighting was over. Most of the volunteers went home. Lincoln and a few others signed up for another twenty days. "I was out of work," he explained, "and there being no danger of more fighting, I could do nothing better than enlist again."[9] On May 29, he was sworn into service as a private by Lieutenant Robert Anderson, later to become the Union Army commander at Fort Sumter in the first battle of the Civil War.

Private Lincoln then reenlisted for a third tour. He was assigned to the Independent Spy Corps of Captain Jacob Early, a Springfield physician and Methodist preacher who had served as a private with Lincoln in the Sangamon Militia. On June 25, Captain Early's Spy Corps discovered the grisly remains of a skirmish with Black Hawk at Kellogg's Grove. A small detail of white scouts had been brutally executed. "I remember just how those men looked," said Lincoln, "as we rode up the little hill where their camp was. The red light of the morning sun was streaming upon them as they lay heads toward us on the ground. Every man had a round red spot on the top of his head about as big as a dollar, where the redskins had taken his scalp. It was frightful but it was grotesque."[10]

The Spy Corps marched into Wisconsin, through settlements named Turtle Village, Lake Koshkonong, White Water, and Burnt Village. They slept on their muskets at night, performing scout duty for General Atkinson and the regular US Army by day.

In the beginning of July, with provisions running out, they found the Wisconsin swamps and dense forests impassable, even on foot. On July 10, Early's Spy Corps returned to White Water on the Rock River to be honorably discharged and sent home with "the special thanks of Brigadier General H. Atkinson, Commander in Chief of the Army of the Illinois frontier."[11]

By now Black Hawk's braves were hungry and war-weary. Sioux and Winnebago Indians were on the army's payroll, helping thwart Black Hawk's tricks. On August 1 at Bad Axe, most of Black Hawk's warriors were massacred. Black Hawk slipped away, but Sioux and Winnebago scouts trailed him and finally delivered him to the white man. Black Hawk remained in the custody of one Lieutenant Jefferson Davis, who would become Lincoln's sworn enemy as president of the Confederate States of America.

The military career of Abraham Lincoln was over. He fought an Indian war without harming a single Indian. He marched with his Illinois brothers hundreds of miles into the rugged bowels of American wild country. He smelled rotting corpses and laid bodies in the ground.

He grew close to the men of Illinois. Men of all kinds and backgrounds became his friends. One particular soldier, Major John Stuart, who was a lawyer from Springfield, gave him some career advice. When Lincoln mentioned that he was interested in studying law, Major Stuart advised him to begin by reading *Blackstone's Commentaries on the Laws of England.*

Years later, Lincoln could find nothing heroic in his military service. When General Lewis Cass became the Democratic candidate for president in 1848 (the same General Cass who signed the old Indian's safe-conduct pass) he made a valiant saga of his own exploits during the Black Hawk War.

This made Lincoln laugh. "Did you know I am a military hero?" he crowed with evident sarcasm. "Yes sir. In the days of the Black Hawk War. I fought, bled, and came away.

"Speaking of General Cass' career reminds me of my own. . . . It is quite certain I did not break my sword, for I had none to break. But I bent a musket pretty badly on one occasion. If Cass broke his sword, the idea is, he broke it in desperation. I bent the musket by accident.

"If General Cass went in advance of me in picking huckleberries, I guess I surpassed him in charges upon the wild onions. If he saw any live fighting Indians, it was more than I did. But I had a good deal of bloody struggles with the mosquitoes, and although I never fainted from loss of blood, I can truly say I was often hungry."

Lincoln concluded his biting satire by mocking his own war effort. "I protest they shall not make fun of me, as they have of General Cass, by attempting to write me into a military hero."[12]

CHAPTER 28

"The only time I ever have
been beaten."

—⸙—

When the candidate returned to New Salem, Election Day was less than a week away. He soon discovered that his three months away from his district was no handicap. "He became very popular whilst in the army," said Rowan Herndon.[1]

His first campaign stop took him to Pappsville, where a crowd of Illinois farmers were inspecting livestock, hogs, bulls, and steers up for auction. "There was a large gathering there on account of a sale of goods," related James Herndon, Rowan's brother. "He was the only candidate there and was called on to make a speech."[2]

The candidate climbed into the wagon bed, where he could see the whole crowd. But before he could speak, a commotion broke out among his fellow citizens. A gang of thugs had pounced, knocking a man down and beating him. From the speaker's platform Lincoln recognized the unfortunate victim; it was his good friend Rowan Herndon.

"I think he was about to commence speaking when the fight commenced," recalled Rowan Herndon. "It was on that day that I whipped Jessy Dodson, and his friends attempted to show foul play."[3]

The candidate stopped his speech and plunged into the crowd to help his friend. "Lincoln pulled me away," he said.[4] "He pitched in and pitched them out like they were boys and told them his friend could whip the whole of them one at a time," said Rowan Herndon. "That ended the fuss."[5]

The crowd cheered when the candidate climbed back into the speaker's box to resume his speech. "Gentlemen and Fellow Citizens," he began. "I presume you all know who I am. I am humble Abraham Lincoln. I have been solicited by many friends to become a candidate for the Legislature. My politics are short and sweet like the old woman's dance. I am in favor of a National Bank. I am in favor of the internal improvement system and a high protective tariff. These are my sentiments and political principles. If elected, I shall be thankful. If not, it will be all the same."[6]

There were more speeches and more rallies for the candidate. "I accompanied him on one of his electioneering trips to Island Grove," said A. Y. Ellis. "He made a speech which pleased his party friends very well, indeed, though some of the Jackson men tried to make sport of him. He told several anecdotes and applied them, as I thought, very well. He also told the boys several stories which drew them after him. I remember them, but modesty and my veneration for his memory forbid me to relate them."[7]

"I well remember how he was dressed," Ellis went on. "He wore flax and tow linen pantaloons—I thought about five inches too short in the legs—and frequently he had but one suspender, no vest or coat. He wore a calico shirt, such as he had in the Black Hawk War, coarse brogans, tan color, blue yarn socks and straw hat, old style, without a band."[8]

Stephen T. Logan, a Springfield lawyer who would later become Lincoln's law partner, saw him for the first time during the '32 campaign. "He was a very tall and gawky and rough looking fellow then. His pantaloons didn't meet his shoes by six inches. But after he began speaking I became very much interested in him. He made a very sensible speech. . . .

"I knew nothing then about his avocation or calling at New Salem. The impression I had at the time was that he was sort of a loafer down there. . . . But one thing we very soon learned was that he was immensely popular. . . . In the election of 1832 he made a very considerable impression upon me as well as upon other people."[9]

"I heard him speak frequently," said Rowan Herndon, "and he was a full match for any man that was on the track."[10]

Rowan Herndon reported on a speech he heard from the lips of candidate Lincoln. "Fellow Citizens," began Lincoln. "I have been told that some of my opponents have said it was a disgrace to have such a looking man as I am stuck up for the legislature. Now I thought this was a free country. That is the reason that I address you today. Had I known to the contrary I should not have consented to run.

"But I will say one thing," the candidate went on. "Let the shoe pinch who it may. When I have been a candidate before you some five or six times and have been beaten every time, I will consider it a disgrace and will be sure never to try it again."

Then he added defiantly, "I am bound to beat that man if I am beat myself."[11]

"And sure enough," said Rowan Herndon, "he was beat."[12]

The top four vote-getters out of thirteen candidates were elected to the state legislature from Sangamon County. John Stuart made it. Lincoln ran eighth. "He was defeated at this election," said Bill Greene, "though the people in and around New Salem precinct voted him 275 out of the 278 votes, so popular was he."[13]

Lincoln's showing was astonishing for a political newcomer with no credentials. Said Jason Duncan, "Mr. Lincoln was in favor of Henry Clay in 1832, voted for him during that memorable campaign, though the New Salem precinct was largely for Jackson. Such was his personal popularity that he obtained a majority, very many Jackson men of the most violent party feelings voting for him on the grounds they believed him an honest and worthy young man."[14]

Still the results were discouraging. He lost this first election. "The only time," said Lincoln, "I ever have been beaten by the people."[15]

Lincoln knew that life had brought him to a crossroad. "He was now without means and out of business," he wrote in his autobiography. He said he was "anxious to remain with his friends who had treated him with so much generosity, especially as he had nothing else-where to go to."[16]

He decided to stay in New Salem and find his fortune there. At the time, he was living with Rowan Herndon and his family. "He came to my house to board soon after his return from the army," his friend recalled. "During his stay at my house my family became much attached to him. He was always at home wherever he went. . . . He most always had one of my children around with him. . . . Very kind to the widows and orphans—chop their wood and read the news from all over the country once a week as we only had a weekly mail."[17]

It was here that young Billy Herndon first came to know Lincoln. Soon he would become his law partner and fifty years later would be writing his biography. Lincoln left a deep impression on the boy. "I had up to this time frequently seen Mr. Lincoln—had often, while visiting my cousins James and Rowan Herndon at New Salem, met him at their house. . . . There was something in his tall and angular frame, his ill-fit-ting garments, honest face, and lively humor that imprinted his individ-uality on my affection and regard. . . . He was my senior by nine years, and I looked up to him, naturally enough, as my superior in every-thing—a thing I continued to do till the end of his days."[18]

Lincoln needed direction for his life. "He studied what he should do," he wrote of himself. "Thought of learning the blacksmith trade. Thought of trying to study law. Rather, thought he could not succeed at that without a better education."[19]

He wanted an occupation that would allow him time to read and study. "What he seemed to want," said Herndon, "was some lighter work, employment in a store or tavern where he could meet the village celebrities, exchange views with strangers, discuss politics, horse-races, cock-fights and narrate to listening loafers his striking and significant stories."[20]

In the fall of 1832, there were four stores in New Salem. Samuel Hill and John McNeil were partners in one. Reuben Radford had a store. So did James Rutledge. The Herndon Brothers ran another store.

"But," said Herndon, "there seemed no favorable opening for him. Clerks in New Salem were not in demand just then."[21]

Soon opportunity came knocking at the door of Abraham Lincoln. He decided to follow in the footsteps of his mentor, Denton Offutt. Lincoln became a merchant and businessman. "My cousins, Rowan and James Herndon, were at that time operating a store," recalled Bill Herndon. "Tiring of their investment and the confinement it necessitated, James sold his interest to an idle, shiftless fellow named William Berry. Soon after, Rowan disposed of his to Lincoln."[22]

Said Rowan Herndon, "I sold him my stock of goods to Lincoln & Berry on credit."[23]

Businesses in new frontier towns did not deal much with money. Enterprises were bought and sold with promissory notes and IOUs. That was how, in the spring of 1833, Abraham Lincoln and William Berry became partners, managing a business enterprise even though they were both paupers.

"I once asked Rowan Herndon what induced him to make such liberal terms in dealing with Lincoln, whom he had known for so short time," said Bill Herndon.

"I believed he was thoroughly honest," Cousin Rowan replied, "and that impression was so strong in me I accepted his note in payment of the whole. He had no money, but I would have advanced him more had he asked for it."[24]

On March 6, 1833, the two businessmen signed a license granted by the Sangamon County Court to keep a tavern and sell liquor. So Lincoln and Berry, according to Abe, "opened as merchants."[25]

CHAPTER 29

"The National Debt."

———∞∞∞———

Business ventures need room to expand. The two merchants purchased the entire stock of merchandise from James Rutledge's store
with a promissory note. Soon the partners acquired the store of Reuben
Radford. Berry & Lincoln now claimed ownership of three of New
Salem's four stores.

The deal for the Radford property was a riotous frontier tale New
Salem style, courtesy of the boys from Clary's Grove. Thomas Reep, one
of the locals, recounted the unlikely details.

"Reuben Radford incurred the enmity of the Clary's Grove Boys
which resulted in Berry and Lincoln securing his stock of goods and
moving into the store," began Reep.[1]

"The circumstances was as follows: Radford was a large man of great
physical strength and announced his ability to look after his own rights
and to protect them. He was told that such an attitude would cause the
Clary's Grove Boys to try him out and they would surely lick him. If one
couldn't then two or three together would.

"On the day in question, Radford, having occasion to go to the
country, left his younger brother in charge of the store, admonishing
him to be careful and directing him to sell the Clary's Grove Boys—in
case any of them came in—but two drinks of liquor.

"Sure enough, the Clary's Grove Boys came and in peace got their two drinks of liquor. Being denied more, they shoved the protesting youth out of their way, stepped behind the counter and helped themselves. . . . They all got 'rip-roaring' drunk and turned things in the store topsy-turvy, broke the crockery and knocked out the windows, leaving chaos and ruin in their wake. Then they leaped on their horses and yelling like wild Indians, left the town for their homes.

"A bunch of them passed a short distance from where Radford was stopping in the country. Hearing their yells, he immediately feared the worst. Leaping on his horse, ran him all the way to New Salem where he dismounted from his panting and lathered steed and rushed into his store. Broken glass and crockery ware covered the floor and the contents seemed to be a total wreck.

"Stepping out, Radford declared that he would sell out to the first man who made him an offer.

"Just at that moment, William Greene, the erstwhile Offutt clerk, came along, having been sent on horseback with some grist to the mill. Hearing Radford's words, he replied—'Sell out to me!'

"Radford replied—'I will. How much will you give?'

"Greene rode up to the side of the store and sticking his head through a broken window, surveyed the contents and offered Radford $400 for the stock, which Radford accepted.

"The news of the purchase traveled fast in New Salem and soon Lincoln came over to see his old friend and new competitor. Looking over the contents, he announced that they must take an inventory. Greene, not understanding the term and guessing that it might mean some sort of celebration along the line followed by the Clary's Grove Boys just before, replied—'Abe, I don't believe this store will stand another one just at this time.'

"Lincoln explained that by inventory he meant the listing of the goods and the setting opposite each item the value thereof. So they at once proceeded to make the inventory.

"Greene paid $23 cash and for the balance gave two notes each for $188.50 which was secured by a mortgage drawn and witnessed by Lincoln. . . .

"Before the inventory was completed, it was evident that the stock would run to nearly $900. Berry and Lincoln bought it from Greene, paying him $265 cash, principally in silver, assuming the payment of his notes for $377 to Radford and by turning over a horse, saddle and bridle owned by Berry. Berry and Lincoln then moved their stock into the new store building and bid fair to make considerable money, as competition had now been reduced to but one other store, that owned and operated by Hill. . . .

"The taking of the inventory and fixing of the papers covering the purchase from Radford and the sale to Berry and Lincoln kept young Greene till quite late that night and when he arrived home the family had retired. His father, however, was awake, waiting for him. . . .

"'So, Billy,' the older Greene said, 'you are a merchant, are ye? You git along to bed now and in the morning I will thrash the merchant out you mighty quick.'

"Young Bill held his peace until he had stirred up the coals and lighted the room with fresh kindling. Then, reaching into his pockets, he began stacking up his silver on the floor with considerable jingle. . .

"'Pap,' said Billy, 'I was a merchant, but I've sold out and cleared this.'

"Whereupon Greene Sr. reached over and awaking his wife said—'Liz, git up and git Billy a fust rate supper. He's had a hard day of it.'" [2]

"I sold to Wm Berry and A Lincoln my grocery store," said Bill Greene. "I gave $400 for it and they gave me $750."[3]

Berry and Lincoln were an odd couple. Neither man had ever shown any aptitude for business. As the chief clerk at Offutt's store, Lincoln could not keep the business from folding. Berry was the son of the Reverend John Berry and had attended Illinois College with Billy Greene. But he picked up none of his father's moral, temperate ways. "It always was a mystery to me," said friend George Spears, "why a man of Mr. Lincoln's integrity would enter into a partnership with such a character."[4]

Berry hung out in the back of the store playing poker and drinking whiskey, pouring free rounds for his friends and finishing off most of it himself. Lincoln was no more attentive to the business. He spent his time reading. Law, grammar, poetry, and ancient history enriched his mind while he was keeping store. He read Gibbon's *Decline and Fall of the Roman Empire* and Rollin's *Ancient History*. He read Robert Burns and Shakespeare. Customers were sure to get an earful about the ideas Lincoln discovered. Remembered Caleb Carman, "Often in conversation he would refer to that great man Shakespeare. Also Lord Byron as being a great man. And Burns . . . And Lord Nelson as being a great Admiral and Naval Commander and Adams and Henry Clay . . . George Washington was the greatest of all of them and was his great favorite."[5]

"As a salesman," said Herndon, "Lincoln was lamentably deficient. He was too prone to lead off into a discussion of politics or morality, leaving someone else to finish the trade which he had undertaken."[6]

The storekeeper continued to read anything he could get his hands on. "Lincoln was fond of short, spicy stories," said Herndon.[7] A. Y. Ellis, who clerked for him, gave him some popular novels like *Cousin Sally Dillard*, *Becky William's Courtship*, and *The Down-Easter and the Bull*.

"He seemed to master his studies with little effort," said R. B. Rutledge, "until he commenced the study of law. In that he became wholly engrossed and began for the first time to avoid the society of men in order that he might have more time for study."[8]

The Law. The subject called him. From the first day he found himself in court, the law excited him. Long discussions with fellow soldier John Stuart during the Black Hawk War encouraged him. Stuart's advice stayed with him: if he wanted to become serious about studying law, he needed to read Blackstone.

"One day," Lincoln remembered, "a man who was migrating to the West drove up in front of my store with a wagon which contained his family and household plunder. He asked me if I would buy an old barrel for which he had no room in his wagon and which he said contained nothing of special value. I did not want it, but to oblige him I bought it and paid him, I think, half a dollar for it. Without further examination, I put it away in the store and forgot all about it.

"Some time after in overhauling things, I came upon the barrel, and emptying it upon the floor to see what it contained, I found at the bottom of the rubbish a complete edition of Blackstone's *Commentaries*. I began to read those famous works, and I had plenty of time. For during the long summer days, when the farmers were busy with their crops, my customers were few and far between. The more I read, the more intensely interested I became. Never in my whole life was my mind so thoroughly absorbed. I read until I devoured them."[9]

New Salem resident Russell Godbey was surprised one day to find Lincoln sitting barefoot on a woodpile attentively reading a book. "I asked him what he was reading," said Godbey.

"I'm not reading," he answered. "I'm studying."

"Studying what?"

"Law, sir."

Said Godbey, "It was really too much for me as I looked at him sitting there proud as Cicero. 'Great God Almighty!' I exclaimed, and passed on."[10]

Meanwhile, the Berry and Lincoln enterprise continued to flounder. "While Lincoln at one end of the store was dispensing political information, Berry at the other end was disposing of the firm's liquors, being the best customer for that article of merchandise himself," said Herndon. "To put it more plainly—Lincoln's application to Shakespeare and Burns was only equaled by Berry's attention to spigot and barrel."[11]

"Of course," said Lincoln, "they did nothing but get deeper and deeper in debt."[12]

"Berry squandered everything and left Lincoln flat," said George Spears.[13]

Finally the doors closed on Berry & Lincoln. Said Abe, "The store winked out."[14]

"They, like their predecessors, were ready to retire," said Herndon. "Two brothers named Trent coming along, they sold to them on liberal terms."[15]

By the time the Trent brothers' notes to Lincoln and Berry came due, they, too, had failed. "One morning in the late fall of 1834 the village awoke," recalled Thomas Reep. "Smoke spirals arose from the chimneys but none from the Trent brothers' store. Its absence and the closed doors attracted the attention of the inhabitants. An examination was made and no one was seen about the building. Further investigation showed the families to have disappeared."[16]

Explained Rowan Herndon, "Lincoln and Berry sold to two brothers by the name of Trent and they ran off leaving Lincoln the burden to bear."[17]

The burden grew exponentially on January 10, 1835. "Berry died," said Row Herndon. "Left Lincoln the debts to pay."[18]

He owed close to $1,100.

"The debt was the greatest obstacle I have ever met in my life," said Lincoln. "I had no way of speculating and could not earn money except by labor. And to earn by labor eleven hundred dollars, besides my living, seemed the work of a lifetime.

"There was, however, but one way," he went on. "I went to the creditors and told them that if they would let me alone, I would give them all I could earn over my living as fast as I could earn it."[19]

Fifteen years later, Lincoln was still saving part of his salary as a Representative in Washington to send to his creditors in New Salem.

"Lincoln paid the last dollar of that debt after he went to Congress [in 1846]," said Rowan Herndon. "I have no doubt of the truth of the matter concerning that debt. For the first time I saw him after his return he told me that he had paid the last of the old debt."[20]

Lincoln joked about it, calling it "The National Debt." [21] It was a backbreaking burden for a young man just starting to make a name for himself. But he persisted until all his debts were paid in full.

CHAPTER 30

"I loved the woman dearly and sacredly."

⊰⊱

"The memory of Ann Rutledge was the saddest chapter in Mr. Lincoln's life," wrote Billy Herndon.[1]

Lincoln fell in love. The story of his doomed relationship was vividly recalled by Lincoln's New Salem friends, who became alarmed when they saw him devastated in grief. After the assassination, when Herndon found New Salem old-timers who knew about Lincoln and Ann Rutledge, here is what they told him:

JOHN JONES:"Having known Mr. Lincoln and been an eyewitness to the events as narrated from my boyhood, I take pleasure in saying they are literally true."[2]

R. B. RUTLEDGE:"My sister Ann was born January 7, 1813 and died August 25, 1835."[3]

JAMES SHORT: "Mr. L. boarded with the parents of Miss Ann Rutledge."[4]

R. B. RUTLEDGE: "Boarded with my father during the years 1833 and 1834 as appears from papers still in the possession of my family."[5]

BILLY GREENE: "In the years 1833 and 4 was in love with a young lady in New Salem by the name of Miss Ann Rutledge."[6]

ROWAN HERNDON: "There was a Miss Rutledge. I have no doubt he would have married if she had of lived."[7]

BILLY GREENE: "He would have married her but she sickened and died."[8]

BILLY HERNDON: "I knew Miss Rutledge myself, as well as her father and other members of the family and have been personally acquainted with every one of the score or more of witnesses whom I at one time or another interviewed on this delicate subject."[9]

MENTOR GRAHAM: "I knew Miss Ann Rutledge . . . Lincoln and her both were studying at my house . . . She was about 20 years, eyes blue, large and expressive. Fair complexion. Sandy or light auburn hair . . . About 5 feet 4 inches. Face rather round—outlines beautiful . . . Good teeth. Mouth well made . . . Weight about 120–130. Hearty and vigorous. Amiable. Kind."[10]

BILLY GREENE: "This young lady was a woman of exquisite beauty but her intellect was quick, sharp, deep and philosophic as well as brilliant. She had a gentle and kind heart as an angel, full of love, kindness and sympathy. She was beloved by everybody and everybody respected and loved her, so sweet and angelic was she."[11]

R. B. RUTLEDGE: "In 1830, my sister being then but seventeen years of age, a stranger calling himself John McNeil came to New Salem."[12]

BILLY HERNDON: "Within three years he owned a farm and a half interest with Samuel Hill in the leading store. He had a good capacity for business."[13]

R. B. RUTLEDGE: "A friendship grew up between McNeil and Ann which ripened apace and resulted in an engagement to marry."[14]

BILLY HERNDON: "McNeil, having disposed of his interest in the store to Hill, determined to return to New York, his native state, for a visit. . . . Before leaving, he made to Ann a singular revelation. He told her the name McNeil was an assumed one—that his real name was McNamar."[15]

R. B. RUTLEDGE: "It seems that his father had failed in business and his son, a very young man, had determined to make a fortune, pay off his father's debts and restore him to his former social and financial standing. With this view, he left his home clandestinely, and in order to avoid pursuit by his parents, changed his name."[16]

JOHN McNAMAR: "I left behind me in New York my parents and brothers and sisters. They are poor and were in more or less need when I left them in 1829. I vowed that I would come west, make a fortune, and go back to help them."[17]

BILLY HERNDON: "He had accumulated up to this time, as near as we can learn, ten or possibly twelve thousand dollars."[18]

R. B. RUTLEDGE: "McNamar left the country on business. Was gone some years."[19]

JOHN McNAMAR: "Circumstances beyond my control detained me much longer away than I intended."[20]

R. B. RUTLEDGE: "At all events, he was absent two or three years."[21]

BILLY HERNDON: "Meanwhile, a different view of the matter was taken by Miss Rutledge. Her friends encouraged the idea of cruel desertion. . . . Some contended that he had undoubtedly committed a crime in his earlier days and for years had rested secure from apprehension under the shadow of an assumed name, while others with equal assurance whispered in the unfortunate girl's ear the old story of a rival in her affections."[22]

A. Y. ELLIS: "She had a secret, too, and a sorrow—the unexplained and painful absence of McNamar."[23]

PARTHENA HILL: "Ann well thought that McNamar was playing off on her."[24]

BILLY HERNDON: "Ann began to lose faith."[25]

R. B. RUTLEDGE: "In the meantime, Mr. Lincoln paid his addresses to Ann. Continued his visits and attentions regularly."[26]

BILLY HERNDON: "Lincoln began to court Miss Rutledge in dead earnest."[27]

GEORGE MILES: "Mrs. Bowling Green says that Mr. Lincoln was a regular suitor of Miss Ann Rutledge for between two and three years."[28]

JOHN JONES:"As to the relation existing between Mr. Lincoln and Ann Rutledge, I have every reason to believe that it was of the tenderest character, as I know of my own knowledge that he made regular visits to her."[29]

JAMES SHORT: "The Rutledges lived about a half a mile from me. Mr. L. came over to see me and them every day or two. I did not know of any engagement or tender passages between Mr. L. and Miss R. at the time. But after her death, which happened in '34 or '35, he seemed to be so much affected and grieved so hardly that I then supposed there must have been something of the kind."[30]

MENTOR GRAHAM: "Lincoln and she was engaged—Lincoln told me so. She intimated to me the same."[31]

JOHN JONES: "It was generally understood that Mr. Lincoln and Ann Rutledge were engaged to be married. She was a very amiable and lovable woman and it was deemed a very suitable match, one in which the parties were in every way worthy of each other."[32]

R. B. RUTLEDGE: "There is no kind of doubt as to the existence of this engagement. David Rutledge [their brother] urged Ann to consummate it but she refused until such time as she could see McNamar, inform him of the change in her feelings, and seek an honorable release."[33]

JAMES McRUTLEDGE: "Ann told me once in coming from a camp meeting on Rock Creek that engagements made too far ahead sometimes failed—that one had failed, meaning her engagement with McNamar—and gave me to understand that as soon as certain studies were completed she and Lincoln would be married."[34]

R. B. RUTLEDGE:"I have no doubt that Ann had fully determined to break off the engagement with McNamar, but presume she had never notified him of the fact, as he did not return until after her death."[35]

JOHN McNAMAR:"Mr. Lincoln was not to my knowledge paying particular attention to any of the young ladies of my acquaintance when I left for my home in New York. There was no rivalry between us on that score. On the contrary, I had every reason to believe him my warm personal friend."[36]

DR. LORENZO MATHENY: "Spring and summer of 1835 was the hottest ever known in Illinois. From the first of March to the middle of July it rained almost every day and the whole country was literally covered with water. When the rain ceased the weather became excessively hot and continued so until sometime in August. About the tenth of August, the people began to get sick."[37]

R. B. RUTLEDGE: "In August 1835 Ann sickened."[38]

PARTHENA HILL:"Mr. Hill told me that Ann's sickness was caused by her complications—two engagements."[39]

BILLY HERNDON: "Late in the summer she took to her bed. A fever was burning in her head. Day by day she sank."[40]

BILLY GREENE:"Lincoln went and saw her during her sickness, just before her death."[41]

BILLY HERNDON: "Her physician had forbidden visitors to enter her room, prescribing absolute quiet. But her brother relates that she kept inquiring for Lincoln so continuously, at times demanding to see him that the family at last sent for him. On his arrival at her bedside the door was closed and he was left alone with her. What was said, what vows and relations were made during this sad interview were known only to him and the dying girl." [42]

JOHN RUTLEDGE:"I have heard mother say that Ann would frequently sing for Lincoln's benefit. She had a clear ringing voice. Early in her illness he called and she sang a hymn for which he always expressed a great preference. It begins—'Vain man, thy fond pursuits forbear.' You will find it in one of the standard hymn books. It was likewise the last thing she ever sung."[43]

BILLY HERNDON:"A few days afterward she became unconscious and remained so until her death."[44]

JOHN JONES: "During her last illness he visited her sick chamber and on his return stopped at my house. It was very evident that he was much distressed and I was not surprised when it was rumored subsequently that his reason was in danger."[45]

ELIZABETH ABELL: "This much I do know. He was staying with us at the time of her death. It was a great shock to him. I never seen a man mourn for a companion more than he did for her. He made a remark one day when it was raining that he could not bear the idea of it raining on her grave."[46]

R. B. RUTLEDGE: "The effect upon Mr. Lincoln's mind was terrible. He became plunged in despair and many of his friends feared that reason would desert her throne."[47]

GEORGE MILES: "Lincoln took her death very hard, so much so, that some thought his mind would become impaired."[48]

HENRY McHENRY:"As to the condition of Lincoln's mind after the death of Miss R, after that event he seemed quite changed. He seemed retired and loved solitude. He seemed wrapped in profound thought, indifferent to transpiring events, had but little to say but would take his gun and wander off in the woods by himself, away from the association of even those he most esteemed. This gloom seemed to deepen for some time so as to give anxiety to his friends in regard to his mind."[49]

HARDIN BALE:"After the death of Miss Rutledge and because of it, Lincoln was locked up by his friends, Samuel Hill and others, to prevent derangement or suicide, so hard did he take her death."[50]

JOHN HILL:"He was fearfully wrought up on her death. My father [Samuel Hill] had to lock him up and keep guard over him for some two weeks I think, for fear he might commit suicide. The whole village engaged in trying to quiet him and reconcile him to the loss."[51]

ELIZABETH ABELL: "That was the time the community said he was crazy. He was not crazy but he was very desponding a long time."[52]

GEORGE MILES: "Bowling Green went to Salem after Lincoln. Brought him to his house and kept him a week or two and succeeded in cheering him—Lincoln—up, though he was quite melancholy for months."[53]

A. Y. ELLIS: "So was Bowling Green, his almost second father. Mr. Green used to say that Lincoln was a man after his own heart and I think myself he was. Mr. Lincoln used to say that he owed more to Mr. Green for his advancement than any other man."[54]

BILLY HERNDON: "In the years that followed, Mr. Lincoln never forgot the kindness of Green through those weeks of suffering and peril. In 1842, when the latter died and Lincoln was selected by the Masonic lodge to deliver the funeral oration, he broke down in the midst of his address."[55]

A. Y. ELLIS: "I saw Mr. L cry. It was at his old friend Bowling Green's Masonic funeral. Mr. L was to deliver an address on the occasion. He was on the stand but when he arose he only uttered a few words and commenced choking and sobbing. He told his listeners that he was unmanned and could not proceed."[56]

BILLY HERNDON: "His voice was choked with deep emotion. He stood a few moments while his lips quivered in the effort to form the words of fervent praise he sought to utter and the tears ran down his yellow and shriveled cheeks. Every heart was hushed at the spectacle. After repeated efforts, he found it impossible to speak and strode away, bitterly sobbing.[57]

Years later, Isaac Cogdal, an old friend from New Salem, came to visit President Lincoln in the White House. "I knew Abe Lincoln the first week he came to Salem in 1831," Cogdal said. Lincoln told him to return to his office after sundown when his visitors would be gone. They could talk then.

"I want to inquire about old times and old acquaintances," Lincoln told him when they were alone. "When we lived in Salem there were the Greens, Potters, Armstrongs and Rutledges. These folks have got scattered all over the world. Some are dead. Where are the Rutledges, the Greens?"

The two friends enjoyed reminiscing. "After we had spoken over old times, persons, circumstances, in which he showed a wonderful memory, I then dared to ask him this question," Cogdal said. It was a personal question, one that dealt with a troubling episode that lingered in the memory of all who knew him in New Salem. Cogdal had heard the rumors. Now he wanted to know if they were true. It remains the only record we have of anyone asking him directly about his most devastating loss.

"Abe," said Cogdal, "is it true that you fell in love with and courted Ann Rutledge?"

Then Lincoln finally opened up, revealing the depth of his feelings. "It is true," he said. "True, indeed I did. I have loved the name of Rutledge to this day. I have kept my mind on their movements ever since and love them dearly."

Cogdal followed up with another question. "Abe, is it true that you ran a little wild about the matter?"

"I did really," Lincoln admitted. "I run off the track."

Then came one of the most startling personal revelations he ever made. "It was my first," he said. "I loved the woman dearly and sacredly. She was a handsome girl. Would have made a good loving wife. Was natural and quite intellectual, though not highly educated. I did honestly and truly love the girl and think often, often of her now."[58]

Thus we have it on good authority from the man himself—that Lincoln carried the heartache of the death of Ann Rutledge for the rest of his days.

CHAPTER 31

"Oh! Why should the spirit of mortal be proud?"

———ꙮ———

"Lincoln is a gloomy man," said law partner John Stuart.[1]
Billy Herndon agreed. "He was a sad looking man. His melancholy dripped from him as he walked."[2]

As the young Illinois lawyer grew in prominence, his mournful bouts of depression became more apparent. Unfathomable dark spells would plague him for the rest of his life. "The cause of this peculiar condition was a matter of frequent discussion among his friends," said Herndon.[3]

Everyone seemed to have a theory.

"Lincoln's melancholy was illogical and unexplainable . . . was ingrained . . . hereditary." This was Henry Whitney's opinion.[4]

"John Stuart said it was due to his abnormal digestion," added Herndon.[5]

"I used to advise him to take blue-mass pills," Stuart said.[6]

Herndon, never shy about speculating, had his own explanation. "As to the cause of this morbid condition" he said, "my idea has always been that it was occult."[7]

"Sometimes it seemed to me a mixed state of abstraction and sadness," said Caleb Carman, who ran a gristmill on the Sangamon River.[8]

"My opinion is that Mr. Lincoln's sadness, melancholy, despair, grew on him," said James Matheny, a Springfield lawyer and groomsman at Lincoln's wedding. "He had two sentiments—one to stick his head in a hollow log and see no one. And the other was to climb up." [9]

The two faces of Abraham Lincoln were well known by those close to him. When he was bright and effusive, they rejoiced in his company, reveled in his good humor, delighted in his laughter. They met his mournful silences mostly by leaving him alone.

A vivid description of Lincoln's shifting moods was offered by his fellow lawyers. "Mr. Lincoln, when not engaged in court, spent a good deal of his time in the clerk's office," Jonathan Birch remembered. "Very often he could be seen there surrounded by a group of lawyers . . . some standing, others seated on chairs or tables, listening intently to one of his characteristic and inimitable stories." [10]

"He was a genial, fun loving young man," observed Robert Wilson, "always the center of the circle wherever he was." [11]

"His eyes would sparkle with fun," said Birch. "When he reached the point in his narrative which invariably evoked the laughter of the crowd, nobody's enjoyment was greater than his." [12]

Those who were with him day by day knew the depth of his secret despair. "He told me that although he appeared to enjoy life rapturously, still he was the victim of terrible melancholy," said Wilson. [13]

Whenever the mysterious cloud descended, it swallowed him in misery. Suddenly he became a changed man. Birch recalled a shocking transformation soon after Lincoln had his friends rollicking in glee. "An hour later, he might be seen in the same place or in some law office nearby. But, alas, how different! His chair, no longer in the center of the room, would be leaning back against the wall, his feet drawn up . . . his hat tipped slightly forward as if to shield his face, his eyes no longer sparkling with fun or merriment but sad and downcast and his hands clasped around his knees. There, drawn up within himself, as it were, he would sit, the very picture of dejection and gloom.

"Thus absorbed have I seen him sit for hours at a time, defying the interruption of even his closest friends. No one ever thought of breaking the spell by speech; for by his moody silence and abstraction, he had thrown about him a barrier so dense and impenetrable no one dared to break through. It was a strange picture and one I have never forgotten." [14]

When these spells of melancholy attacked, his friends would grow deeply concerned for Lincoln's well-being and safety. Lincoln was keenly aware of the great danger to himself. "He sought company and indulged in fun and hilarity without restraint," said Wilson. "Still, when by himself, he told me that he was so overcome with mental depression, that he never dare carry a knife in his pocket." [15]

"In May 1834 Mr. Lincoln at this time was about twenty-four or five years old," said Wilson. "Six feet and four inches high in his stockings . . . stoop shouldered, his legs were long, feet large, arms long, longer than any man I ever knew. When standing straight and letting his arms fall down his sides, the points of his fingers would touch a point lower on his legs by nearly three inches than was usual with other persons." [16]

"It was shortly after this," said Herndon, "that Dr. Jason Duncan placed in Lincoln's hands a poem called *Immortality*. The piece starts out with the line—'Oh! Why should the spirit of mortal be proud.' Lincoln's love for this poem has certainly made it immortal. He committed these lines to memory." [17]

Lawrence Weldon practiced law with Lincoln. He remembered hearing Lincoln recite the poem early one morning. What struck him was the profound effect it had on the man.

"In traveling on the circuit he was in the habit . . . of rising earlier than his brothers of the bar," Weldon said. "On such occasions, he was wont to sit by the fire, having uncovered the coals, and muse, ponder and soliloquize. . . . On one of these occasions . . . sitting in the posture described, he quoted aloud and at length the poem entitled *Immortality*. When he had finished he was questioned as to the authorship and where it could be found. He has forgotten when he learned it but not the Author [William Knox]. Said that to him it sounded as much like true poetry as anything he had ever heard." [18]

Lincoln was known to recite the poem so often that people thought he wrote it. "I am not the author," an appreciative Abraham Lincoln marveled. "I would give all I am worth and go in debt to be able to write so fine a piece as I think that is." [19]

IMMORTALITY

William Knox

Oh, why should the spirit of mortal be proud?
Like a swift fleeting meteor, a fast-flying cloud,
A flash of the lightning, a break of the wave,
He passes from life to his rest in the grave.

The leaves of the oak and the willow shall fade,
Be scattered around and together be laid;
And the young and the old, the low and the high,
Shall molder to dust, and together shall lie.

The infant a mother attended and loved;
The mother that infant's affection who proved;
The husband, that mother and infant who blessed:
Each, all, are away to their dwelling of rest.

The maid on whose cheek, on whose brow, in whose eye,
Shone beauty and pleasure—her triumphs are by;
And the memory of those who loved her and praised,
Are alike from the minds of the living erased.

The band of the king that the scepter hath borne,
The brow of the priest that the mitre hath worn,
The eye of the sage, and the heart of the brave,
Are hidden and lost in the depths of the grave.

The peasant, whose lot was to sow and to reap,
The herdsman, who climbed with his goats up the steep,
The beggar, who wandered in search of his bread,
Have faded away like the grass that we tread.

The saint, who enjoyed the communion of Heaven,
The sinner, who dared to remain unforgiven,
The wise and the foolish, the guilty and just,
Have quietly mingled their bones in the dust.

So, the multitude goes—like the flower or the weed
That withers away to let others succeed;
So the multitude comes—even those we behold,
To repeat every tale that has often been told.

For we are the same that our fathers have been;
We see the same sights that our fathers have seen;
We drink the same stream, we feel the same sun,
And run the same course that our fathers have run.

The thoughts we are thinking, our fathers would think;
From the death we are shrinking, our fathers would shrink;
To the life we are clinging, they also would cling—
But it speeds from us all like a bird on the wing.

They loved—but the story we cannot unfold;
They scorned—but the heart of the haughty is cold;
They grieved—but no wail from their slumber will come;
They joyed—but the tongue of their gladness is dumb.

They died—aye, they died—we things that are now,
That walk on the turf that lies over their brow,

And make in their dwellings a transient abode,
Meet the things that they met on their pilgrimage road.

Yea, hope and despondency, pleasure and pain,
Are mingled together in sunshine and rain;
And the smile and the tear, the song and the dirge,
Still follow each other, like surge upon surge.

'Tis the wink of an eye—'tis the draught of a breath,
From the blossom of health to the paleness of death,
From the gilded saloon to the bier and the shroud,
Oh, why should the spirit of mortal be proud?[20]

CHAPTER 32

"Did you vote for me?"

———— ∞∞∞ ————

As Berry & Lincoln enterprises collapsed and died, Abe felt the pinch of his empty pockets. "Lincoln was earning no money," said Herndon. [1]

"He had a running board bill to pay and nothing to pay it with," a friend added. [2]

He took odd jobs as a laborer, splitting rails and doing construction work and farming. Then came his first big break—an opportunity to serve in a government post. Said Abe, "Was appointed postmaster at New Salem." [3]

Lincoln was commissioned on May 7, 1833. He was chosen to replace Samuel Hill, his business rival, after the women of New Salem complained to postal authorities that Hill would make them wait for the mail while he served liquor to the men in his store. The Democratic administration of President Andrew Jackson allowed the post to go to Lincoln even though he was a Clay man, "the office being too insignificant to make . . . politics an objection," observed Abe. [4]

A stagecoach to Springfield made regular stops at New Salem once a week. Letter writers used no stamps or envelopes. They tried to squeeze all the message they could write on one page, writing sideways or diagonally to save postage. Then they folded the page and sealed it with wax. A fee was charged according to the number of pages and the distance traveled. The person receiving the letter was expected to pay the postage. The postmaster calculated the charge, marking it on the upper right-hand corner of the folder page. The rates for each page were 6¢ for 30 miles or less, 10¢ for up to 80 miles, 12½¢ for up to 150 miles, 18½¢ for 400 miles or less. Over 400 miles was 25¢ per page.

Once a week, Lincoln made the rounds to deliver the mail. "Mr. Lincoln used to tell me that when he had a call to go to the country . . . he placed inside his hat all the letters belonging to people in the neighborhood and distributed them along the way," said Herndon.[5]

"He carried his office around in his hat," cracked one New Salemite.[6]

Everyone welcomed the mail, especially when the mailman was "Honest Abe." Folks liked to stop and talk with him. They would read their letters together and discuss what it said. If the customer received a newspaper, Abe could tell him where to find the most interesting stories, since he had already read every newspaper that came through his office.

As postmaster, Lincoln received a modest salary and the privilege of mailing letters for free, a practice called franking. Postal regulations were quite strict on the matter. "If any person shall frank any letter or letters other than those written by himself or by his order on the business of the office, he shall, on conviction thereof, pay a fine of ten dollars."[7]

The postmaster conducted his office in a genial manner, not allowing mere formalities to get in the way of service to his customers. One private letter, from Matthew Marsh to his brother George, illustrates Lincoln's freewheeling policy. "The Postmaster is very careless about leaving his office open and unlocked during the day," complained Marsh. "Half the time I go in and get my papers without anyone being there, as was the case yesterday.

"The letter was only marked twenty-five," Marsh observed, "and even if he had been there and known it was double he would not have charged me any more. Luckily, he is a very clever fellow and a particular friend of mine. If he is there when I carry this to the office I will get him to frank it."[8]

Marsh's letter was folded and sealed. Sure enough, on the outside of the letter in Lincoln's own hand was marked: "Free. A. Lincoln, P.M. New Salem, Ill. Sept. 22." [9]

Once, Lincoln became miffed at one of his patrons who wanted a receipt for fees paid. "At your request," Lincoln wrote, "I send you a receipt from the postage on your paper. I am somewhat surprised at your request. I will however comply with it. The law requires newspaper postage to be paid in advance and now that I have waited a full year you choose to wound my feelings by insinuating that unless you get a receipt I will probably make you pay it again." [10]

Another government job beckoned for Lincoln. "Someone, probably a Democrat who voted for him in the preceding fall, recommended him to John Calhoun, then surveyor of the county, as suitable material for an assistant," said Herndon. [11]

The county surveyor's office was swamped with requests from landowners. Settlers now flooding the prairie needed division lines to mark the boundaries of their farms. Speculators wanted their tracts of land parceled into lots. Towns needed to be laid out. Roads needed to be planned. Surveying was a skill that proved to be in great demand on the frontier.

Lincoln took the job. "This procured bread and kept soul and body together," he said. [12]

Lincoln had no experience in the art of surveying and was thoroughly unfamiliar with its underlying principles and procedures. Calhoun lent him some books on surveying and told him to study hard until he felt confident that he could get to work.

Lincoln called on New Salem's school teacher, Mentor Graham, for help. "Perhaps received more assistance from Mentor Graham than any other person," said R. B. Rutledge of Lincoln. [13]

"In the month of July 1833, Mr. Lincoln came and lived with me and continued with me about six months," recalled Mentor Graham. "I was then teaching school. I taught him the rules of surveying. I do not think that Mr. Lincoln knew anything of arithmetic, especially geometry and trigonometry before he came to my house." [14]

The two went at the books with solemn resolution. Mentor Graham's daughter remembers how her father and Lincoln became engrossed in the numbers. "Mr. Lincoln knew nothing much originally about surveying," said Mrs. Elizabeth Bell. "After he had surveyed a piece of land, getting corners, distances, directions etc, he would call at our house and get my father to calculate the figures and get the number of acres. My father and Lincoln would sit till midnight calculating." [15]

"It was here," said Graham, "that he commenced to study the English Grammar with me. [16] He studied to see the subject matter clearly and to express it truly and strongly. I have known him to study for hours the best way of three to express an idea. [17]

"I have taught in my life four or six thousand pupils as school master," avowed his admiring teacher, "and no one ever surpassed him in rapidly acquiring the rudiments and rules of English Grammar." [18]

Some nights Abe worked alone, absorbed in his books until daylight. Besides grammar, he studied decimal fractions, logarithms, trigonometry, scaling of maps, and the use of mathematical instruments. He caught sleep in short stretches and barely took time to eat.

"He studied surveying under Mentor Graham," said Henry McHenry. "He still continued reading law at the same time. He read so much, was so studious, took so little physical exercise. Was so laborious in his studies that he became emaciated and his best friends were afraid that he would craze himself, make himself deranged from his habits of study which were incessant." [19]

After weeks of serious study, Lincoln reported to Calhoun and announced that he was ready. He bought a horse, saddle, and bridle on credit and acquired a compass, chain, and other surveying equipment. Lincoln set out to measure and mark property lines all over Sangamon County.

"It has never been denied that his surveys were exact and just and he was so manifestly fair that he was often chosen to settle disputed questions of corners and measurements," Herndon said.[20]

Henry McHenry remembers an argument over the exact location of an old street corner. "After a good deal of disputing," he reported, "we agreed to send for Lincoln and to abide by his decision.

"He came with compass, flag-staff and chain . . . and surveyed the whole section. When in the neighborhood of the disputed corner by actual survey, he called for his staff and driving it in the ground at a certain spot said: 'Gentlemen, here is the corner.'

"We dug down into the ground at the point indicted and lo! There we found about six or eight inches of the original stake, sharpened at the end and beneath which was the usual piece of charcoal placed there by Rector, the surveyor who laid the ground off for the government many years before." [21]

He laid the lines for towns in New Boston, Bath, Albany, and Huron. He surveyed roads and county lines. Wherever he went, he made friends. "Not only did his wit, kindliness and knowledge attract people, but his strange clothes and uncouth awkwardness advertised him—the shortness of his trousers causing particular remark and amusement," said Coleman Smoot, who became justice of the peace in Sangamon County. "Soon the name 'Abe Lincoln' was a household word." [22]

When he surveyed the town of Petersburg, he let one street go crooked. It was the street near Jemima Elmore's house, a widow whose husband served with Lincoln in the Black Hawk War. He drew the boundary line around her property to make sure it did not cut her house in half.

For the first time in his life, Lincoln was making a comfortable living. His salary of three dollars a day was a royal sum in an economy where the governor of the state earned a thousand dollars a year and decent board and lodging went for a dollar a week. But he was never allowed to enjoy the fruits of his labor. His creditors found him.

On April 7, 1834, a merchant named Peter Van Bergen sued Lincoln and Berry. He held a note signed by the two principles for $379.82. Jimmy Short explains: "Radford sold out his stock of goods to W. G. Greene and Greene sold out to Lincoln and Berry. Lincoln and Berry gave their note . . . to Greene and Greene assigned it to Radford. Radford assigned it to Peter Van Bergen." [23]

The judge ordered Lincoln to pay Van Bergen his share, set at $154. When Lincoln admitted he didn't have the money, the court moved to take possession of all his personal belongings.

"An execution was issued and levied upon Lincoln's horse, saddle, bridle, compass, chain and other surveyor's instruments," said Jimmy Short. "Mr. L. was then very much discouraged and said he would let the whole thing go by the board." [24]

Lincoln was crushed. Suddenly, after such a promising start to his career he was unable to continue.

"I did all I could to put him in better spirits," Jimmy Short said. [25] On the day Lincoln's wares went up for public auction, his friend was there to help.

"When the sale came off—which Mr. Lincoln did not attend—I bid on the above property at $120," Jimmy said. "Immediately gave it up again to Mr. L." [26]

Through the generosity of his friend, Lincoln was back in business. But his good fortune did not last long. He was in danger of being separated from his horse. "My father sold Lincoln the horse," recalled Tom Watkins. "My recollection is that Lincoln agreed to pay him fifty dollars for it. Lincoln was a little slow in making the payments and after he had paid all but ten dollars, my father, who was a high strung man, became impatient and sued him for the balance.

"I have always been sorry Father sued," admitted Watkins.[27]

Somehow, Lincoln managed to come up with enough money to prevent the repossession of his horse.

On April 19, 1834, the name Abraham Lincoln appeared once again in the *Sangamo Journal*. "Mr. Lincoln was persuaded by his old friend Bowling Green to become a candidate for the State Legislature," said A. Y. Ellis. [28] This time, he ran as a candidate of the Whig Party along with his political mentor, John Stuart.

"I have Lincoln's word for it that it was more of a hand shaking campaign than anything else," said Herndon. [29]

"He came to my house near Island Grove during the harvest," remembered Rowan Herndon. "There were some thirty men in the field. He got his dinner and went out in the field where the men were at work. I gave him an introduction and the boys said that they could not vote for a man unless he could make a hand."

"Well, boys," crowed Lincoln, "if that is all, I am sure of your votes."

Said Rowan Herndon, "He took hold of the cradle and led the way all the round with perfect ease. The boys were satisfied and I don't think he lost a vote in the crowd." [30]

When Doc Barrett saw Lincoln, he complained to Rowan Herndon, "Can't the party raise no better materials than that?"

"I said go tomorrow and hear all before you pronounce judgment," Rowan recalled. "When he come back, I said—'Doc, what say you now?'"

"Why sir! He is a perfect take-in," Doc replied. "He knows more than all of them put together." [31]

Election Day was August 4. This time, Lincoln finished second, outpolling his friend John Stuart, who finished fourth, good enough to seat them both in the Illinois State Legislature.

The next session of the Illinois legislature was scheduled to begin on December 1, 1834. The new lawmaker made his preparations to leave New Salem and take his place in the government. He arranged with friend Caleb Carman to care for his cats, the two loves of his life, Jane and Susan.

"I will tell you about Lincoln and his two cats," said Carman. "When living with me in Salem we had two kittens, Lincoln's favorite pets. He would take them up in his lap and play with them and hold their heads together to say that Jane had a better countenance than Susan had. . . . He went to Vandalia to the legislature and left very strict orders for the cats to be well taken care of." [32]

As an elected representative, Lincoln showed a newfound awareness of his public image. He knew he had to do something about it.

"After he was elected to the legislature, he came to my house one day," related Coleman Smoot.

"Smoot," he said. "Did you vote for me?"

"I did."

"Well," said Lincoln, "You must loan me money to buy suitable clothing. I want to make a decent appearance in the legislature."

Said Smoot, "I then loaned him $200, which he returned to me according to promise." [33]

Lincoln spent $60 on a fine cloth suit, the first one he ever owned. Then as November drew to a close, he boarded a stagecoach for the seventy-five-mile journey to the state capital at Vandalia. Abraham Lincoln, now twenty-five, was ready to begin his career as servant of the people.

Bibliography

Angle, Paul. Editor. *The Lincoln Reader*. Rutgers University Press, 1947.

Atkinson, Eleanor. *The Boyhood of Lincoln*. The McClure Co., 1908.

Barton, William E. *The Life of Abraham Lincoln*. 2 Vols. Bobbs-Merrill, 1925.

Basler, Roy P., Editor. *Collected Works of Abraham Lincoln*. 9 Vols. Rutgers University Press, 1953.

Beveridge, Albert. *Abraham Lincoln, 1809–1858*. 2 Vols. Houghton-Mifflin Co., 1928.

Callow, Philip. *From Noon to Starry Night: A Life of Walt Whitman*. Ivan R. Dee, Publisher, 1992.

Current, Richard N. *The Lincoln Nobody Knows*. Hill and Wang, 1958.

Donald, David. *Lincoln*. Simon & Schuster, 1995.

Donald, David. *Lincoln's Herndon*. Alfred A. Knopf, 1948.

Franklin, Benjamin. *The Autobiography of Benjamin Franklin*. The Spencer Press, 1936.

Herndon, William H. Collected Papers, Library of Congress.

Herndon, William H. and Weik, Jesse W. *Abraham Lincoln: The True Story of a Great Life*. 2 Vols. D. Appleton & Co., 1892.

Herndon, William H. and Weik, Jesse W. *Herndon's Lincoln*, David Freeman Hawke, ed. Bobbs-Merrill, 1970.

Herndon, William H. and Weik, Jesse W. *Herndon's Life of Lincoln*. Da Capo Press, 1984.

Hertz, Emanuel. *The Hidden Lincoln.* Viking Press, 1938.

Hertz, Emanuel. *Lincoln Talks.* Viking Press, 1939.

Holzer, Harold. *Lincoln Seen and Heard,* University Press of Kansas, 2000.

Jennison, Keith W. *The Humorous Mr. Lincoln.* Bonzano Books, 1965.

Luthin, Reinhold. *The Real Lincoln.* New York, 1960.

Neely, Mark. E. *The Abraham Lincoln Encyclopedia.* McGraw-Hill, 1982.

Nicolay, John G. and Hay, John. *Abraham Lincoln: A History.* 10 Vols. Century Co., 1890.

Oates, Stephen B. *With Malice Toward None.* New American Library, 1977.

Oates, Stephen B. *Abraham Lincoln: The Man Behind the Myths.* New American Library, 1984.

Rankin, Henry B. *Personal Recollections of Abraham Lincoln.* G. P. Putnam's Sons, 1916.

Rice, Allen Thorndike. Editor. *Reminiscences of Abraham Lincoln.* North American Publishing Co., 1886.

Sandburg, Carl. *Abraham Lincoln: The Prairie Years.* 2 Vols. Harcourt Brace and Co., 1926.

Sandburg, Carl. *Abraham Lincoln: The War Years.* 4 Vols. Harcourt Brace and Co., 1939.

Sandburg, Carl. *Abraham Lincoln: The Prairie Years and The War Years.* Harcourt Brace Jovanovich, 1954.

Scripps, John Locke. *Life of Abraham Lincoln.* Chicago Press and Tribune, May 19, 1860. Reprint: Indiana University Press, 1961.

Stern, Philip Van Doren. Editor. *The Life and Writings of Abraham Lincoln.* Random House, 1940.

Tarbell, Ida M. *The Early Life of Abraham Lincoln.* McClure Co., 1896. Reprint: A. S. Barnes & Co., 1974.

Tarbell, Ida M. *The Life of Abraham Lincoln.* 2 Vols. McClure & Phillips and Co., 1900.

Thomas, Benjamin P. *Lincoln's New Salem.* Alfred A. Knopf, 1934.

Thomas, Benjamin P. *Abraham Lincoln.* Alfred A. Knopf, 1952.

Van Natter, Francis Marion. *Lincoln's Boyhood.* Public Affairs Press, 1963.

Warren, Louis A. *Lincoln's Youth, Indiana Years, Seven to Twenty-One, 1816–1830.* Indiana Historical Society, 1959.

Weems, Mason Locke. *A History of the Life and Death, Virtues and Exploits of General George Washington.* The World Publishing Co., Reprint: 1965. Original: 1809.

Whitman, Walt, *Leaves of Grass.* Doubleday and Co., 1926.

Whitman, Walt, *Walt Whitman's Civil War.* Walter Lowenfels, ed. Alfred A. Knopf, 1971.

Wilson, Douglas. *Honor's Voice: The Transformation of Abraham Lincoln.* Vintage Books, 1999.

Wilson, Douglas and Davis, Rodney, ed. *Herndon's Informants, Letters, Interviews and Statements about Abraham Lincoln.* University of Illinois Press, 1998.

Notes

INTRODUCTION: "I SAW HIM THIS MORNING ABOUT 8:30"

1. Walt Whitman, *Walt Whitman's Civil War*, Walter Lowenfels, ed., Alfred A. Knopf, 1971, p. 3.
2. Whitman, *Walt Whitman's Civil War*, p. 4.
3. Whitman, *Walt Whitman's Civil War*, p. 293.
4. Whitman, *Walt Whitman's Civil War*, p. 14.
5. Whitman, *Walt Whitman's Civil War*, p. 10.
6. Whitman, *Walt Whitman's Civil War*, p. 14.
7. ibid
8. Philip Callow, *From Noon to Starry Night: A Life of Walt Whitman*, Ivan P. Dee, Inc., 1992, p. 304.
9. Whitman, *Walt Whitman's Civil War*, p. 257. (Whitman's Journal, Aug. 12, 1863)
10. Whitman, *Walt Whitman's Civil War*, p. 257–258. (Whitman's Journal, Aug. 12, 1863)
11. ibid
12. Whitman, *Walt Whitman's Civil War*, p. 264. (Whitman's Journal, March 4, 1864)

13. Stephen B. Oates, *With Malice Toward None: A Life of Abraham Lincoln*; preface to the Harper Perennial Edition, Harper & Row, 1994, p. xvi.

14. Douglas L. Wilson, *Honor's Voice: The Transformation of Abraham Lincoln*, Vintage Books, 1998, p. 6.

15. ibid

16. Wilson, p. 10.

17. Michiko Kakutani, "Lincoln as the Visionary with His Eye on the Prize," *New York Times*, October 25, 2005.

18. David Donald, *Lincoln's Herndon*, Alfred A. Knopf, 1948, p. 300. (Herndon to Weik, Dec. 21, 1885)

19. Douglas L. Wilson and Rodney O. Davis, *Herndon's Informants*, University of Illinois Press, 1998, p. 57. (Scripps to Herndon, June 24, 1865)

20. ibid

21. Abraham Lincoln, *The Life and Writings of Abraham Lincoln*, Random House, 1940, Philip Van Doren Stern, ed., p. 564.

22. Emanuel Hertz, *The Hidden Lincoln*, The Viking Press, 1938, p. 120.

23. Hertz, *The Hidden Lincoln*, p. 439.

24. Wilson, p. 11.

25. Paul M. Angle, Editor's Preface, *Herndon's Lincoln*, Da Capo Press, 1942, p. xxxix.

26. Hertz, *The Hidden Lincoln*, p. 64.

27. Hertz, *The Hidden Lincoln*, p. 63. (Herndon to Lamon, Feb. 25, 1870)

28. Angle, p. xl.

29. Donald, *Lincoln's Herndon*, p. 193.

30. Donald, *Lincoln's Herndon*, p. 347.

31. Angle, p. xxxviii.

32. Wilson, p. 12.

33. Hertz, *The Hidden Lincoln*, p. 12.

34. Hertz, *The Hidden Lincoln*, p. 13.

35. Hertz, *The Hidden Lincoln*, p. 267. (Herndon to Bartlett, Feb. 27, 1891) *This was the last letter Herndon ever wrote. He died March 18, 1891.*

36. Abraham Lincoln, *Collected Works of Abraham Lincoln*, Roy P. Basler, ed., III: p. 59.

37. Herndon and Weik, *Herndon's Life of Lincoln*, Da Capo Press, 1983, p. 353.

38. Carl Sandburg, *The War Years*, Harcourt, Brace and World, 1939, II: p. 306.

CHAPTER 1. "MY GOOD FRIEND IS GONE"

1. David Donald, *Lincoln*, Simon & Schuster, 1995, p. 576.

2. Carl Sandburg, *Abraham Lincoln*, Harcourt, Brace, Jovanovich, 1954, p. 684.

3. Sandburg, *Abraham Lincoln*, p. 685.

4. David Donald, *Lincoln's Herndon*, Alfred A. Knopf, 1948, p. 165. (Herndon to Caroline Dall, May 26, 1865)

5. William H. Herndon and Jesse W. Weik, *Herndon's Life of Lincoln*, Da Capo Press, 1984, p. 323.

6. Emanuel Hertz, *The Hidden Lincoln*, The Viking Press, 1938, p. 64. (Herndon to Ward Hill Lamon, Feb. 25, 1870)

7. Douglas C. Wilson and Rodney O. Davis, *Herndon's Informants*, University of Illinois Press, 1998 p. 152. (Richard J. Oglesby to Herndon, Jan. 5, 1866)

8. Donald, *Lincoln's Herndon*, p. 200.

9. Donald, *Lincoln's Herndon*, p. 364.

10. Wilson and Davis, p. xvi. (Herndon to Charles Hart, Dec. 12, 1866)

11. Hertz, *The Hidden Lincoln*, p. 71. (Herndon to Lamon, March 6, 1870)

12. Herndon and Weik, *Herndon's Life of Lincoln*, p. vii.

13. Hertz, *The Hidden Lincoln*, p. 84. (Herndon to Weik, Oct. 8, 1881)

14. Wilson and Davis, p. xiv. (Herndon to Josiah Holland, May 26, 1865)

15. Wilson and Davis, p. xiv. (Herndon to Josiah Holland, June 8, 1865)

16. Hertz, *The Hidden Lincoln,* p. 440.

17. Donald, *Lincoln's Herndon,* p. 184. (Herndon to Josiah Holland, June 8, 1865)

CHAPTER 2. "I HAVE HEARD MUCH OF THIS BLESSED GOOD WOMAN"

1. Wilson and Davis, p. 242. (Dennis Hanks to Herndon, April 2, 1866)

2. Eleanor Atkinson, *The Boyhood of Lincoln,* The McClure Co., 1908, p. 3. (Interview with Dennis Hanks, January 1889)

3. Hertz, *The Hidden Lincoln,* p. 94. (Herndon to Weik, April 14, 1885)

4. Donald, *Lincoln's Herndon,* p. 308. (Herndon to Weik, May 6, 1885)

5. Hertz, *The Hidden Lincoln,* p. 94. (Herndon to Weik, April 14, 1885)

6. ibid

7. Wilson and Davis, p. 199. (Dennis Hanks to Herndon, Feb. 10, 1866)

8. Wilson and Davis, p. 220. (Dennis Hanks to Herndon, Feb. 12, 1866)

9. Wilson and Davis, p. 199. (Dennis Hanks to Herndon, Feb. 10, 1866)

10. Wilson and Davis, p. 37. (Dennis Hanks to Herndon June 13, 1865)

11. Wilson and Davis, p. 199. (Dennis Hanks to Herndon, Feb. 10, 1866)

12. Wilson and Davis, p. 149. (Dennis Hanks to Herndon, Dec. 1865)

13. Wilson and Davis, p. 144. (Dennis Hanks to Herndon, Dec. 12, 1865)

14. Wilson and Davis, p. 176. (Dennis Hanks to Herndon, Jan. 26, 1866)

15. Albert Beveridge, *Abraham Lincoln,* Houghton-Mifflin Co., 1928, p. 5.

16. Wilson and Davis, p. 109. (Herndon interview with Sarah Bush Lincoln, Sept. 8, 1865)

17. Hertz, *The Hidden Lincoln,* p. 84–85.

18. Wilson and Davis, *Herndon's Informants,* p. 109. (Herndon interview with Sarah Bush Lincoln, Sept. 8, 1865)

19. Wilson and Davis, p. 117. (Herndon interview with Nathaniel Grigsby, Sept. 14, 1865)

20. Wilson and Davis, p. 116. (Herndon interview with Nathaniel Grigsby, Sept. 14, 1865)

CHAPTER 3. "INJUNS!"

1. Albert Beveridge, *Abraham Lincoln*, Houghton-Mifflin Co., 1928, p. 8.

2. Ida Tarbell, *The Early Life of Abraham Lincoln*, original, S. S. McClure, 1896; reprinted, A. S. Barnes & Co., 1974, p. 24.

3. Tarbell, *The Early Life of Abraham Lincoln*, p. 23.

4. Wilson and Davis, p. 234. (Charles Friend to Herndon, March 19, 1866)

5. Carl Sandburg, *Abraham Lincoln: The Prairie Years*, Harcourt, Brace and Co., 1926, p. 15.

6. Wilson and Davis, p. 439. (A. H. Chapman to Herndon, 1865–1866)

7. Wilson and Davis, p. 36. (Dennis Hanks to Herndon, June 13, 1865)

8. Wilson and Davis, p. 96. (A. H. Chapman to Herndon, Sept. 8, 1865)

9. Abraham Lincoln, *The Life and Writings of Abraham Lincoln*, p. 600.

10. Wilson and Davis, p. 113. (Nat Grigsby to Herndon, Sept. 12, 1865)

11. Wilson and Davis, p. 176. (Dennis Hanks to Herndon, Jan. 26, 1866)

12. Wilson and Davis, p. 37. (Dennis Hanks to Herndon, June 13, 1865)

13. Wilson and Davis, p. 97. (A. H. Chapman to Herndon, Sept. 8, 1865)

14. Wilson and Davis, p. 646. (Weik interview with Harriet Chapman, 1886)

15. Wilson and Davis, p. 149. (Dennis Hanks to Herndon, Dec. 1865)

16. Wilson and Davis, p. 28. (Erastus Wright interview with Dennis Hanks, June 8, 1865)

17. Atkinson, *The Boyhood of Lincoln*, p. 11. (Atkinson interview with Dennis Hanks, Jan. 1889)

18. Wilson and Davis, p. 37. (Dennis Hanks to Herndon, June 13, 1865)

19. Wilson and Davis, p. 96. (A. H. Chapman to Herndon, Sept. 8, 1865)

20. Sandburg, *The Prairie Years*, p. 6.

21. Wilson and Davis, p. 98. (A. H. Chapman to Herndon, Sept. 8, 1865)

22. Wilson and Davis, p. 102. (A. H. Chapman to Herndon, Sept. 8, 1865)

23. Wilson and Davis, p. 67. (Samuel Haycraft to Herndon, June 1865)

24. Wilson and Davis, p. 123. (William Wood to Herndon, Sept. 15, 1865)

25. Sandburg, *The Prairie Years*, p. 6.

CHAPTER 4. "PURTY AS A PITCHER"

1. Louis A. Warren, *Lincoln's Youth, Indiana Years, Seven to Twenty-One*, original, Indiana Historical Society, 1959; reprinted, Greenwood Press, 1976, p. 6.

2. Carl Sandburg, *Abraham Lincoln: The Prairie Years and The War Years,* Harcourt, Brace, Jovanovich, 1954, p. 5.
3. Wilson and Davis, p. 585. (Statement by Charlotte Hobart Vawter, granddaughter of Sarah Mitchell in *Louisville Courier-Journal,* February 20, 1874)
4. Wilson and Davis, p. 242. (Dennis Hanks to Herndon, April 2, 1866)
5. Wilson and Davis, p. 221. (Dennis Hanks to Herndon, Feb. 28, 1866)
6. Atkinson, p. 11.
7. Wilson and Davis, p. 37. (Dennis Hanks to Herndon, June 13, 1865)
8. Wilson and Davis, p. 454. (John Hanks to Herndon, 1865–1866)
9. Wilson and Davis, p. 615. (John Hanks to Weik, June 12, 1887)
10. Herndon and Weik, p. 3.
11. ibid
12. Hertz, p. 73. (Herndon to Lamon, March 6, 1870)
13. Herndon and Weik, p. 3.
14. Warren, p. 240.
15. Tarbell, p. 235.
16. Tarbell, p. 233.

CHAPTER 5. "NANCY'S GOT A BOY BABY"

1. Atkinson, p. 6.
2. Atkinson, p. 7.
3. Atkinson, p. 8.
4. Beveridge p. 3
5. Wilson and Davis, p. 38. (Dennis Hanks to Herndon, June 13, 1865)
6. Atkinson, p. 9.
7. Wilson and Davis, p. 726. (Dennis Hanks to Jesse W. Weik, Oct. 28, 1886)

8. Francis Marion Van Natter, *Lincoln's Boyhood,* Public Affairs Press, 1963, p. 7.

9. Van Natter, p. 14.

10. Atkinson, p. 11.

11. Wilson and Davis, p. 257. (E. R. Burba to Herndon, May 25, 1866)

12. Atkinson, p. 13.

13. Ida Tarbell, *The Life of Abraham Lincoln,* McClure & Phillips and Co., 1900, Vol. I, p. 17.

14. Nicolay and Hay, *Abraham Lincoln: A History,* Vol. I, p. 27.

15. Wilson and Davis, p. 37. (Dennis Hanks to Herndon, June 13, 1865)

16. John Locke Scripps, *Life of Abraham Lincoln,* original, Chicago Press and Tribune, May 19, 1860; reprinted, Indiana University Press, p. 32.

17. Henry Rankin, *Personal Recollections of Abraham Lincoln,* 1916, p. 325.

18. Abraham Lincoln, *Collected Works,* II: p. 217.

19. Wilson and Davis, p. 235. (Charles Friend to Herndon, June 13, 1865)

20. Tarbell, *The Early Life of Abraham Lincoln,* p. 44.

21. Tarbell, *The Early Life of Abraham Lincoln,* p. 45.

22. Wilson and Davis, p. 676. (Charles Friend to Herndon, Aug. 1889)

CHAPTER 6. "IT WAS A WILD REGION"

1. Keith W. Jennison, *The Humorous Mr. Lincoln,* Bonzano Books, 1965, p. 1.

2. Wilson and Davis, p. 38. (Dennis Hanks to Herndon, June 13, 1865)

3. Abraham Lincoln, *The Life and Writings of Abraham Lincoln,* Philip Van Doren Stern, ed., p. 600.

4. Warren, p. 12.

5. Warren, p. 13.

6. ibid

7. Wilson and Davis, p. 38. (Dennis Hanks to Herndon, June 13, 1865)

8. Wilson and Davis, p. 97. (A. H. Chapman to Herndon, Sept. 8, 1865)

9. Wilson and Davis, p. 38. (Dennis Hanks to Herndon, June 13, 1865)

10. ibid

11. William H. Herndon and Jesse W. Weik, *Herndon's Life of Lincoln*, original, Da Capo Press, Inc., 1942, p. 20. (Originally published as *Abraham Lincoln: The True Story of a Great Life*, D. Appleton and Co., 1892.)

12. Wilson and Davis, p. 97. (A. H. Chapman to Herndon, Sept. 8, 1865)

13. Beveridge, p. 38.

14. Wilson and Davis, p. 111. (Nat Grigsby to Herndon, Sept. 12, 1865)

15. Wilson and Davis, p. 98. (A. H. Chapman, Written Statement, Sept. 8, 1865)

16. Wilson and Davis, p. 39. (Dennis Hanks to Herndon, June 13, 1865)

17. Wilson and Davis, p. 93. (Nat Grigsby to Herndon, Sept. 4, 1865)

18. Wilson and Davis, p. 235. (Dennis Hanks to Herndon, March 22, 1866)

19. Abraham Lincoln, *The Life and Writings of Abraham Lincoln*, p. 565.

20. Atkinson, p. 15.

CHAPTER 7. "CONSTANTLY HANDLING THAT MOST USEFUL INSTRUMENT"

1. Wilson and Davis, p. 39. (Dennis Hanks to Herndon, June 13, 1865)

2. Wilson and Davis, p. 229. (Dennis Hanks to Herndon, March 12, 1866)
3. Abraham Lincoln, *The Life and Writings of Abraham Lincoln*, p. 601.
4. Wilson and Davis, p. 217. (David Turnham to Herndon, Feb. 21, 1866)
5. Abraham Lincoln, *Collected Works,* I: p. 386.
6. Wilson and Davis, p. 217. (David Turnham to Herndon, Feb. 21, 1866)
7. Abraham Lincoln, *The Life and Writings of Abraham Lincoln*, p. 600.
8. Atkinson, p. 12.
9. Van Natter, p. 5.
10. Wilson and Davis, p. 513. (Harriet Chapman to Herndon, Dec. 10, 1866)
11. Wilson and Davis, p. 245. (Elizabeth Crawford to Herndon, April 19, 1866)
12. Hertz, p. 279.
13. Atkinson, p. 37.
14. Abraham Lincoln, *The Life and Writings of Abraham Lincoln*, p. 601.
15. Herndon and Weik, p. 51.
16. Herndon and Weik, p. 52.
17. Herndon and Weik, p. 51.

CHAPTER 8. "I AM GOING AWAY FROM YOU, ABRAHAM"

1. Wilson and Davis, p. 229. (Dennis Hanks to Herndon, March 12, 1866)
2. Van Natter, p. 12.
3. Wilson and Davis, p. 98. (A. H. Chapman to Herndon, March 12, 1866)
4. ibid

5. Atkinson, p. 19.
6. Wilson and Davis, p. 123. (William Wood to Herndon, Sept. 15, 1865)
7. Wilson and Davis, p. 40. (Dennis Hanks to Herndon, June 13, 1865)
8. Warren, p. 54.
9. Wilson and Davis, p. 40. (Dennis Hanks to Herndon, June 13, 1865)
10. Atkinson, p. 16.
11. ibid
12. Warren, p. 55.
13. Warren, p. 56.
14. Hertz, p. 73. (Herndon to Lamon, March 6, 1870)
15. Wilson and Davis, p. 40. (Dennis Hanks to Herndon, June 13, 1865)

CHAPTER 9. "HERE'S YOUR NEW MAMMY"

1. Wilson and Davis, p. 236. (Dennis Hanks to Herndon, March 22, 1866)
2. Atkinson, p. 19.
3. Henry B. Rankin, *Personal Recollections of Abraham Lincoln,* G. P. Putnam's Sons, 1916, p. 320.
4. Atkinson, p. 19.
5. Wilson and Davis, p. 82. (John Helm to Herndon, August 1, 1865)
6. Wilson and Davis, p. 98. (A. H. Chapman to Herndon, Sept. 8, 1865)
7. Wilson and Davis, p. 85. (Samuel Haycraft to Herndon, July 5, 1865)
8. ibid
9. Wilson and Davis, p. 68. (Samuel Haycraft to Herndon, June 1865)
10. Wilson and Davis, p. 503. (Samuel Haycraft to Herndon, Dec. 7, 1866)

11. Wilson and Davis, p. 85. (Samuel Haycraft to Herndon, July 5, 1865)

12. Wilson and Davis, p. 503. (Samuel Haycraft to Herndon, Dec. 7, 1866)

13. Sandburg, *Abraham Lincoln, The Prairie Years,* p. 26.

14. Atkinson, p. 20.

15. Wilson and Davis, p. 99. (A. H. Chapman to Herndon, Sept. 8, 1865)

16. Atkinson, p. 21.

17. Wilson and Davis, p. 99. (A. H. Chapman to Herndon, Sept. 8, 1865)

18. Wilson and Davis, p. 41. (Dennis Hanks to Herndon, June 13, 1865)

19. Wilson and Davis, p. 145. (Harriet Chapman to Herndon, Sept. 8, 1865)

20. Wilson and Davis, p. 41. (Dennis Hanks to Herndon, June 13, 1865)

21. Wilson and Davis, p. 106. (Sarah Bush Lincoln to Herndon, Sept. 8, 1865)

22. Wilson and Davis, p. 99. (A. H. Chapman to Herndon, Sept. 8, 1865)

23. Wilson and Davis, p. 41. (Dennis Hanks to Herndon, June 13, 1865)

24. Atkinson, p. 22.

25. Wilson and Davis, p. 41. (Dennis Hanks to Herndon, June 13, 1865)

26. Wilson and Davis, p. 99. (A. H. Chapman to Herndon, Sept. 8, 1865)

27. Atkinson, p. 22.

28. Atkinson, p. 21.

29. Wilson and Davis, p. 99. (A. H. Chapman to Herndon, Sept. 8, 1865)

30. Atkinson, p. 22.

31. Wilson and Davis, p. 99. (A. H. Chapman to Herndon, Sept. 8, 1865)
32. Atkinson, p. 21.
33. Wilson and Davis, p. 99. (A. H. Chapman to Herndon, Sept. 8, 1865)
34. Wilson and Davis, p. 107. (Sarah Bush Lincoln to Herndon, Sept. 8, 1865)
35. Warren, p. 194.

CHAPTER 10. "LAND O' GOSHEN, THAT BOY AIR A' GROWIN'"

1. Wilson and Davis, p. 121. (David Turnham to Herndon, Sept. 15, 1865)
2. Sandburg, *Abraham Lincoln, The Prairie Years,* p. 26.
3. Atkinson, p. 35.
4. Warren, p. 143.
5. Wilson and Davis, p. 124. (William Wood to Herndon, Sept. 15, 1865)
6. Warren, p. 142.
7. Wilson and Davis, p. 110. (Matilda Johnston Moore to Herndon, Sept. 8, 1865)
8. Warren, p. 153.
9. Wilson and Davis, p. 110. (Matilda Johnston Moore to Herndon, Sept. 8, 1865)
10. Warren, p. 154.
11. Warren, p. 249.
12. ibid
13. Wilson and Davis, p. 94. (Nat Grigsby to Herndon, Sept. 4, 1865)
14. Wilson and Davis, p. 123. (William Wood to Herndon, Sept. 15, 1865)
15. Beveridge, p. 61.
16. Wilson and Davis, p. 146. (Dennis Hanks to Herndon, Dec. 2, 1965)

17. Wilson and Davis, p. 120. (Joseph Richardson to Herndon, Sept. 14, 1865)
18. Atkinson, p. 40.
19. Warren, p. 197.
20. Wilson and Davis, p. 130. (Green Taylor to Herndon, Sept. 16, 1865)
21. Beveridge, p. 93.
22. Herndon and Weik, p. 41.
23. Wilson and Davis, p. 130. (Green Taylor to Herndon, Sept. 16, 1865)
24. Wilson and Davis, p. 113. (Nat Grigsby to Herndon, Sept. 12, 1865)
25. Warren, p. 210.
26. Atkinson, p. 35.
27. Herndon and Weik, p. 23.
28. Herndon and Weik, p. 25.
29. Sandburg, *Abraham Lincoln, The Prairie Years,* p. 29.

CHAPTER 11. "A REAL EDDICATION"

1. Atkinson, p. 17.
2. Sandburg, p. 23.
3. Leonard Swett, *Reminiscences of Abraham Lincoln,* Allen Thorndike Rice, ed. North American Publishing Co., 1886, p. 458.
4. Abraham Lincoln, *Collected Works,* III: p. 512. (Lincoln to J. W. Fell, Dec. 20, 1859)
5. Wilson and Davis, p. 37. (Dennis Hanks to Herndon, June 13, 1865)
6. Atkinson, p. 18.
7. Wilson and Davis, p. 67. (Samuel Haycraft to Herndon, June 1865)
8. Swett, p. 455.
9. Warren, p. 11.

10. Atkinson, p. 17.
11. Wilson and Davis, p. 112. (Nat Grigsby to Herndon, Sept. 12, 1865)
12. Wilson and Davis, p. 93. (Nat Grigsby to Herndon, Sept. 4, 1865)
13. Wilson and Davis, p. 112. (Nat Grigsby to Herndon, Sept. 12, 1865)
14. Wilson and Davis, p. 94. (Nat Grigsby to Herndon, Sept. 4, 1865)
15. Beveridge, p. 70.
16. Wilson and Davis, p. 241. (E. R. Burba to Herndon, March 31, 1866)
17. Warren, p. 169.
18. Wilson and Davis, p. 112. (Nat Grigsby to Herndon, Sept. 12, 1865)
19. Wilson and Davis, p. 131. (Anna Caroline Roby Gentry, Sept. 17, 1865)
20. Herndon and Weik, p. 35.
21. Wilson and Davis, p. 131. (Anna Caroline Roby Gentry, Sept. 17, 1865)
22. Wilson and Davis, p. 132. (Anna Caroline Roby Gentry, Sept. 17, 1865)
23. Book of Daniel, 3:1, 3:11–12
24. Warren, p. 83.
25. Warren, p. 102.
26. Warren, p. 243.
27. Warren, p. 128.
28. Abraham Lincoln, *The Life and Writings of Abraham Lincoln,* p. 601.
29. Wilson and Davis, p. 131. (Anna Caroline Roby Gentry, Sept. 17, 1865)

CHAPTER 12. "MIGHTY DARNED GOOD LIES"

1. Atkinson, p. 26.
2. Wilson and Davis, p. 455. (John Hanks to Herndon, 1865–1866)

3. Wilson and Davis, p. 512. (Harriet Chapman to Herndon, Dec. 10, 1866)
4. Atkinson, p. 27.
5. Wilson and Davis, p. 118. (John Romine to Herndon, Sept. 14, 1865)
6. Wilson and Davis, p. 109. (Matilda Johnston Moore to Herndon, Sept. 8, 1865)
7. Wilson and Davis, p. 121. (David Turnham to Herndon, Sept. 15, 1865)
8. Wilson and Davis, p. 455. (John Hanks to Herndon, 1865–1866)
9. Warren, p. 46.
10. Sandburg, *The War Years,* II: 309.
11. Hertz, *Lincoln Talks,* p. 339.
12. Atkinson, p. 24.
13. Atkinson, p. 23.
14. Atkinson, p. 25.
15. *The Autobiography of Benjamin Franklin,* The Spencer Press, 1936, p. 8.
16. Franklin, p. 13.
17. Franklin, p. 14.
18. Wilson and Davis, p. 662. (Oliver Terry to Weik, July 1888)
19. ibid
20. ibid
21. ibid
22. Wilson and Davis, p. 125. (Elizabeth Crawford to Herndon, Sept. 15, 1865)
23. Wilson and Davis, p. 662. (Oliver Terry to Weik, July 1888)
24. ibid
25. Mason Locke Weems, *A History of the Life and Death, Virtues and Exploits of General George Washington,* The World Publishing Co., 1965, p. 21–25.
26. Warren, p. 110–111.
27. Beveridge, p. 83

CHAPTER 13. "SOMETHIN' PECULIARSOME"

1. Atkinson, p. 28.
2. Wilson and Davis, p. 39. (Dennis Hanks to Herndon, June 13, 1865)
3. Atkinson, p. 29.
4. Wilson and Davis, p. 39. (Dennis Hanks to Herndon, June 13, 1865)
5. Atkinson, p. 29.
6. Wilson and Davis, p. 105. (Dennis Hanks to Herndon, Sept. 8, 1865)
7. Wilson and Davis, p. 107. (Sarah Bush Lincoln to Herndon, Sept. 8, 1865)
8. Atkinson, p. 35.
9. Wilson and Davis, p. 455. (John Hanks to Herndon, 1865–1866)
10. Wilson and Davis, p. 102. (A. H. Chapman to Herndon, Sept. 8, 1865)
11. Atkinson, p. 37.
12. Wilson and Davis, p. 123. (Dennis Hanks to Herndon, Sept. 15, 1865)
13. Wilson and Davis, p. 107. (Sarah Bush Lincoln to Herndon, Sept. 8, 1865)
14. Wilson and Davis, p. 245. (Elizabeth Crawford to Herndon, April 19, 1866)
15. Wilson and Davis, p. 108. (Sarah Bush Lincoln to Herndon, Sept. 8, 1865)
16. Wilson and Davis, p. 42. (Dennis Hanks to Herndon, June 13, 1865)
17. Wilson and Davis, p. 126. (Elizabeth Crawford to Herndon, Sept. 16, 1865)
18. Sandburg, *Abraham Lincoln, The Prairie Years*, p. 42.
19. Atkinson, p. 23.
20. Atkinson, p. 27.

21. Tarbell, p. 32.

22. Wilson and Davis, p. 107. (Sarah Bush Lincoln to Herndon, Sept. 8, 1865)

23. Wilson and Davis, p. 108. (Sarah Bush Lincoln to Herndon, Sept. 8, 1865)

24. Wilson and Davis, p. 474. (Joseph Richardson to Herndon, 1865–1866)

25. Beveridge, p. 78.

26. ibid

27. Wilson and Davis, p. 107. (Sarah Bush Lincoln to Herndon, Sept. 8, 1865)

28. Herndon and Weik, p. 39.

29. Wilson and Davis, p. 107. (Sarah Bush Lincoln to Herndon, Sept. 8, 1865)

30. Herndon and Weik, p. 39.

31. Wilson and Davis, p. 107. (Sarah Bush Lincoln to Herndon, Sept. 8, 1865)

32. ibid

33. Herndon and Weik, p. 36.

34. Wilson and Davis, p. 105. (Dennis Hanks to Herndon, Sept. 8, 1865)

35. Warren, p. 131.

36. Warren, p. 245.

37. Wilson and Davis, p. 499. (Joshua Speed to Herndon, Dec. 6, 1866)

38. Wilson and Davis, p. 105. (Dennis Hanks to Herndon, Sept. 8, 1865)

CHAPTER 14. "CHRONICLES OF REUBEN"

1. Wilson and Davis, p. 38. (Dennis Hanks to Herndon, June 13, 1865)

2. Wilson and Davis, p. 456. (John Hanks to Herndon, 1865–1866)

3. Wilson and Davis, p. 113. (Nat Grigsby to Herndon, Sept. 12, 1865)
4. ibid
5. Tarbell, *The Early Life of Lincoln,* p. 67.
6. Wilson and Davis, p. 249. (Elizabeth Crawford to Herndon, May 3, 1866)
7. ibid
8. Wilson and Davis, p. 169. (Nat Grigsby to Herndon, Jan. 21, 1866)
9. Wilson and Davis, p. 114. (Nat Grigsby to Herndon, Sept. 12, 1865)
10. Wilson and Davis, p. 105. (Dennis Hanks to Herndon, Sept. 8, 1865)
11. Herndon and Weik, p. 35.
12. Warren, p. 154.
13. Warren, p. 157.
14. Warren, p. 155.
15. Wilson and Davis, p. 131. (Anna Caroline Gentry [Kate Roby] to Herndon, Sept. 17, 1865)
16. Wilson and Davis, p. 518. (David Turnham to Herndon, Dec. 17, 1865)
17. Sandburg, *Abraham Lincoln, The Prairie Years,* p. 460.
18. Tarbell, *The Early Life of Lincoln,* p. 26.
19. Wilson and Davis, p. 119. (Joseph Richardson to Herndon, Sept. 14, 1865)
20. Hertz, p. 155. (Herndon to Weik, Jan. 8, 1887)
21. Wilson and Davis, p. 119. (Joseph Richardson to Herndon, Sept. 14, 1865)
22. Hertz, p. 155. (Herndon to Weik, Jan. 8, 1887)
23. Wilson and Davis, p. 120. (Joseph Richardson to Herndon, Sept. 14, 1865)
24. ibid
25. Wilson and Davis, p. 154. (S. Crawford to Herndon, Jan. 8, 1866)

26. Warren, p. 196.
27. Wilson and Davis, p. 114. (Nat Grigsby to Herndon, Sept. 12, 1865)
28. Wilson and Davis, p. 127. (Elizabeth Crawford to Herndon, Sept. 16, 1865)
29. Wilson and Davis, p. 169. (Nat Grigsby to Herndon, Jan. 21, 1866)
30. Wilson and Davis, p. 152. (Elizabeth Crawford to Herndon, Jan. 4, 1866)
31. ibid

CHAPTER 15. "WHY DOST THOU TEAR MORE BLESSED ONES HENCE?"

1. Wilson and Davis, p. 147. (Dennis Hanks to Herndon, Dec. 27, 1865)
2. Sandburg, *The Prairie Years,* p. 266.
3. Wilson and Davis, p. 119. (Joseph Richardson to Herndon, Sept. 14, 1865)
4. Wilson and Davis, p. 389. (R. B. Rutledge to Herndon, Oct. 1866)
5. Herndon and Weik, p. 38.
6. Wilson and Davis, p. 120. (Joseph Richardson to Herndon, Sept. 14, 1865)
7. Herndon and Weik, p. 37.
8. ibid
9. Wilson and Davis, p. 470. (James H. Matheny, 1865–1866)
10. Lincoln, *Collected Works,* I: p. 378. (Lincoln to Andrew Johnston, April 18, 1846)
11. ibid.
12. Warren, p. 173.
13. ibid
14. ibid
15. ibid

16. Lincoln, *Collected Works,* I: p. 384. (Lincoln to Andrew Johnston, Sept. 6, 1846)
17. Herz, *The Hidden Lincoln*, p. 68. (Herndon to Lamon, Feb. 25, 1870)
18. Herz, *The Hidden Lincoln*, p. 110. (Herndon, Dec. 4, 1885)
19. Lincoln, *Collected Works,* I: p. 385. (Lincoln to Andrew Johnston, Sept. 6, 1846)

CHAPTER 16. "I CAN SEE THE QUIVERING AND SHINING OF THAT HALF-DOLLAR YET"

1. Wilson and Davis, p. 129. (Green Taylor to Herndon, Sept. 16, 1865)
2. ibid
3. Warren, p. 145.
4. ibid
5. Wilson and Davis, p. 100. (A. H. Chapman to Herndon, Sept. 8, 1865)
6. Tarbell, *The Early Life of Abraham Lincoln,* p. 64.
7. Leonard Swett, *Reminiscences of Abraham Lincoln,* North American Publishing Co., 1886; Allen Thorndike Rice, ed., p. 458.
8. Warren, p. 145.

CHAPTER 17. "RIVER MAN"

1. Warren, p. 176.
2. Warren, p. 179
3. Lincoln, *Collected Works,* IV: p. 62.
4. ibid
5. Wilson and Davis, p. 131. (Anna Roby Gentry to Herndon, Sept. 17, 1865)
6. Lincoln, *Collected Works,* IV: p. 62.
7. Swett, p. 462.
8. Warren, p. 181.

9. Warren, p. 185.
10. Atkinson, p. 39.
11. ibid
12. Wilson and Davis, p. 124. (William Wood to Herndon, Sept. 15, 1865)

CHAPTER 18. "SNOWBIRDS"

1. Wilson and Davis, p. 124. (William Wood to Herndon, Sept. 15, 1865)
2. ibid
3. Atkinson, p. 41.
4. Wilson and Davis, p. 456. (John Hanks to Herndon, 1865–1866)
5. William H. Herndon and Jesse Weik, *Herndon's Lincoln: The True Story of a Great Life ... The History and Personal Recollections of Abraham Lincoln,* Volume 1, Belford, Clarke, 1889, p. 87.
6. Sandburg, *Abraham Lincoln, The Prairie Years,* p. 55.
7. Tarbell, *Life of Lincoln,* p. 45.
8. Warren, p. 204.
9. ibid
10. Atkinson, p. 41.
11. Wilson and Davis, p. 244. (Dennis Hanks to Herndon, April 18, 1866)
12. Warren, p. 208.
13. ibid
14. Atkinson, p. 41.
15. Lincoln, *Collected Works,* IV: p. 63. (Lincoln to Scripps, June 1, 1860)
16. Warren, p. 208.
17. Wilson and Davis, p. 103. (A. H. Chapman to Herndon, Sept. 8, 1865)
18. Atkinson, p. 41.
19. Herndon, p. 57.
20. Tarbell, *Life of Lincoln,* p. 48.

21. Sandburg, p. 57.

22. Lincoln, *Collected Works*, IV: p. 63. (Lincoln to Scripps, June 1, 1860)

23. Tarbell, *The Early Life of Abraham Lincoln*, p. 99

24. Wilson and Davis, p. 456. (John Hanks to Herndon, 1865–1866)

25. Atkinson, p. 42.

26. Lincoln, *Collected Works*, IV: p. 63. (Lincoln to Scripps, June 1, 1860)

27. Wilson and Davis, p. 456. (John Hanks to Herndon, 1865–1866)

28. Atkinson, p. 42.

29. Wilson and Davis, p. 456. (John Hanks to Herndon, 1865–1866)

30. Lincoln, *Collected Works*, IV: p. 63. (Lincoln to Scripps, June 1, 1860)

31. ibid

32. ibid

33. Tarbell, *Life of Lincoln*, p. 53.

CHAPTER 19. "I FOUND HIM NO GREEN HORN"

1. Herndon and Weik, p. 68.

2. ibid

3. Wilson and Davis, p. 73. (James Short to Herndon, July 7, 1865)

4. Wilson and Davis, p. 456. (John Hanks to Herndon, 1865–1866)

5. ibid

6. Lincoln, *Collected Works*, IV: p. 63. (Lincoln to Scripps, June 1, 1860)

7. Wilson and Davis, p. 456. (John Hanks to Herndon, 1865–1866)

8. Lincoln, *Collected Works*, IV: p. 63. (Lincoln to Scripps, June 1, 1860)

9. Wilson and Davis, p. 456. (John Hanks to Herndon, 1865–1866)

10. Wilson and Davis, p. 429. (Caleb Carman to Herndon, Nov. 30, 1866)

11. Sandburg, *Abraham Lincoln, The Prairie Years*, p. 59.

12. Tarbell, *Life of Lincoln*, p. 52.

13. Tarbell, p. 53.
14. Wilson and Davis, p. 457. (John Hanks to Herndon, 1865–1866)
15. Wilson and Davis, p. 373. (Caleb Carman to Herndon, Oct. 12, 1866)
16. ibid
17. Wilson and Davis, p. 429. (Caleb Carman to Herndon, Nov. 30, 1866)
18. Tarbell, p. 53–55.

CHAPTER 20. "I"LL HIT IT HARD"

1. John Locke Scripps, *The Life of Abraham Lincoln*, Indiana University Press, 1961, p. 53. (Lincoln to Scripps, Autobiographical sketch, about June 1, 1860)
2. Herndon and Weik, p. 63.
3. Wilson and Davis, p. 44. (John Hanks to Herndon, June 13, 1865)
4. Herndon and Weik, p. 63.
5. Wilson and Davis, p. 254. (Coleman Smoot to Herndon, May 7, 1866)
6. Scripps, p. 53. (Lincoln to Scripps, Autobiographical sketch, about June 1, 1860)
7. Herndon and Weik, p. 63.
8. Wilson and Davis, p. 457. (John Hanks to Herndon, 1865–1866)
9. Wilson and Davis, p. 17. (William Greene to Herndon, May 30, 1865)
10. Herndon and Weik, p. 62.
11. Wilson and Davis, p. 254. (Coleman Smoot to Herndon, May 7, 1866)
12. Wilson and Davis, p. 457. (John Hanks to Herndon, 1865–1866)
13. Herndon and Weik, p. 63.
14. Sandburg, *Abraham Lincoln: The Prairie Years*, p. 60.
15. ibid
16. ibid
17. ibid

18. ibid
19. ibid
20. Wilson and Davis, p. 457. (John Hanks to Herndon, 1865–1866)
21. Herndon, p. 64.
22. Wilson and Davis, p. 457. (John Hanks to Herndon, 1865–1866)
23. *The Life and Writings of Abraham Lincoln*, Philip Van Doren Stern, ed., The Modern Library, NY, 1940, p. 392. (Lincoln to Joshua Speed, Aug. 4, 1855)
24. *The Life and Writings of Abraham Lincoln*, Philip Van Doren Stern, ed. (Lincoln to Mary Speed, Sept. 27, 1841), p. 253.
25. *The Life and Writings of Abraham Lincoln*, Philip Van Doren Stern, ed. (Lincoln to Joshua Speed, Aug. 4, 1855), p. 392.
26. Wilson and Davis, p. 429. (Caleb Carman to Herndon, Nov. 30, 1866)
27. Lincoln, *Collected Works*, XI: p. 56. (Lincoln speech to Indiana Regiment, March 17, 1865)
28. Wilson and Davis, p. 458. (John Hanks to Herndon, 1865–1866)
29. Wilson and Davis, p. 439. (A. H. Chapman to Herndon, 1865–1866)
30. ibid
31. ibid
32. Wilson and Davis, p. 456. (John Hanks to Herndon, 1865–1866)
33. Atkinson, p. 43.

CHAPTER 21. "A KIND OF DRIFTWOOD"

1. Lincoln, *Life and Writings*, p. 603. (Lincoln to Scripps June 1, 1860)
2. Wilson and Davis, p. 80. (L. M. Greene to Herndon, July 30, 1865)
3. Herndon and Weik, p. 65.
4. Wilson and Davis, p. 384. (R. B. Rutledge to Herndon, Nov. 1, 1866)
5. Wilson and Davis, p. 382. (R. B. Rutledge to Herndon, Nov. 1, 1866)
6. Douglas L. Wilson, *Honor's Voice*, Vintage Books, NY, 1998, p. 25.

7. Benjamin Thomas, *Lincoln's New Salem*, Alfred A. Knopf, NY, 1954, p. 41.
8. Thomas, p. 42.
9. Sandburg, *Abraham Lincoln: The Prairie Years,* p. 97.
10. Herndon and Weik, p. 65.
11. Lincoln, *Life and Writings*, p. 603. (Lincoln to Scripps June 1, 1860)
12. Barton, p. 161.
13. Wilson and Davis, p. 8. (Mentor Graham to Herndon, May 29, 1865)
14. Lincoln, *Life and Writings*, p. 603. (Lincoln to Scripps June 1, 1860)
15. Herndon and Weik, p. 69.

CHAPTER 22. "THE BEST FELLER THAT EVER BROKE INTO THIS SETTLEMENT"

1. Wilson and Davis, p. 381. (R. B. Rutledge to Herndon, Nov. 1, 1866)
2. Herndon and Weik, p. 68.
3. Wilson and Davis, p. 17. (William Greene to Herndon, May 30, 1865)
4. Herndon and Weik, p. 68.
5. Wilson and Davis, p. 17. (William Greene to Herndon, May 30, 1865)
6. Herndon and Weik, p. 68.
7. Sandburg, p. 78.
8. Herndon and Weik, p. 69.
9. Wilson and Davis, p. 539. (Jason Duncan to Herndon, 1866–1867)
10. Wilson and Davis, p. 73. (James Short to Herndon, July 7, 1865)
11. Herndon and Weik, p. 69.
12. Wilson, p. 20.
13. Wilson and Davis, p. 370. (Mentor Graham to Herndon, Oct. 10, 1866)
14. Herndon and Weik, p. 69.

15. Wilson and Davis, p. 386. (R. B. Rutledge to Herndon, Nov. 1, 1866)
16. Wilson and Davis, p. 73. (James Short to Herndon, July 7, 1865)
17. Wilson and Davis, p. 369. (Henry McHenry to Herndon, Oct. 10, 1866)
18. Wilson and Davis, p. 366. (J. G. Greene to Herndon, Oct. 5, 1866)
19. Herndon and Weik, p. 69.
20. Wilson and Davis, p. 386. (R. B. Rutledge to Herndon, Nov. 1, 1866)
21. Wilson and Davis, p. 73. (James Short to Herndon, July 7, 1865)
22. Wilson and Davis, p. 369. (Henry McHenry to Herndon, Oct. 10, 1866)
23. ibid
24. Wilson and Davis, p. 703. (James Harriott interview, undated)
25. Wilson and Davis, p. 369. (Henry McHenry to Herndon, Oct. 10, 1866)
26. Wilson and Davis, p. 386. (R. B. Rutledge to Herndon, Nov. 1, 1866)
27. Wilson and Davis, p. 369. (Henry McHenry to Herndon, Oct. 10, 1866)
28. Wilson, p. 20.
29. Wilson and Davis, p. 387. (R. B. Rutledge to Herndon, Nov. 1, 1866)
30. Wilson and Davis, p. 7. (J. Rowan Herndon to Herndon, May 28, 1865)
31. Wilson and Davis, p. 73. (James Short to Herndon, July 7, 1865)
32. Wilson and Davis, p. 386. (R. B. Rutledge to Herndon, Nov. 1, 1866)
33. Wilson, p. 20.
34. Wilson and Davis, p. 73. (James Short to Herndon, July 7, 1865)
35. Wilson and Davis, p. 402. (J. M. Rutledge to Herndon, Nov. 1, 1866)
36. Wilson, p. 20.

37. Wilson and Davis, p. 386. (R. B. Rutledge to Herndon, Nov. 1, 1866)

38. Wilson and Davis, p. 369. (Henry McHenry to Herndon, Oct. 10, 1866)

39. Wilson and Davis, p. 386. (R. B. Rutledge to Herndon, Nov. 1, 1866)

40. Wilson and Davis, p. 402. (J. M. Rutledge to Herndon, Nov. 1, 1866)

41. Wilson and Davis, p. 80. (L. M. Greene to Herndon, July 30, 1865)

42. Wilson and Davis, p. 402. (J. M. Rutledge to Herndon, Nov. 1, 1866)

43. Wilson and Davis, p. 369. (Henry McHenry to Herndon, Oct. 10, 1866)

44. Wilson and Davis, p. 386. (R. B. Rutledge to Herndon, Nov. 1, 1866)

45. Wilson and Davis, p. 80. (L. M. Greene to Herndon, July 30, 1865)

46. Wilson and Davis, p. 386. (R. B. Rutledge to Herndon, Nov. 1, 1866)

47. Wilson and Davis, p. 74. (James Short to Herndon, July 7, 1865)

48. Wilson, p. 20.

49. Sandburg, *Abraham Lincoln: The Prairie Years,* p. 79.

50. Wilson and Davis, p. 525. (Hannah Armstrong to Herndon, 1866)

51. Wilson, p. 35.

52. Wilson and Davis, p. 539. (Jason Duncan to Herndon, 1866–1867)

53. Wilson, p. 20.

54. Wilson and Davis, p. 385. (R. B. Rutledge to Herndon, Nov. 1, 1866)

55. Wilson and Davis, p. 450. (Russell Godbey to Herndon, 1865–1866)

CHAPTER 23. "SOMETHING THAT WAS KNOTTY"

1. Wilson and Davis, p. 605. (Parthena Hill to Herndon, March 1887)

2. ibid
3. Wilson and Davis, p. 14. (Henry McHenry to Herndon, May 29, 1865)
4. Wilson and Davis, p. 9. (Mentor Graham to Herndon, May 29, 1865)
5. Wilson and Davis, p. 539. (Jason Duncan to Herndon, 1866–1867)
6. Wilson and Davis, p. 14. (Henry McHenry to Herndon, May 29, 1865)
7. Wilson and Davis, p. 76. (Mentor Graham to Herndon, July 15, 1865)
8. Herndon and Weik, p. 103.
9. ibid
10. Herndon and Weik, p. 94.
11. Wilson and Davis, p. 161. (A. Y. Ellis, Jan. 1866)
12. Wilson and Davis, p. 497. (R. B. Rutledge to Herndon, Dec. 4, 1866)
13. Wilson and Davis, p. 202. (Robert Wilson to Herndon, Feb. 10, 1866)
14. Herndon and Weik, p. 94.
15. Wilson and Davis, p.174. (A. Y. Ellis to Herndon, Jan. 23, 1866)
16. Wilson and Davis, p. 69. (J. Rowan Herndon to Herndon, July 3, 1865)
17. Wilson and Davis, p. 442. (H. E. Dummer, 1865–1866)
18. Sandburg, *Abraham Lincoln: The Prairie Years*, p. 30.
19. Warren, p. 245.
20. Wilson, p. 95.
21. Herndon and Weik, p. 70.
22. ibid
23. Wilson and Davis, p. 10. (Mentor Graham to Herndon, May 29, 1865)
24. Herndon and Weik, p. 71.
25. Wilson and Davis, p. 539. (Jason Duncan to Herndon, 1866–1867)
26. Wilson and Davis, p. 384. (R. B. Rutledge to Herndon, Nov. 1, 1866)

27. Wilson and Davis, p. 426. (R. B. Rutledge to Herndon, Nov. 30, 1866)

28. Wilson and Davis, p. 498. (R. B. Rutledge to Herndon, Dec. 4, 1866)

29. Wilson and Davis, p. 92. (J. Rowan Herndon to Herndon, Aug. 16, 1865)

30. Wilson and Davis, p. 426. (R. B. Rutledge to Herndon, Nov. 30, 1866)

31. Wilson and Davis, p. 497. (R. B. Rutledge to Herndon, Dec. 4, 1866)

32. Wilson and Davis, p. 92. (J. Rowan Herndon to Herndon, Aug. 16, 1865)

33. Wilson and Davis, p. 90. (N. W. Branson interview with J. Short, Aug. 3, 1865)

34. Wilson and Davis, p. 92. (J. Rowan Herndon to Herndon, Aug. 16, 1865)

35. Wilson and Davis, p. 90. (N. W. Branson interview with J. Short, Aug. 3, 1865)

36. Wilson and Davis, p. 91. (J. Rowan Herndon to Herndon, Aug. 16, 1865)

37. Thomas, p. 69.

CHAPTER 24. "I AM YOUNG AND UNKNOWN"

1. Wilson and Davis, p. 384. (R. B. Rutledge to Herndon, Nov. 1, 1866)

2. Wilson and Davis, p. 539. (Jason Duncan to Herndon, 1866–1867)

3. Wilson and Davis, p. 384. (R. B. Rutledge to Herndon, Nov. 1, 1866)

4. ibid

5. Wilson and Davis, p. 451. (James Gourley, 1865–1866)

6. Wilson and Davis, p. 350. (David Davis, Sept. 20, 1866)

7. Wilson and Davis, p. 540. (Jason Duncan to Herndon, 1866–1867)

8. Wilson and Davis, p. 539. (Jason Duncan to Herndon, 1866–1867)
9. Lincoln, *Life and Writings*, p. 604.
10. Wilson and Davis, p. 253. (John McNeil, May 5, 1866)
11. Lincoln, *Complete Works,* I: p. 5.

CHAPTER 25. "THEY SURELY THOUGHT IT WAS A DREAM"

1. Wilson and Davis, p. 34. (J. Rowan Herndon to Herndon, June 11, 1865)
2. Herndon and Weik, p. 73.
3. ibid
4. Wilson and Davis, p. 34. (J. Rowan Herndon to Herndon, June 11, 1865)
5. ibid
6. Wilson and Davis, p. 704. (James Matheny to Herndon, undated)
7. Wilson and Davis, p. 34. (J. Rowan Herndon to Herndon, June 11, 1865)
8. ibid
9. ibid
10. Lincoln, *Life and Writings*, p. 603.
11. Herndon and Weik, p. 71.
12. Thomas, p. 61.
13. Wilson and Davis, p. 580. (James Hall to Herndon, Sept. 17, 1873)
14. Scripps, p. 51.
15. Barton, p. 169

CHAPTER 26. "CAPTAIN ABRAHAM LINCOLN'S COMPANY OF THE FIRST REGIMENT OF THE BRIGADE OF VOLUNTEERS"

1. Tarbell, *Life of Lincoln*, p. 75.
2. Wilson and Davis, p. 6. (J. Rowan Herndon to Herndon, May 28, 1865)

3. Tarbell, *Life of Lincoln*, p. 74.

4. Barton, p. 174.

5. Tarbell, *Life of Lincoln*, p. 74.

6. Rice, p. 464.

7. Wilson and Davis, p. 368. (William Greene to Herndon, Oct. 9, 1866)

8. ibid

9. Tarbell, *Life of Lincoln*, p. 74.

10. Sandburg, *The Prairie Years*, p. 90.

11. Rice, p. 465.

12. Lincoln, *Life and Writings*, p. 566. (Lincoln to Jesse Fell, Dec. 20, 1859)

13. Rice, p. 464.

14. Tarbell, *Life of Lincoln*, p. 86.

15. Herndon and Weik, p. 78.

16. Rice, p. 218.

17. Wilson and Davis, p. 78. (David Pantier to Herndon, July 21, 1865)

18. ibid

19. ibid

20. Sandburg, *The Prairie Years*, p. 91.

21. Wilson and Davis, p. 372. (Royal Clary to Herndon, Oct. 1866)

22. Wilson and Davis, p. 18. (William Greene to Herndon, May 30, 1865)

23. ibid

24. Herndon and Weik, p. 79.

25. ibid

26. Wilson and Davis, p. 18. (William Greene to Herndon, May 30, 1865)

27. Wilson and Davis, p. 372. (Royal Clary to Herndon, Oct. 1866)

28. Wilson and Davis, p. 18. (William Greene to Herndon, May 30, 1865)

29. Wilson and Davis, p. 372. (Royal Clary to Herndon, Oct. 1866)

30. Wilson and Davis, p. 18. (William Greene to Herndon, May 30, 1865)
31. ibid
32. Wilson and Davis, p. 363. (William Miller to Herndon, Sept. 1866)
33. ibid
34. Wilson and Davis, p. 19. (William Greene to Herndon, May 30, 1865)
35. ibid
36. Wilson, p. 30.
37. Wilson and Davis, p. 19. (William Greene to Herndon, May 30, 1865)
38. Wilson, p. 30.
39. Wilson and Davis, p. 19. (William Greene to Herndon, May 30, 1865)
40. Wilson, p. 30
41. Wilson and Davis, p. 19. (William Greene to Herndon, May 30, 1865)
42. Wilson, p. 30.
43. Wilson and Davis, p. 19. (William Greene to Herndon, May 30, 1865)
44. Wilson, p. 30.

CHAPTER 27. "CHARGES UPON THE WILD ONIONS . . . BLOODY STRUGGLES WITH THE MOSQUITOES"

1. Wilson and Davis, p. 371. (Royal Clary to Herndon, Oct. 1866)
2. Wilson and Davis, p. 362. (William Miller to Herndon, Sept. 1866)
3. ibid
4. Tarbell, *Life of Lincoln*, p. 79.
5. ibid
6. Wilson and Davis, p. 554. (George Harrison to Herndon, Jan. 29, 1867)

7. Wilson and Davis, p. 555. (George Harrison to Herndon, Jan. 29, 1867)
8. Sandburg, *The Prairie Years and the War Years*, p. 31.
9. Herndon and Weik, p. 82.
10. Beveridge, p. 123.
11. Sandburg, *The Prairie Years and the War Years*, p. 31.
12. Lincoln, *Complete Works,* I: p. 509. (Speech in the US House of Representatives, July 27, 1848)

CHAPTER 28. "THE ONLY TIME I EVER HAVE BEEN BEATEN"

1. Wilson and Davis, p. 6. (J. Rowan Herndon to Herndon, May 28, 1865)
2. Wilson and Davis, p. 16. (James Herndon to Herndon, May 29, 1865)
3. Wilson and Davis, p. 51. (J. Rowan Herndon to Herndon, June 21. 1865)
4. ibid
5. Wilson and Davis, p. 7. (J. Rowan Herndon to Herndon, May 28, 1865)
6. Wilson and Davis, p. 171. (A. Y. Ellis to Herndon, Jan. 1866)
7. ibid
8. Wilson and Davis, p. 170. (A. Y. Ellis to Herndon, Jan. 1866)
9. Thomas, p. 86.
10. Wilson and Davis, p. 7. (J. Rowan Herndon to Herndon, May 28, 1865)
11. ibid.
12. ibid
13. Wilson and Davis, p. 20. (William Greene to Herndon, May 30, 1865)
14. Wilson and Davis, p. 540. (Jason Duncan to Herndon, 1866–1867)
15. Lincoln, *Life and Writings*, p. 566. (Lincoln to Jesse Fell, Dec. 20, 1859)

16. Lincoln, *Life and Writings*, p. 604. (Lincoln to Scripps, June 1, 1860)
17. Wilson and Davis, p. 7. (J. Rowan Herndon to Herndon, May 28, 1865)
18. Herndon and Weik, p. 146.
19. Lincoln, *Life and Writings*, p. 604. (Lincoln to Scripps, June 1, 1860)
20. Herndon and Weik, p. 88.
21. ibid
22. ibid
23. Wilson and Davis, p. 7. (J. Rowan Herndon to Herndon, May 28, 1865)
24. Herndon and Weik, p. 88.
25. Lincoln, *Life and Writings*, p. 604. (Lincoln to Scripps, June 1, 1860)

CHAPTER 29. "THE NATIONAL DEBT"

1. Thomas P. Reep, *The Lincoln Reader*, Paul Angle, ed., Rutgers University Press, 1947, p. 52.
2. Reep, p. 52–54.
3. Wilson and Davis, p. 20. (William Greene to Herndon, May 30, 1865)
4. Wilson and Davis, p. 375. (George Spears to Herndon, Oct. 17, 1866)
5. Wilson and Davis, p. 504. (Caleb Carman to Herndon, Dec. 8, 1866)
6. Herndon and Weik, p. 95.
7. Herndon and Weik, p. 93.
8. Wilson and Davis, p. 426. (R. B. Rutledge to Herndon, Nov. 30, 1866)
9. Tarbell, *The Early Life of Abraham Lincoln*, p. 168.
10. Herndon and Weik, p. 92.
11. Herndon and Weik, p. 90.
12. Lincoln, *Life and Writings*, p. 604. (Lincoln to Scripps, June 1, 1860)

13. Wilson and Davis, p. 375. (George Spears to Herndon, Oct. 17, 1866)
14. Lincoln, *Life and Writings*, p. 604. (Lincoln to Scripps, June 1, 1860)
15. Herndon and Weik, p. 90.
16. Reep, p. 54.
17. Wilson and Davis, p. 378. (J. Rowan Herndon to Herndon, Oct. 28, 1866)
18. Wilson and Davis, p. 51. (J. Rowan Herndon to Herndon, June 21. 1865)
19. Tarbell, *The Early Life of Abraham Lincoln*, p. 188.
20. Wilson and Davis, p. 51. (J. Rowan Herndon to Herndon, June 21. 1865)
21. Tarbell, *The Early Life of Abraham Lincoln*, p. 188.

CHAPTER 30. "I LOVED THE WOMAN DEARLY AND SACREDLY"

1. Herndon and Weik, p. 105.
2. Wilson and Davis, p. 387. (John Jones to Herndon, Oct. 22, 1866)
3. Wilson and Davis, p. 383. (R. B. Rutledge to Herndon, Nov. 1, 1866)
4. Wilson and Davis, p. 73. (James Short to Herndon, July 7, 1865)
5. Wilson and Davis, p. 382. (R. B. Rutledge to Herndon, Nov. 1, 1866)
6. Wilson and Davis, p. 21. (William Greene to Herndon, May 30, 1865)
7. Wilson and Davis, p. 69. (J. Rowan Herndon to Herndon, July 3, 1865)
8. Wilson and Davis, p. 175. (William Greene to Herndon, Jan. 23, 1866)
9. Herndon and Weik, p. 105.
10. Wilson and Davis, p. 242. (Mentor Graham to Herndon, April 2, 1866)

11. Wilson and Davis, p. 19. (William Greene to Herndon, May 30, 1865)
12. Wilson and Davis, p. 383. (R. B. Rutledge to Herndon, Nov. 1, 1866)
13. Herndon and Weik, p. 107.
14. Wilson and Davis, p. 383. (R. B. Rutledge to Herndon, Nov. 1, 1866)
15. Herndon and Weik, p. 108.
16. Wilson and Davis, p. 383. (R. B. Rutledge to Herndon, Nov. 1, 1866)
17. Herndon and Weik, p. 108.
18. ibid
19. Wilson and Davis, p. 409. (R. B. Rutledge to Herndon, Nov. 21, 1866)
20. Wilson and Davis, p. 252. (John McNamar to Herndon, May 5, 1866)
21. Wilson and Davis, p. 383. (R. B. Rutledge to Herndon, Nov. 1, 1866)
22. Herndon and Weik, p. 109.
23. Herndon and Weik, p. 110.
24. Wilson and Davis, p. 605. (Parthena Hill to Herndon, March 1887)
25. Herndon and Weik, p. 110.
26. Wilson and Davis, p. 383. (R. B. Rutledge to Herndon, Nov. 1, 1866)
27. Herndon and Weik, p. 111.
28. Wilson and Davis, p. 236. (George U. Miles to Herndon, Mar. 23, 1866)
29. Wilson and Davis, p. 387. (John Jones to Herndon, Oct. 22, 1866)
30. Wilson and Davis, p. 73. (James Short to Herndon, July 7, 1865)
31. Wilson and Davis, p. 242. (Mentor Graham to Herndon, April 2, 1866)
32. Wilson and Davis, p. 387. (John Jones to Herndon, Oct. 22, 1866)

33. Wilson and Davis, p. 383. (R. B. Rutledge to Herndon, Nov. 1, 1866)

34. Wilson and Davis, p. 409. (R. B. Rutledge to Herndon, Nov. 21, 1866)

35. ibid

36. Wilson and Davis, p. 252. (John McNamar to Herndon, May 5, 1866)

37. Wilson, p. 117. (Dr. Lorenzo Matheny, doctoral dissertation, 1836)

38. Wilson and Davis, p. 383. (R. B. Rutledge to Herndon, Nov. 1, 1866)

39. Wilson and Davis, p. 604. (Parthena Hill to Herndon, March 1887)

40. Herndon and Weik, p. 112.

41. Wilson and Davis, p. 21. (William Greene to Herndon, May 30, 1865)

42. Herndon and Weik, p. 112.

43. ibid

44. ibid

45. Wilson and Davis, p. 387. (John Jones to Herndon, Oct. 22, 1866)

46. Wilson and Davis, p. 557. (Elizabeth Abell to Herndon, Feb. 15, 1867)

47. Wilson and Davis, p. 383. (R. B. Rutledge to Herndon, Nov. 1, 1866)

48. Wilson and Davis, p. 236. (George U. Miles to Herndon, March 23, 1866)

49. Wilson and Davis, p. 155. (Henry McHenry to Herndon, Jan. 8, 1866)

50. Wilson and Davis, p. 13. (Hardin Bale to Herndon, May 29, 1865)

51. Wilson, p. 121. (John Hill to Tarbell, Feb. 17, 1896)

52. Wilson and Davis, p. 557. (Elizabeth Abell to Herndon, Feb. 15, 1867)

53. Wilson and Davis, p. 236. (George U. Miles to Herndon, March 23, 1866)

54. Wilson and Davis, p. 501. (A. Y. Ellis to Herndon, Dec. 6, 1866)

55. Herndon and Weik, p. 113.
56. Wilson and Davis, p. 173. (A. Y. Ellis to Herndon, Jan. 23, 1866)
57. Herndon and Weik, p. 114.
58. Wilson and Davis, p. 440. (Includes the entire conversation between Cogdal and Lincoln: Isaac Cogdal to Herndon, 1865–1866)

CHAPTER 31. "OH! WHY SHOULD THE SPIRIT OF MORTAL BE PROUD?"

1. Wilson and Davis, p. 63. (John Stuart to Herndon, June 1865)
2. Herndon and Weik, p. 473.
3. ibid
4. Wilson and Davis, p. 626. (Henry Whitney to Herndon, Aug. 23, 1887)
5. Herndon and Weik, p. 473.
6. ibid
7. ibid
8. Wilson and Davis, p. 374. (Caleb Carman to Herndon, Oct. 12, 1866)
9. Wilson and Davis, p. 432. (James Matheny to Herndon, Nov. 1866)
10. Wilson and Davis, p. 727. (Jonathan Birch to Herndon, 1887)
11. Wilson and Davis, p. 201. (Robert L. Wilson to Herndon, Feb. 10, 1866)
12. Wilson and Davis, p. 727. (Jonathan Birch to Herndon, 1887)
13. Wilson and Davis, p. 205. (Robert L. Wilson to Herndon, Feb. 10, 1866)
14. Wilson and Davis, p. 727. (Jonathan Birch to Herndon, 1887)
15. Wilson and Davis, p. 205. (Robert L. Wilson to Herndon, Feb. 10, 1866)
16. Wilson and Davis, p. 201. (Robert L. Wilson to Herndon, Feb. 10, 1866)
17. Herndon and Weik, p. 114.

18. Wilson and Davis, p. 88. (Lawrence Weldon to Herndon, Aug. 1, 1865)

19. Lincoln, *Collected Works* I: p. 378.

20. Sandburg, *Abraham Lincoln: The Prairie Years*, p. 197–198.

CHAPTER 32. "DID YOU VOTE FOR ME?"

1. Herndon and Weik, p. 97.

2. ibid

3. Lincoln, *Life and Writings*, p. 604. (June 1, 1860)

4. ibid

5. Herndon and Weik, p. 101.

6. ibid

7. Thomas, p. 96.

8. ibid

9. Thomas, p. 97.

10. ibid

11. Herndon and Weik, p. 97.

12. Lincoln, *Life and Writings*, p. 604. (June 1, 1860)

13. Wilson and Davis, p. 384. (R. B. Rutledge to Herndon, Nov. 1, 1866)

14. Wilson and Davis, p. 10. (Mentor Graham to Herndon, May 29, 1865)

15. Wilson and Davis, p. 606. (Elizabeth Bell to Herndon, March 1887)

16. Wilson and Davis, p. 10. (Mentor Graham to Herndon, May 29, 1865)

17. Herndon and Weik, p. 99.

18. Wilson and Davis, p. 10. (Mentor Graham to Herndon, May 29, 1865)

19. Wilson and Davis, p. 14. (Henry McHenry to Herndon, May 29, 1865)

20. Herndon and Weik, p. 99.

21. Herndon and Weik, p. 100.

22. Thomas, p. 112.

23. Wilson and Davis, p. 74. (James Short to Herndon, July 7, 1865)

24. ibid

25. ibid

26. ibid

27. Tarbell, *Life of Lincoln*, p. 104.

28. Wilson and Davis, p. 171. (A. Y. Ellis to Herndon, Jan. 23, 1866)

29. Herndon and Weik, p. 103.

30. Wilson and Davis, p. 8. (Rowan Herndon to Herndon, May 28, 1865)

31. ibid

32. Wilson and Davis, p. 504. (Caleb Carman to Herndon, Dec. 8, 1866)

33. Wilson and Davis, p. 254. (Coleman Smoot to Herndon, May 7, 1866)